FRIEND OR FOE?

Friend or Foe?

Russians in American Film and Foreign Policy, 1933–1991

Michael Strada
and
Harold Troper

The Scarecrow Press, Inc.
Lanham, Md., & London
1997

SCARECROW PRESS, INC.

Published in the United States of America
by Scarecrow Press, Inc.
4720 Boston Way
Lanham, Maryland 20706

4 Pleydell Gardens, Folkestone
Kent CT20 2DN, England

PN
1995.9
S665
S76
1997

Copyright © 1997 by Michael Strada and Harold Troper

British Library Cataloguing in Publication Information Available

Library of Congress Cataloging-in-Publication Data

Strada, Michael J.
    Friend or foe? : Russians in American film and foreign policy,
1933–1991 / Michael J. Strada and Harold R. Troper.
      p.   cm.
    Filmography: p.
    Includes bibliographical references and index.
    ISBN 0-8108-3245-3 (cloth : alk. paper)
    1. Soviet Union in motion pictures.   2. National characteristics,
Russian, in motion picture.   3. United States—Relations—Soviet
Union.   4. Soviet Union—Relations—United States.   I. Troper,
Harold R.   II. Title.
PN1995.9.S665S76   1997
791.43'6247—dc21
                                      96-42928
                                      CIP

ISBN 0-8108-3245-3 (cloth : alk. paper)

Contents

Preface

More than a decade ago a curious event sparked our interest in Hollywood's Russians, much as shooting stars spark the night sky. In 1986, poet Yevgeny Yevtushenko and some colleagues from the Soviet Writers Union held a rare Western-style press conference. As the hastily assembled Moscow press corps scribbled notes, the cream of Soviet letters took dead aim at Hollywood. Recent American films like *Rocky IV* (1985), *Red Dawn* (1984), and *Invasion, USA* (1985), Yevtushenko charged, represented a cultural orgy of Russian bashing tantamount to "war-nography." What had packed audiences into theater seats and pushed up popcorn sales was berated as crude profiteering, even warmongering, at the expense of Soviet-American relations.

These charges appear extreme, yet because they emanated from the official Soviet Writers Union, they turned into global headlines. In the process, fundamental questions were raised, such as, How have Hollywood films depicted Russians? Have they influenced American attitudes toward the Soviet Union? When one of the authors was asked precisely these questions by a local radio station after the Moscow press conference, he had no answers, definitive or otherwise. An examination of film literature found only a few brief pieces on Hollywood's historical depiction of Russians—hardly sufficient for such a complex topic.

Even the most cursory examination of cinematic Russians reveals that the always uneasy and often fractious Soviet-American relationship was clearly mirrored in Hollywood's portrayal of Russians and the Soviet Union during nearly sixty years of filmmaking. Other questions also arise. For example, what messages do celluloid Russians communicate to the Americans who view them, and do such messages affect superpower relations?

Hollywood's Russians

Hollywood's attitudinal pendulum has swung as wildly as Russo-American relations. When relations were tense, Hollywood fed off those tensions by creating villainous Russians. Movie junkies will recall psychopathic terrorist Mikhail Rostov delighting in the murder of innocent families in *Invasion, USA* (1985), and evil KGB Colonel Nikita Biroshilov deriving fiendish pleasure from the torture of Korean War POWs in *Prisoner of War* (1954). Also memorable is Viktor Rostavili, a drug kingpin eagerly pushing the profitable limits of sadism in *Red Heat* (1988).

The list goes on. *World War III* (1982) features megalomanic coup leader Alexei Rodinsky blithely risking nuclear annihilation to gain a Cold War advantage over the United States. KGB loose cannon Nikolai Dalchimsky stretches the definition of personal fulfillment by blowing up cities beginning with letters needed to engrave his name in blood across America's landscape in *Telefon* (1977). Dissolute, black-clad Soviet fisherman Red Skain is a seagoing brigand who cheats, lies, and steals to defeat his American competitors in *Spawn of the North* (1939).

If relations warmed up, filmic Russians—mostly female—hit the other extreme by nuzzling up to perfection. Pacifist ballerina Nina Ivanova turns into a heroic World War II partisan in *Days of Glory* (1944). Young Russian pianist Nadia Petrovna marries a touring American conductor, and together they make beautiful music while battling Nazi invaders in *Song of Russia* (1944). In *Ninotchka* (1939), hard-edged Nina Yakushova melts like butter when exposed to the warmth of a western Adonis, so becoming the prototype for a spate of subsequent cinematic clones. A humble yet saintly Catholic priest, Kiril Lakota, the implausible first Russian pope in *The Shoes of the Fisherman* (1969), spends much of the Church's money delivering the Chinese from starvation and the world from the brink of nuclear annihilation.

While most Russian characters projected onto the big screen look predictable and uncomplicated, a few defy convention, like the clever investigator, Arkady Renko, in *Gorky Park* (1984); the lovable musician, Vladimir Ivanov, who defects in Bloomingdale's department store in *Moscow on the Hudson* (1985); and the tender Lara, Yuri

Zhivago's worldly yet spiritual companion on his wrenching odyssey through war-ravaged Russia in *Dr. Zhivago* (1965).

If Tinseltown's Russians consist of diverse types, so do the films in which they appear. A few are gems that stand the test of time and continue to sparkle, but most are not. Many of these films seem trite, even mindless, and quickly fade from memory. The handful warranting attention as aesthetic achievements begin with Ernst Lubitsch's masterful direction of *Ninotchka* (1939), which exudes a European sophistication enabling Greta Garbo to work her magical screen presence. Stanley Kubrick's conviction and creative instincts blossom in his sardonic comedy, *Dr. Strangelove* (1964), which breaks with Hollywood norms by daring audiences to look, without blinking, into the nuclear fireball.

Canadian-born director Norman Jewison's plea for America to lighten up, *The Russians Are Coming, The Russians Are Coming* (1966), continues to work as delightful Cold War parody three decades after its release. Warren Beatty's sympathetic look at American socialists and the Russian Revolution through the eyes of American journalist John Reed in *Reds* (1982) is epic in scope and courage. Director Paul Mazursky's *Moscow on the Hudson* (1985) examines people tossed about by forces larger than themselves and coping as best they can. It celebrates their feelings and foibles with an introspection almost nonexistent in Shadowland's other Russian-genre films. No Hollywood motion picture captures the deep-seated Russian sense of futility in the face of conditions beyond human control that is depicted in *Dr. Zhivago* (1965).

Film and National History

But what do these Russian-genre films—good and bad—say about America? Much. Hollywood movies constitute rich repositories of the inner life of the nation. One can peel them back to reveal popular fears and obsessions, not unlike the stratified layers of earth that archaeologists dig through to uncover artifacts of earlier ages. This book follows Hollywood films through six decades of official Soviet-American relations from 1933, when the United States recognized the Soviet Union, until 1991, when the Soviet Union collapsed.

Others have understood Hollywood films as windows on the American mind-set. Albert Auster and Leonard Quart argue that movies tap the genuine social tone of a given era,[1] while Mark Carnes believes film serves as "a great repository of historical consciousness in these United States of Amnesia."[2] Similarly, Peter Rollins declares Hollywood an "unwitting recorder of national moods."[3] This certainly rings true for American foreign policy and Hollywood film. They track each other through time as compulsively as symmetrical sundials.

Subtlety is not a quality esteemed by films produced in the dream factories located around Culver City, California. To the degree that a recurrent American mind-set assumes anything worth doing must be worth overdoing, examples of excessiveness in American foreign policy and in Hollywood film work in tandem.[4] What explains this? The American character's exaggerative tendencies constitute the proclivities of an equal opportunity overachiever, reflecting something deeper than political philosophy and swallowing up liberals and conservatives alike.

America's twentieth-century worldview has turned on the idea of political freedom expressed as the right of national self-determination. America's self-image, deeply rooted in its unique national psyche, is liberty's defender against bullies.[5] Very early on, America had defined itself as the world's first new nation, or in Thomas Jefferson's words, "the last best hope of mankind." Herman Melville's hyperbole later sketched a "peculiar, chosen people, the Israel of our times; who bear the ark of the liberties of the world."[6]

This libertarian bugle call sounded throughout the land as Americans rushed into continental expansion during the nineteenth century. It echoed through the era of massive immigration and urbanization, sounding the need for order and unity in an increasingly diverse and complex society.[7] A strong sense of benevolence and exceptionalism periodically dictated to Americans that their nation assume a unique mission in the world beyond their borders.[8] Woodrow Wilson set the moral tone for the American century by proclaiming that "the world must be made safe for democracy," in what must have seemed to many of America's World War I allies as well-meaning naivete.[9] It was a call Americans were to hear again and again. America's idealistic, self-declared, twentieth-century role has been that of freedom's defender from international aggressors—villains like Hitler, Tojo, Mao, Castro, Ho Chi Minh, Noriega, and Saddam Hussein.[10]

But no villain captured the American imagination for as long as Stalin and his Kremlin successors. Perceptive British historian Peter Boyle sees America's Soviet policy resulting from "American political culture as much as concern with U.S. national security." In this milieu, ideological zeal and emotion have proven as crucial as rational calculations of security based on Soviet military capabilities.[11]

Russian-Genre Films

The scant research exploring a link between Hollywood films about Russians and America's foreign policy has focused on the World War

II era. Its main conclusion is that World War II movies were influenced by a combination of political pressure applied by Washington and the studios' desire to appear patriotic while making money: doing well while doing good.[12] This seems understandable. As for wartime political pressure, America found itself in an all-out war for survival. And just as Washington mobilized America's military resources, it mobilized industry to the national cause, the film industry included. Hollywood studios are very big businesses, not to be confused with the United Way or other philanthropic organizations, since the profitability gremlin never eases its grip on studio executives.

But wartime film production constitutes a single-case scenario. The relationship between film and American policy in other periods proves far more resistant to explanation. As the course of world events often snaked through unexpected turns, the policies emanating from both Washington and Moscow became characterized by abrupt shifts. So too did Tinseltown's films. Thus, to understand how Hollywood's Russian-genre films follow the flag—and why they vary from season to unique season—we must know when the flag was headed where, and why. At the end of the day, while films surely serve as escapist entertainment, they also represent rich cultural artifacts, revealing more about their times than their creators consciously realize.[13]

Concerning film criticism, one caveat seems necessary. Whereas most film critics embrace single films of quality, this study looks to a broader message inherent in a set of films: their attitudinal center of gravity. This highlights plot, which in Martin Scorsese's opinion dwells near the core of America's national cinema. He recalls "being reared on American films, which means the story and narrative. In most cases, everything is at the service of the narrative."[14] We take Scorsese's theme and repeat it like a celluloid mantra.

Linguistic Liberties

The nature of our subject suggests a few linguistic ground rules. Russians were officially described by Soviet ideology as but one of fifteen major nationality groups living in fifteen Socialist republics making up the Soviet Union. However, the truth was much less egalitarian. In the Soviet period, like imperial Russia of the Romanov tsars before it, Russia dominated the union. It constituted 75 percent of the landmass of the Soviet Union, and remains the world's largest country, spanning eleven time zones.[15] Russians, as a people, comprised half the population of the Soviet Union. More importantly, however, they controlled the social, political, and economic life of the country as denizens of the heartland. More than 120 languages were spoken in the country, but Russian was required in all schools, party functions, and official communications.[16]

The line between Russians as a distinct ethnic group and Russia as a pseudonym for the Soviet Union is blurred in American cinema. Most films treat all ethnic groups as Russians, with a rare Ukrainian or Byelorussian tossed in.[17] For these reasons, we often use the term "Russians" when we ought to employ the more technical term, "Soviets."[18] Likewise, the United States frequently is referred to as "America."

While assessing the aesthetic value of Russian-genre films is not our main goal, a simple reality cannot be avoided: some are good, a few are great, while many others will remain forever stinkers. Nevertheless, our rating system addresses not film quality, but point of view. The categories identify favorable (FAV), middling (MID), and critical (CRI) attitudes toward Russians and Soviet society.[19]

Methodological note: All films were screened for this project except a few early marginal films (identified in filmography). For these, we rely on written screenplays from the New York State Motion Picture Archive, the world's largest such collection, and on print reviews. Films in this book depict Russians as protagonists or express views about the U.S.S.R. and its citizens. British or British-American ventures widely distributed in the U.S. (such as James Bond movies), are included, but not documentary films.

Our main interest is in the product of the film industry rather than the creative intentions of writers and directors. Nevertheless, we address the input side of films to provide context and depth for important pictures. Although sporadic and time bound, box-office figures are discussed for successful pictures; major award winners are also identified. We use the concept of hindsight bellwether films to identify two or three important films typifying each era of Soviet-American relations.

The great majority of movies fit comfortably into their respective eras. Since it is not unusual for two years to elapse between the conception and the release of a movie, the issue of lag time raises interesting questions. Most relevant to us is how a film meshes with the national mood upon its release rather than how it was seen at its inception. Also, since it is the center of gravity of many films that we seek, a rare lack of fit for a specific picture becomes less meaningful.

Acknowledgments

Finishing a book can seem a bit like exiting from purgatory, given its repetitive rituals. Fortunately, angels assigned to this project arrived in three waves: inspirational, editorial, and logistical. Creative catalysts included Peter Boyle, Mark Carnes, Robert Dallek, Sam Keen, Peter Makuck, Sophia Peterson, Peter Rollins, and John Stoessinger. Uniquely entertaining among inspirational forces was Oscar Homolka, the late character actor who enlivened six Russian-genre films.

Our efforts benefited greatly from the editorial eyes of Arthur Barbeau, Alice Javersak, Ann Levine, Virgil Peterson, and David Thomas. Research logistics provided unexpected zigs and zags, and we owe debts of gratitude to Clyde Campbell, Jennifer Cross, Robert Fyne, Ed Jacobs, David Javersak, Rosey Miller, and Allan Ramsey. Terri Geeskin, stills archivist at the Museum of Modern Art, assisted in selecting photographs.

The West Virginia Humanities Council and West Liberty State College Foundation provided crucial summer research fellowships. Special thanks go to Linda Strada, not only for patience and support, but for research leads to which only librarians seem privy. We sincerely appreciate the professionalism and good cheer of the helpful individuals comprising Scarecrow Press. For any mistake of fact or judgment? It was the other guy—the one with six letters in his last name.

Chapter One

1933–1940: Ambivalence

Metro-Goldwyn-Mayer and director Ernst Lubitsch could not have found a better location for the final scene of *Ninotchka* (1939) than Istanbul. This legendary city of intrigue—belonging to neither East nor West—provides the cinematic neutral space in which love can bridge the political divide. Here, in one passionate embrace, *Ninotchka*'s central characters, the once stiff Soviet woman loyal only to the Revolution, and her opposite, the suave nobleman and borderline libertine, the antithesis of a revolutionary ideologue, can sweep aside barriers of class and doctrine. Both Stalin and the free market be damned. What really counts is that two lovers finally merge as one.

The denouement of *Ninotchka* unwinds simply enough. Ministry of Trade official Nina Yakushova, "Ninotchka," arrives in Istanbul to investigate the actions of three bumbling Soviet trade emissaries from whom Moscow has not heard in some time. When Ninotchka meets with the three, who else should be present but Count Leon D'Algout? She had fallen in love with this suave raconteur during an earlier trade mission in Paris. Once back in Moscow, she tried to put him out of her mind. As the two now talk, Leon not only reaffirms his love for Ninotchka but also details his battle with the unfeeling Soviet bureaucracy, which thwarted his every effort to be at her side.

> Leon. [*Referring to Soviet red tape*] Trying to keep me away from you! It couldn't be done. Naturally I couldn't go on forever punching passport officials in the nose [*as he tried to get into Russia*]—but I found a way didn't I? Darling, I had to see you. I wrote and wrote but all my letters came back.

1

Ninotchka. The one I got they wouldn't let me read. [*Carried away by emotion*] It began, "Ninotchka, my darling," and ended, "Yours, Leon." [Revealing total government censorship]

Leon. [*With great feeling and sincerity*] I won't tell you what came between . . . I'll prove it. It will take a long time, Ninotchka . . . at least a lifetime.

[*Ninotchka is torn. She must choose between two loves, a man and a country. She knows what she wants, but it is painful to embrace one and forego the other.*]

Ninotchka. But Leon, I am only here for a few days.

Leon. If you don't stay with me, I'll have to continue my fight. I'll travel wherever Russian commissions are. I'll turn them all into Buljanoffs, Iranoffs, and Kopalskis [i.e., *the three trade officials seduced by the West into opening a restaurant*] The world will be crowded with Russian restaurants. I'll de-populate Russia. Once you saved your country by going back [*with money to feed starving peasants*]. This time you can save it by staying here.

Ninotchka. Well, when it is a choice between my personal interest and the good of my country, how can I waiver? No one shall say Ninotchka was a bad Russian. [*Spoken with tongue-in-cheek irony suggesting disjunction between words and deeds*]

[*Leon takes her in his arms, they kiss*]

Leon. Darling![1]

[*Fade to black. The end.*]

This "love conquers all" film-ending conversation exudes playful romanticism. It also does what American-Soviet relations, despite a hopeful beginning, failed to do: cement a strong, lasting relationship. On celluloid Leon and Ninotchka would share what the Soviets and westerners were unable to achieve during the 1930s. America, for all its sympathy with the struggles of the Russian people, could not put aside barriers of mistrust cemented by ideological, diplomatic, and cultural differences. Neither in darkened theaters nor in Washington's corridors of power did relations with the Soviet Union rank high on the list of pressing American issues. Coping with a sense of national drift and hopelessness, the twin legacies of the economic collapse during the Dirty Thirties, remained the singular national priority.

A Sanguine Franklin Roosevelt

In March of 1933, America took a leap of faith; it placed its trust in the promises of a former New York governor to accomplish what had eluded others—cranking up a stalled economy and returning the American dream to Americans. A lost nation held its breath as newly elected Democratic president Franklin Roosevelt took the oath of office. Reading his political compass, FDR intoned that America had nothing to fear but fear itself and attacked the mood of deep despair and grinding poverty that had become the lot of millions. And some dared hope that, just perhaps, Roosevelt could lead America to the promised land, which had eluded the now banished Republicans. But not all looked to Roosevelt with hope. Some feared he would unleash a whirlwind of radical reform, toss aside the existing social structure, and replace it with a new collectivist order.

Far-fetched as it seems today, even while many hoped for an economic miracle, others worried about a social revolution. Roosevelt delivered neither. Instead of a miracle he offered experimentation. In place of social revolution he provided federal intervention. But to the many millions of Americans convinced that something needed to be done, he represented action. The problems of America were too large, the pain of its people too great, for the state to stand around with its hands in its pockets, waiting for conditions to turn around by themselves. It was time for government to put the nation on the right track; and if its efforts did not work, it would be time to try something else. The only way to find out whether something worked was to try it. During his chaotic first term in office, FDR licensed so many innovative experiments that some were convinced he intended to transform America three letters at a time—WPA, NRA, CCC, TVA.

Roosevelt's initial focus remained fixed on the domestic front. He was comfortable there, and, besides, the nation's most pressing problems resided there. A party man through and through, FDR knew how to manage Democratic party machinery, which worked well for him. He had far less interest and experience in foreign affairs. But neither was he blind to the possibility that international trade initiatives could further his domestic agenda. And for a president who wanted, above all, to put Americans back to work, any untapped market for American goods seemed worth pursuing. More immediately interested in economics than ideology, FDR eyed the possibility of increased exports and reopened diplomatic relations with the Soviet Union. To the pleasure of liberals who had long advocated normalizing relations, Franklin Roosevelt extended diplomatic recognition to the Bolshevik government on 16 November 1933. Expectations of Russo-American cooperation mounted rapidly, then fell just as quickly.

Washington's Russians

For those who lobbied FDR to open relations with the Soviet government, the welcome prospect of increased trade was not the only potential reward. While Russia looked to American businessmen like a wide-open (albeit exotic) market, Moscow was also a potential security partner. Although they were obsessed with domestic problems, it was becoming harder for Americans to ignore the bellicose sounds coming from the expansionist regimes in Berlin and Tokyo. Talk of formal alliances against Germany and Japan may have struck most Americans as premature, yet liberals argued that room existed for discussing possible strategic options with the Soviets.

A smaller group of Americans wished to build bridges to the Soviet Union for more ideological reasons. The American left included some strident believers who viewed the Soviet system as a hopeful model, latching onto its vaunted egalitarian ethos as a potential alternative to the harsh realities of capitalism without safety nets in Depression era America. While most would eventually become disillusioned, in the early 1930s many dared hope that America might learn from the Soviet socialist experiment.

Ephemeral Optimism

The optimistic new era in American-Soviet relations faded fast, as initial hopes for cooperation soon gave way to suspicion and verbal sparring. The slide from the apex of recognition in 1933 to the nadir of the Molotov-Von Ribbentrop Pact of 1939 was marked by one unresolved dispute after another. Underlying it all, a deep-seated mistrust of the Soviet system existed in the corridors of American power, contributing to a sense of inertia and ambivalence. This unease was reciprocated in kind. The experience of America's first ambassador to the Soviet Union, William Bullitt, exemplified America's nosedive into disillusionment. He arrived in Moscow in 1934, filled with enthusiasm and confidence. Bullitt hoped to oversee the construction of a new American embassy in the Soviet capital as a tangible sign of good will. The Russians, however, frustrated his plans at every turn.

Neither Bullitt nor his staff came prepared for the gray Soviet lifestyle. The usually pampered Western diplomatic corps found creature comforts in very short supply. What was available was poor in quality, overpriced, or available only on the black market. Americans came to know the black market well, especially the black market in currency. The inflated official value of the ruble forced American diplomats to smuggle currency into the country. There was one other problem that discomfited officials quickly learned about—Soviet xenophobia made spying on the private lives of diplomats a fact of daily life. To remain positive about the Soviet Union was difficult for diplomats who were constantly tailed by Soviet agents.[2]

Bullitt's greatest frustration sprang from his inability to gain Soviet cooperation in resolving the first item on his list of American grievances against the Soviets: repayment of tsarist debts. The Soviet regime simply refused to honor any financial claim against the old tsarist government. When Roosevelt hastily reached an agreement to recognize the Soviet Union, he believed he had reached a "gentleman's agreement" with Soviet Foreign Minister Maxim Litvinov on debt repayments, but Roosevelt was wrong. What he took to be Soviet agreement to pay, the Soviets understood as an agreement to talk about paying. And for all the talk, the Soviets had no intention of paying tsarist debts to the United States or anyone else, using the ambiguous language of the Roosevelt-Litvinov understanding to cover their intransigence. FDR felt betrayed. Ambassador Bullitt was so incensed over the Soviet refusal to settle the debt issue that he sent a "stinging message of rebuke" to the Soviet government and reduced American embassy staff in protest.[3] These protests accomplished nothing except to further erode Bullitt's already fading confidence in Soviet intentions.

What of trade? After all, if any overriding rationale existed for opening relations with the Soviet Union, it was to forge trade links. This too proved a disappointment. Trade became tied to the unresolved debt problem when the 1934 Johnson Act forbade American credits and loans to countries that had defaulted on American loans. Furthermore, since the Soviet ruble was not a convertible currency on international money markets, long-term bartering arrangements were required for any trade with the Soviets. Bartering proved difficult to negotiate and, together with the unavailability of credits, made trade almost impossible to organize. Nor were the Soviets prepared to make much effort in this regard. Soviet state monopoly over trade meant that those few American businessmen who persisted despite these problems confronted the daunting Stalinist bureaucracy; even the most patient capitalists eventually drowned in the sea of red tape that Soviet authorities seemed either incapable or not interested in bridging.

But perhaps these structural problems were moot. The reality was that in spite of early hopes, little Soviet money existed to buy American goods and even less American consumer demand existed for Soviet products. Although a 1935 agreement had extended "most favored nation" status to the Soviets, by the late 1930s, levels of trade plunged well below those of the 1920s. Nor did diplomatic relations increase one-on-one American-Soviet contacts. Just the opposite. Threatened by the prospect of an inflow of alien ideas, Stalin slammed shut the door to the outside world and the trickle of American tourism ground to a halt. Citizen contacts ended along with economic relations.

Public Perceptions

Whatever sympathy Americans felt for the Soviet Union when FDR came to power quickly faded. Opinion polls revealed growing mistrust of the Soviets and a failure of Stalinist propaganda to attract any more than a small—if dedicated—band of sympathizers in the United States. But these sympathizers generated concern beyond their numbers. While Moscow had pledged not to spread revolutionary propaganda in America, the Soviets continued to expand such efforts in the 1930s via their international arm, the Comintern, and through the small but active American Communist Party. In 1935, following the "popular front" strategy cobbled together at the Seventh Congress of the Comintern, the ACP launched an outreach program aimed at American institutions, hoping to use a common front to infiltrate in the manner of the "Trojan horse."[4]

But if the popular front was designed to attract American attention, it was the horror of Stalin's brutal purges that most gripped the American imagination. Widely covered by the American press, the purges reshaped American attitudes. Not that opinion of the purges was uniform. Some conservatives reveled in Comrade Ivan's pain, portraying it as the natural consequence of collectivist experimentation and warning that Roosevelt was heading in the same direction. Others, including some liberals who had been grateful to the Soviet Union for supporting Republican Spain in the civil war that erupted in 1936, "were still shaken by press revelations of the purges."[5] In the end, talk of a common front floundered on the rocks of home grown Stalinist repression.

Only the most doctrinaire remained unmoved by the spectacle of three Soviet "show trials" in 1936, 1937, and 1938. Most were shocked by press reports of the carefully orchestrated public trials, but few grasped the nature of these trials: a systematic effort by Stalin to eliminate every last vestige of independent thought among political, economic, technical, creative, and military elites. Nevertheless, what Americans read in the daily press seemed bad enough. It eroded most remaining sympathy for the Soviet Union and caused many to question the motives of the ACP.

The ultimate act of Kremlinesque deceit, in American eyes, came toward the end of the decade. Even many of those who continued to sympathize with the Soviet experiment were jolted by the unilateral Soviet absorption of the Baltic states, the unprovoked invasion of democratic Finland, and, most of all, the Nazi-Soviet nonaggression pact. On 3 May 1939 Stalin fired the moderate Litvinov as foreign minister and appointed Vyacheslav Molotov. The move signaled a strategic shift in Soviet policy. As far as Stalin was concerned, no deal remained to be made with the West that would benefit Moscow. Other ways must be sought to secure Soviet borders in the event of another German war. Stalin took an unprecedented step. He opened the door to accommodation with his sworn enemy, Nazi Germany. It took Molotov and Germany's Von Ribbentrop less than three months to conclude a nonaggression pact. Hitler, knowing he would avoid war on two fronts, at least temporarily, relied on his "Unholy Alliance" with Stalin to launch World War II, invading Poland on 1 September 1939.

What was in the pact for the Kremlin? It should not be supposed that Moscow forged a deal with the Nazi devil except as a last resort. Stalin knew only too well that if war exploded on his western front, his was ill-prepared to take on the Germans. Furthermore, Stalin believed that the western democracies secretly wanted exactly such a war: Germany and the Soviet Union having a go at one another, with the West counting casualties. The Soviets needed to put off war with Germany, or, at the very least, to build strategic advantage for the confrontation with Germany that might be coming. Stalin had gutted the officer corps from top to bottom, and it would take some time to restructure an effective fighting machine. The wily Georgian needed time and strategic depth. He hoped the nonaggression pact would buy both, at least long enough to give the Nazis second thoughts about taking on the massive Soviet Union.

A secret protocol in the treaty specified that within two weeks of any German attack on Poland, the Soviets would move in to claim their partitioned section of eastern Poland. Stalin would also take the Baltic states of Lithuania, Latvia, and Estonia as well as part of Rumania. A fortnight after Germany's invasion of Poland and the British and French declarations of war on Germany, the Soviets claimed their territorial prize. Emboldened by his acquisitions and hoping to firm up his northwestern flank, Stalin also ordered an attack on Finland in November 1939. The Finns—buoyed by a strong American condemnation of Soviet aggression—fought courageously against larger forces and received 100 million dollars in aid from America. When Finland took its case to the League of Nations, the United States worked with the League toward expulsion of the Soviet Union, and on 2 December 1939 President Roosevelt declared a "moral embargo" against the Soviets.

Vagueness in Roosevelt's Soviet Policy

FDR's Russian policy resulted in few positive gains and was marred by many unresolved disputes. But at least one prestigious observer believes that Roosevelt's many foreign policy critics fail to appreciate the "constraints under which he had to work in foreign affairs."[6] Things might have been different if FDR would have had a freer hand to deal with the Soviet Union, but alas, he did not. Proponents of isolationism dominated Congress throughout the 1930s. They resisted and resented every foreign policy initiative that might either commit the United States or enhance the foreign policy role of the president. Even a suggestion that FDR might try to circumvent the draconian neutrality laws led two congressmen to publicly threaten FDR with impeachment. If not intimidated by these threats, the president dared not ignore them. Relations with Moscow were less important for FDR than winning congressional approval for New Deal domestic programs. Best to avoid battling with Congress over foreign policy, since the president needed all the energy he could muster in coming battles over contentious domestic issues.

During his second administration, however, with the Nazi threat looming larger, FDR turned more and more to convincing the Congress and the public that Germany constituted a singular danger to world order. Holding fast to this view, he staked the allied future on bringing Stalin into the anti-Nazi camp. Thus, while many demanded that the Soviets be shunned or even punished for their foreign policy adventures, Roosevelt, the activist in domestic affairs, seemed willing to passively tolerate Soviet excesses. In retrospect, some observers consider this policy less passive than inconsistent. The oscillations in FDR's foreign policy are regarded by his detractors as signs of confusion—not diplomatic prudence. One critic lamented Roosevelt's "hopscotch mind," or his readiness to abandon unpopular positions for ones more in tune with public opinion.[7] FDR, some charge, forever bounced between Woodrow Wilson's moralism and Theodore Roosevelt's pragmatism, without remaining faithful to either. Still others believe that FDR gave ear to too many liberal nonexperts including his wife, Eleanor, Harry Hopkins, and Joseph Davies, while shutting out more hard-line Soviet specialists in the State Department like Loy Henderson, Charles Bohlen, and George Kennan.

More moderate assessments of FDR's policy refuse to equate his passivity on the Soviet Union with incompetence. They believe that Roosevelt's cautious Soviet policy was warranted by the circumstances. For example, they argue that Roosevelt rejected domestic political pressure to break off relations with the Soviet Union because he hoped to nurture a Soviet "counterweight" to the larger and more immediate Nazi threat, not because he was soft on the Russians.[8] By this reading, the president was not indecisive or blind to the excesses of the Soviet Union as much as he was a juggler, attempting to prop up a faltering anti-Nazi war effort through innovations like the extension of lend-lease assistance, first to the British and then to the Soviets.

The bold and imaginative innovator of the domestic New Deal, leading public opinion rather than reacting to it, FDR nevertheless did not cast a very long shadow as the prudent but cautious foreign policy statesman. Yet his supporters argue well that the president's steady approach represented a reasonable response to a chaotic international environment. His single-minded conviction that Nazi Germany represented the greater danger enabled him to avoid the potential mistake of painting America into a lonely corner by acting precipitately against the Soviet Union in the international arena. He also knew the American people. His sixth sense told him how far and how fast he could push public opinion in a isolationist era. In the end, if Roosevelt was a juggler, he was a cunning juggler who always kept his eye on the ball.

Sources of Policy Ambivalence

Thus, in spite of an isolationist Congress, America's Soviet policy in the 1930s increasingly mirrored FDR's personal worldview. FDR instinctively felt torn between his sympathy for progressive activism and countervailing deep-seated doubts about the Soviet system, doubts shared by most of the American public. As the prime mover of New Deal liberalism, Roosevelt initially hoped that the Soviet experiment might evolve into a humane social alternative. However, he would not move beyond the bounds of public opinion, and Russia's leadership scored low marks among Americans. In fact, polls taken in the mid-thirties showed that Stalin was more disliked than Hitler. FDR dared not slough off this distaste or venture far ahead of American opinion on the Soviet Union. He knew that neither Congress nor the public could be counted on to support an assertive foreign policy; the very era itself seemed genetically tilted toward isolationism. Although large and heterogeneous, America has frequently enjoyed a consensus of opinion on foreign policy issues, which only serves to highlight the differences between Roosevelt and the Congress concerning the Soviets during the 1930s.

How did all this play itself out in American-Soviet relations? For one thing, it rendered FDR unable to aggressively pursue a collective security agreement with the Soviet Union, despite early signals from Moscow that it would welcome movement in this direction. Americans, FDR knew, would have none of it. A second reason for Roosevelt's ambivalence was his well-known tendency to distrust experts and to depend on irregular sources of advice. On matters related to the Soviets the pragmatic FDR leaned heavily upon a few trusted confidantes who proved more idealistic than tough-minded. As a result, he discounted more hard-headed critical assessments emanating from the State Department.

The president's need to balance American grievances with Russia against the imperative of shoring up anti-Nazi forces represents a final consideration. This was neither easy nor universally popular on the domestic scene. Stalin's distrust of liberal democratic values and his ultimate rejection of open dialogue with the West created problems for Roosevelt. And even as Generalissimo Stalin mistrusted the motives of Western leaders, fearing they were setting up the Soviets for unilateral war with Germany, the president's conviction that Germany was the greater threat to both American security and world peace convinced him to leave open a scenario including Stalin as a partner in the allied cause. This often dictated a "look the other way" response, contributing to ambivalence in American policy and infuriating Roosevelt's critics. Unwilling to sidle up too closely to the Russian bear but unable to ignore its place in any concerted struggle against Germany, FDR juggled.

Not trusting the West, Stalin played for time. As the decade closed, he relied on the nonaggression pact with the Nazis. When war broke out, both giants were ephemerally sheltered from the fray—the United States behind its wall of neutrality legislation and the Soviet Union by its misbegotten nonaggression treaty with Hitler. However, neither American neutrality nor the Unholy Alliance would hold back the tide of war swirling them into a whirlpool of common cause. But that remained in the future as the decade closed.

Hollywood's Golden Age

At first blush, nothing seems further from American foreign policy than the tinsel of 1930s Hollywood, which appeared in sharp relief against the era's backdrop of international upheaval and devastating economic depression. Both Tinseltown's films and American policy were greatly affected by the prevailing fears of the American mind-set, but Hollywood was not decimated by the Great Depression of the 1930s. It thrived. Why was this the case? The answer is somewhat counterintuitive: precisely *because* social conditions crumbled so badly in the thirties, fantasy became a necessity and Hollywood cornered the market on fantasy. The public had a "thirst for reassurance," and Hollywood possessed the necessary elixir.[9] Tinseltown represented the essence of escapism, and its "bijous were darkened havens against the storm outside."[10]

Contemporary America takes movies for granted. With video rentals available in every gigaplex, films have lost some of their magic. This disillusionment makes it more difficult to appreciate the centrality of movie theaters to the cultural life of America in the 1930s. Rather than cutting expenses, Hollywood responded to the depression by lavishly producing big-budget escapist films, which the studios found to be a better financial investment than several riskier low-budget films.[11]

Hollywood in the 1930s was dominated by the big studios—particularly Metro-Goldwyn-Mayer, Paramount, and Warner Brothers.[12] Each major studio functioned like a self-sufficient city. Each produced films in sound and color, and each boasted an entire stable of stars constituting a new breed of American idol. Hard-boiled loners like Humphrey Bogart, James Cagney, Edward G. Robinson, and Clark Gable ruled as male leads. Bogart in particular symbolized a popular ambivalence toward society and authority. The leading female counterparts, including such stars as Greta Garbo, Marlene Dietrich, Jean Harlow, and Carole Lombard, conveyed a new "morally ambivalent attitude towards sex."[13]

All of this shaped what is regarded as Hollywood's Golden Age. Movie critic Judith Crist, who came of age in the 1930s, refers to the decade as "the worst of times in the real world and the best of times in Shadowland."[14] Film served as a unifying national beacon for the ninety million Americans faithfully flocking to the movies every week. While delayed gratification was forced on much of America during the Great Depression, this did not include films. By 1935, over 75 percent of theaters enticed customers into the seats with double features. The B movie, or bottom of the bill, ran just over an hour. Studios churned out Bs at the amazing rate of one per week. Creativity became a luxury in the headlong rush to crank out the quota of product with formulaic patterns, low budgets, and fresh actors. The end of one production often ran right over into the next. Comedies, lavish musicals, swashbuckling adventure films, and historical dramas filled the screens of countless movie theaters in a seemingly endless stream. Among them appeared a number of films depicting Russians.

Ambivalent Cinematic Russians

Hollywood's Russian-genre films during the 1930s, like America's Soviet policy, have a suspicious and mildly critical streak about them, but, above all else, they exhibit ambivalence. As relations with the Soviet Union deteriorated throughout the decade, cinematic unease about the Russians rose. The American psyche, nevertheless, refused to make up its mind about the Soviet Union or the Russians in any way not readily reversible. Even films finding fault with the Soviet system failed to cast the blanket of negativism so as to cover the Russian people as a whole. Some Russians, the salt of the earth, were allowed to have heart even as their political system appeared heartless.

The period's movies portray Russians in a punchless way that hindsight illuminates like a lighthouse. Suspicion and cautious criticism of Soviet excesses, tempered by ambivalence toward the Russian people, comes across in a variety of ways. Hollywood avoided deciding whether it liked Russians or not; instead, it dealt with them in light romantic comedies, juxtaposing good and bad Russian characters, submitting them to massive personal metamorphoses or using vague endings devoid of opinion.

Referring to *Public Deb Number 1* (1939), one critic expresses a frustration that could serve as the motif for the entire epoch: "This is what has us stymied: which side is this picture on?"[15] The uncertainty of filmic images portraying Russians fits the sense of "escapism" and "evasion of politics" generally characteristic of Hollywood's 1930s pictures.[16] Despite great public controversy about the Soviets and despite the unease over the American-Soviet relationship, films of the 1930s leave the viewer uncertain as to how Americans should feel about Russians. The overall center of gravity of these pictures is middling and noncommittal. Only two films are on balance favorable to the Soviet Union or the Russian people, and a very few are openly critical. The great majority keep both feet firmly planted on both sides of the fence.

Consciously or unconsciously, the message and style of Hollywood's Russian-genre films of the thirties underscore a mood of avoidance. One common convention consists of using light romantic comedies that gently criticize the Soviet system to deliver the subtext message: neither the criticism nor the Soviet Union should be taken too seriously.[17] Another well-worn motif is the personal metamorphosis. Like Scrooge's conversion to goodness on the night before Christmas, Russian characters who are exposed to the light of Western experience change before the viewer's eyes. Filmgoers might well ask, Will the *real* Russians please stand up?[18]

A final convention embraced by Hollywood is the romantic melodrama. As audiences had already come to expect from Hollywood, "love conquers all," despite obstacles that only Tinseltown could dream up.[19] Sexism is also laid on with a trowel. In film after film, the tough and ideologically committed Russian female melts like butter in the embrace of some Westerner's arms. In the tussle between Marx and marriage, marriage always wins out. The relevant subtext message reads that ideology is only skin deep. Given the right inducements, such as a handsome American or reasonable facsimile, Russian women become starry-eyed romantics.[20] Apolitical plots pervade most Russian-genre movies. The Soviet Union represents more of a costume-laden photo opportunity than an ideological haven. Good Russians and bad Russians countervail one another, but the good win out in the end.

Bellwether Films

Each era produces several bellwether films that provide an understanding of how films portrayed the Soviet Union and its people. These pictures are not necessarily produced early in the period and their plots are not recycled. Rather, these films are bellwether films because when viewed with their contemporaries years later they stand out as important films that typify the era. For the thirties, the hindsight bellwether films are *Ninotchka* and *Tovarich*.

Film buffs commonly refer to the "Lubitsch touch."[21] Exactly what the term means remains elusive, but whatever it means, Ernst Lubitsch's *Ninotchka* (1939) displays its playful mockery of the Soviet system as balanced against an embrace of some of its likable citizens. The German-born Lubitsch was fortunate to settle in at Paramount Studios where his creative juices were allowed to flow freely. Founded earlier by Adolph Zukor, Paramount was profitable and was the only major studio in the 1930s not dominated by a traditional studio boss, providing Lubitsch artistic freedom not possible in other studios. In that milieu he felt comfortable in bringing artists such as Rouben Mamoulian and Josef von Sternberg to the studio, giving it a decidedly European flavor, as did the presence of his influential head designer Hans Dreier, formerly of Germany's Universum-Film AG (known as UFA), which had challenged Hollywood before the Nazi era. But Lubitsch's highly successful transition from Europe to Hollywood was most facilitated by his precise, planned (almost programmed) manner of filmmaking. As he put it, "How vital it is for every scene, every action, to be detailed down to the very last raising of an eyelid."[22]

An admitted admirer of Greta Garbo, Lubitsch had long wanted to make a film with the Swedish star. His opportunity arrived in 1939 in a movie that Garbo personally campaigned for. In her mid-1930s films, Garbo had "drowned, crashed to her death, perished before a firing squad, thrown herself under a train, and expired of tuberculosis."[23] Enough of death. Threatening to return to her homeland if not allowed to star in a comedy, Garbo showed particular interest in a promising light Hungarian script about a dedicated communist woman finding love in Paris. By the late thirties Garbo had become one of the giants of Hollywood stardom. Rising above humble origins, Garbo studied at the Royal Dramatic Theater Academy in Stockholm, where she developed a professional and personal relationship with director Mauritz Stiller. Both were brought to Hollywood by Metro-Goldwyn-Mayer supremo Louis B. Mayer. While Stiller could not make it in the Hollywood system, Garbo achieved greatness. The shy and eccentric Garbo completed twenty-seven films, retiring three years after *Ninotchka* at only thirty-six years of age.[24]

Louis B. Mayer opposed casting Garbo in such an untried comedy role, especially since the topic of communism was "repugnant to him." Mayer was accustomed to having his way and relented on Garbo starring in *Ninotchka* only when Paramount agreed to lend the masterful Lubitsch to direct the film. Backed by a close association with Chase National Bank, M-G-M's three parts had been consolidated by New York tycoon Marcus Lowe. Under its corporate symbol of the roaring lion, M-G-M emerged as the richest, biggest, and most productive of the studios. However, Mr. Mayer epitomized filmmaking's constant tension between business and art. Although "an astute and ruthless businessman, Mayer was no artist." It was the frail but brilliant Irving Thalberg, not Mayer, who maintained the high level of sophistication at M-G-M. Despite dying at age thirty-seven from heart disease, the introverted Thalberg—called by some the "boy wonder"—exerted great aesthetic influence while at M-G-M.[25]

Once Mayer approved Garbo to star in *Ninotchka*, the Lubitsch-Garbo chemistry proved magical. Lubitsch's "flair for witty imagery gives his pictures a laconic and yet scintillating quality," and *Ninotchka* stands out as one of his best efforts.[26] It was praised by critics and rewarded with Academy nominations for best picture and best actress. Although regarded today as something of a cinematic classic, *Ninotchka* was not a major public hit in its day. None of the 1930s films about Russians were big money makers. But if it did not keep cash registers ringing, *Ninotchka* provided delightfully escapist entertainment and reflected many of the decade's avoidance contrivances by superficially satirizing the Soviet system while stroking some of its irresistible denizens.

Ninotchka is set in the exciting and romantic Paris of the 1920s, with its elegant bourgeois charms and colorful inhabitants, all of which are important to the film's seductive story line. The story begins as the Soviet Union has just experienced "another crop failure" and the government has dispatched three representatives to Paris in an effort to sell jewels to raise badly needed cash. The jewels were confiscated from prerevolutionary Grand Duchess Swana, who just happens to be an émigré living in Paris.

The trio of emissaries are harmless bumblers easily distracted by Parisian creature comforts. When their marketing mission gets waylaid in the cafes and bistros of Paris, the Kremlin sends a seasoned professional in the person of envoy extraordinaire Nina Yakushova (Greta Garbo) to bring the stalled negotiations to a favorable conclusion. Nina Yakushova, a doctrinaire Marxist and true believer, is a fish out of water in Paris. Contrasted with the soft charms of Paris, the Soviet envoy is tough as nails and exhibits all the subtlety of steel wool. But there is something about Nina that the Soviet system has repressed but not destroyed. As the movie audience knows full well, it is only a matter of time before the charms of Paris and Mr. Right combine to break through the Soviet agent's self-assured, intellectually cool, and emotionally detached veneer to reveal the beautiful, soft woman inside.

OK, everyone knows how the movie will end. The audience still enjoys watching the plot work itself out. No sooner does Nina Yakushova arrive in Paris to unload the jewels than the Grand Duchess Swana (Ina Claire) begins furtive machinations to recover her prerevolutionary property. Assisting is her debonair friend, French Count Leon D'Algout, played by Melvyn Douglas in a piece of ideal casting. The handsome Douglas excelled at playing dapper men-about-town, and Count Leon D'Algout is nothing if not a man-about-town.[27]

When Nina accidentally meets Leon, the two at first seem like fire and water, but the magical chemistry between them soon brings the plot to a quick boil. The cerebral Nina and the visceral Leon prove again—if proof is necessary—that screen opposites attract. At first Nina seems only curious about this man who is so different from any she has known in the Soviet Union. He is, she notes with cool dispassion, "an interesting subject of study" and "the unfortunate product of a doomed culture." Doomed culture or not, this is Paris à la Hollywood back lot, so you can bet your last croissant that destiny will bring Nina and Leon together.

It only takes one lingering kiss for everything to change, at least for Nina. In something well short of a Kafkaesque metamorphosis, Nina becomes Ninotchka, sourpuss begins smiling, introvert becomes spontaneous, ascetic becomes near hedonist, and hard-edged ideologue becomes light-headed romantic. A new woman is born.[28] Greta Garbo so luminously portrays Ninotchka and Melvyn Douglas so convincingly plays Count D'Algout that, in the darkened theater where almost every implausibility seems credible, this change comes as naturally as love itself. But the course of love is not always smooth. Ninotchka is still torn. What of the hunger of her people? What of the jewels for cash?

What of her own inner conflict? Duty calls. Ninotchka returns to Russia. But there is no unhappy ending for Leon and Ninotchka. Leon and the power of Hollywood love eventually resolve the problem of the jewels, the food shortage, and the constraints of socialist realism. The lovers are reunited. But for Ninotchka it is farewell to Russia, as she joins Leon in the West, where almost all Russian-genre happy endings occur.

Don't look to *Ninotchka* to reveal anything of the actual Soviet Union of the day. You will not find it. The famine, the state's need for cash, and even Nina's ideological commitment are not offered for audience reflection. They only serve as props to keep the story moving. The shallow quality of *Ninotchka* fits what Andrew Sarris describes as Lubitsch's interest in presenting characters who are little more than superficial and what Jean-Pierre Coursodon sees similarly as the famed director's "amused detachment" toward his main characters.[29]

And if the lead characters are one-dimensional, the image of the Soviet Union lacks even that. Indeed, *Ninotchka* carefully employs most of the 1930s movie conventions that were used to avoid making any commitment about the Russians one way or the other: personal metamorphosis, melodrama, light romantic comedy, and female defection. But no other movie of the era treats the controversial Soviet system so delicately. Rather than condemning or praising the Soviet system, it pokes fun at it—including Soviet repression and its bureaucracy—and the "political humor is fairly superficial."[30] In the wake of Stalin's well-publicized purges, an uneasy edge may well have accompanied audience laughter when Ninotchka exclaims that "the last mass trials were a great success; there will be fewer but better Russians."

But that is as close as Lubitsch gets to any hard-edged political message. At most, the film distinguishes between the excesses of the Soviet system and the humanity of individual Russians. *Ninotchka*'s essence coalesces around the idea that people are similar the world over "and decent enough at heart."[31] In fact, it is "so good-humored and toothless," remarks film historian Ted Sennett, that it is more of "an affectionate spoof than true satire."[32]

Like Ninotchka, *Tovarich* (1937) also uses personal metamorphosis, light romantic comedy, and mixed messages to sidestep taking a clear position about the Soviet Union or Russians. Adapted from a Broadway production, *Tovarich* emphasizes the comedic aspects of the original play.[33] *Tovarich* shares so many of the same plot markers as *Ninotchka* that one might think the two films had been written together. Once again we find down-at-the-heels former tsarist royalty in Paris squaring off against another batch of Soviet agents. There is the same Soviet famine and the same hope to use wealth from prerevolutionary Russia to feed the starving peasants. And, of course, there is another transmutation of the central Russian characters in a fablelike script. Also like *Ninotchka*, *Tovarich* is the product of a foreign-born director. Growing up in a middle-class family in Saint Petersburg, Anatole Litvak soaked up the city's rich cultural life, even managing to attend university during the revolution and civil war. He received a doctorate in 1921. Litvak worked briefly as assistant director in Leningrad's Nordkino studio but fled the postrevolutionary Soviet Union to Germany's UFA studio under mysterious circumstances in 1925. With the rise of Nazism in the early 1930s, Litvak, a Jew, escaped to Hollywood and Warner Brothers Studio.

Each major Hollywood studio created its own culture and catered to a special audience. It has been said that Metro made films for the middle class, Paramount for the upper class, and Warner Brothers for the working class; the latter was constantly forced to cut corners, leading to the nickname "cinema of poverty."[34] *Tovarich* conveys something of that feel. Warner Brothers provided Litvak, one of many excellent film directors who fled Nazism, with three major stars—Claudette Colbert, Charles Boyer, and Basil Rathbone—and the script for *Tovarich* adapted from a successful Jacques Deval play about White Russian refugees in Paris. Litvak did the rest.

Jack Warner, the youngest of the four Warner brothers and the only one born in North America, founded the studio that remained a Hollywood outsider for most of the 1920s. By the next decade the four brothers had become big players, which was a long way from New Castle, Pennsylvania, where their local theater charged a nickel in 1906 for three films, with Jack singing in between. Jack Warner was a scrapper who fought with everyone, including his top stars. Early innovations in sound technology and a series of lively musicals, especially those spectacular Busby Berkeley geometric patterns, also helped to create the WB image.

In *Tovarich*, the Grand Duchess Tatiana (Claudette Colbert) and her consort Prince Mikail Ouratieff (Charles Boyer) play exiled and poverty-stricken White Russian nobility living in Paris. Once masters of a large household, they are now reduced to working as servants in order to support themselves. They feel out of place in urbane, bustling, impersonal Paris and become easy prey to the machinations of unsavory commoners. Tatiana, as played sympathetically by Claudette Colbert, comes across as particularly impractical, romantic, and vulnerable. Somewhat spoiled and childlike early in the film, she gradually emerges as a mature, high-minded altruist. Her life is anything but easy. In the film's first minutes, she impulsively shoplifts vegetables from a market and is embarrassed when caught by a local gendarme, who is then convinced to release her by the understanding grocer. Charles Boyer's portrayal of the supportive Prince Mikail is similarly charming and high-minded.

The foil to these likable royal émigrés—underscoring the picture's mixed messages about Russian characters—is the scurrilous Soviet Commissar Gorotchenko, played by Basil Rathbone, described by one film historian as the "best all-round villain the movies ever had."[35] Commissar Gorotchenko's connection to the Ouratieffs reaches back to the turmoil of the 1917 revolution when Gorotchenko tortured the noble Mikail with lighted cigarettes and, as he puts it, "questioned Tatiana indelicately." Nevertheless, Basil Rathbone's Gorotchenko character is seen by a charitable critic as "not without a certain charm, in spite of his villainy."[36]

A sublime irony underscores the young couple's desperate financial situation: they control a four-hundred-billion-franc fortune in gold left to them in trust by the last tsar, Nicholas II, who intended to use it to resurrect the monarchy. Naturally, their noble bearing prohibits Tatiana and Mikail from touching a single franc, despite their humbled, plebeian circumstances. Enter the evil Gorotchenko. Despite the way in which their paths crossed earlier, Gorotchenko has the audacity to call on the Ouratieffs in Paris. With a request that is reminiscent of *Ninotchka*, he suggests that the Ouatieffs donate the tsarist fortune to feed millions of starving peasants in the motherland.

What to do? *Tovarich* oozes of moral dilemma. Should the young couple hold tight to the tsar's monarchist dream, or should they feed starving peasants, which may ensure the survival of the Soviet system? Both choices seem right, and both have regrettable consequences. Such ambivalence led one film historian to note that "Litvak's exceptional ability to carry political water on both shoulders has never been better."[37] While *Tovarich* offers muted criticism of Soviet society, like *Ninotchka*, it does so benignly enough for another critic to attribute a "sentimentally warm quality" to the film.[38] In the end, the Ouratieffs do the right thing: they spend the fortune to feed Russia's hungry.

The plot of *Tovarich*, like that of *Ninotchka*, seems little more than a vehicle for an "innocents abroad" comedy resulting in personal transformation of the weak into the strong. Under the light comedy there remains a mixed, ambivalent message about Russians. As caricatured by Hollywood, they are a passionate people, given to extemes of good and evil, innocence, and corruption. On one side of the celluloid appear characters like Gorotchenko who show no remorse whatever at using torture to further the cause of revolution. On the other side appear characters like Tatiana and Mikail, who are prepared to sacrifice their cherished monarchical hopes to feed starving Russian peasants. Altruism is filtered through knowledge that it will prop up the Soviet system and leave them in exile. Bottom line? It's hard to know what to make of these Russians.

Other Middling Films

Two other films, *Once in a Blue Moon* and *British Agent*, hit the same ambivalent note. Ben Hecht conceived the story, wrote the screenplay, then produced and directed *Once in a Blue Moon* (1936). Generally known as a witty but eccentric talent, Hecht wrote "about half of the most entertaining movies to come out of Hollywood."[39] Numerous light satirical comedies of the 1930s bear Hecht's imprint; still more seem modeled on his style. He also contributed to the final screenplay for *Gone With the Wind*. Although Hecht wrote more than one hundred screenplays, he directed only seven times.

Once in a Blue Moon fits with Paramount's image as a producer of comedy with a European twist.[40] Comedian Jimmy Savvo portrays sweet, innocent Gabbo the Great with Chaplinesque pathos. Gabbo the Great, an itinerant clown, gets caught up in the tumultuous Russian Civil War (1918–1921). Typical of 1930s pictures, the film's motif is innocent buffoonery, tinged around the edges with a light-hearted satirical tone. Trying to escape the violence of civil war, apolitical Gabbo the Great makes his way across Russia in a crudely painted circus wagon drawn by his loyal horse, history once again serving as a pretext for comedy rather than reflection. When he meets a fleeing aristocratic family, Gabbo offers his traveling show as cover. A madcap run for the border ensues.

The Bolsheviks are the heavies. At one point they arrest Gabbo and find counterfeit rubles with which he hopes to buy a house in Paris for the family's lovely daughter, his secret love, Princess Ilena (Edwina Armstrong). When the clown is unjustly imprisoned, his many fans mobilize an army of the country's children who unite to free him in a comic rescue. Later, the clown proves himself a hero when he rescues a band of White Army soldiers captured by the Bolsheviks. But Gabbo and his beloved, the daughter of the aristocrats, are accidentally separated, and all surely seems lost. But not to fear: the clown exhibits bravery reserved for the strongest of men, leading to his reunion with Ilena, his true love. Once again Hollywood avoids political statements, either profound or superficial. While *Once in a Blue Moon* plays out against the Russian Civil War, it is presented through the naive and apolitical eyes of Gabbo the Great. Although mildly endorsing the underdog, the Whites over the Reds, Ben Hecht still treats the events of the day as neutrally and as colorlessly as a children's summer camp. Critic Bosley Crowther attacked the film for not making a larger statement, but found Jimmy Savvo's comedic presence endearing.[41]

If Paramount avoided the political, Warner Brothers (First National) often embraced it. Considered the most socially conscious studio, it shared a natural affinity with the Democratic Party, while M-G-M leaned toward the Republicans. Michael Curtiz was a Warner director strongly identified with the "social problem film."[42] Despite never really mastering the English language, Curtiz made an incredible forty-four pictures during the 1930s.

In the case of *British Agent* (1934), the social problem—the Russian Revolution—gets hauled out as another improbable historical prop for love to conquer over. Of course, protagonists need to overcome major obstacles, the bigger the better. In *British Agent* the obstacle is the chaos of World War I, the Russian Revolution, and the tension created by incompatibile worldviews. Pulling this all together in one plot is no problem for director Michael Curtiz, considered so much a part of the studio system that film historian Jean-Pierre Coursodon believes Warner Brothers warrants status as "coauthor" of many Curtiz pictures.[43]

Rather than skirting Russian politics, the convoluted plot of *British Agent* dives in and makes a melodramatic mockery of it. *British Agent* begins with the eight-month struggle between the provisional government of Alexander Kerensky and its Bolshevik opposition led by V.I. Lenin; it ends with events surrounding the 1918 Treaty of Brest-Litovsk, which took the new Soviet Union out of the war against Germany. As the film opens, the Kerensky government expresses its commitment to keeping Russia in World War I, but Lenin's Bolsheviks want out.

The British government fears that a Russian withdrawal from the war would allow Germany to redeploy troops to the western front. On 7 November 1917 Kerensky's provisional government is ousted; Lenin takes power, handing the British a diplomatic headache. At first refusing to recognize Lenin's Soviet regime, the British have no ambassador in Moscow to plead for continued Russian involvement in the war. What can the British do under such circumstances? They can hastily recruit British businessman Stephen Locke (Leslie Howard)—who happens to be in Moscow at the time—as "unofficial emissary."

Stephen Locke's daunting and dangerous mission is nothing less than to persuade the Russians to stay in the war, or at least not sign a peace treaty with Germany. These great war and peace issues end up as mere contrivances around which the movie builds an unlikely love affair between the Oxford-educated Locke and a dark-eyed Slavic beauty named Elena (Kay Francis). Elena, a Bolshevik firebrand, first encounters Locke accidentally in a 1917 clash between the Bolsheviks and the forces of the provisional government. She has wounded a government soldier during the shooting and is helped to escape by a sympathetic Stephen Locke.

When Elena later encounters Stephen in a cafe, they talk and soon discover that they disagree over all things political. Elena's credentials, however, include more than mere Bolshevik revolutionary. She also serves as a spy for the Party and soon finds herself under orders to report on his activities. While their personal politics remain at odds, their hearts soon beat to the same rhythm. Their relationship flowers amidst danger and intrigue. When Elena is ordered to set up Stephen to be murdered, she must choose between their love and the Party. Tough choice, but her love for Stephen is stronger than her revolutionary zeal: she decides to die with her beloved rather than betray him.

They are saved at the last moment when a soft-hearted cinematic Lenin regains consciousness after a failed assassination attempt. His near-death experience has shown him the light. He orders "all political prisoners released" and "the terror stopped." Stephen and Elena are permitted to leave for England, and, to no one's surprise, live well thereafter. Unfortunately for Britain, Lenin does not oblige Stephen by staying in the war. Stephen may have lost the diplomatic war, but he won the battle of love. Critic Andre Sennwald sees the whole film as a loser. He understates the case, observing wryly that *British Agent* has a "vigorous melodramatic style."[44] Besides trivializing two revolutions, the World War, the role of Lenin and besides using all matters political as pawns for a love affair, *British Agent* underscores Hollywood's aversion toward politics and its ambivalence about Russians in the 1930s.

But lest you think you have heard enough about love conquering all, Russian-style, many other middling movies fit this useful mold. *After Tonight* (1933), an RKO Radio production based on a story by Jane Murfin and directed by George Archainbaud, features a demure and capable Russian spy named Carla (Constance Bennett). Set in World War I Austria immediately before the Russian Revolution, *After Tonight* finds the beautiful Carla, "an extraordinarily versatile Russian spy," assigned to steal vital information on Austrian war activities. Code-named agent K14, she works as a seamstress, cabaret singer, and nurse during the film, but her real talents lie in the use of invisible ink, secret jewelry compartments, and seductive womanly wiles to further her secret trade.[45]

Like so many other of Hollywood's Russian women, she turns to putty in the hands of the right man, in this case Austrian Captain Rudolph Ritter (Gilbert Roland). He meets Carla by accident and, unaware of her true identity, is smitten instantly. The plot follows a labyrinthine course, but in the end, war and politics cannot keep the lovers apart: Carla and Rudolph—Russian spy and Austrian patriot—blissfully united.

RKO had no patent on beautiful and versatile Russian spies. M-G-M found one of its own in Russian Countess Olga Mironova (Luise Rainer). And wouldn't you know it, in *The Emperor's Candlesticks* (1937), another lightweight story of intrigue, espionage, and hidden compartments, she finds love in the arms of a competing secret agent. Similar to *After Tonight*, this film has the two spies jockeying with one another across much of Europe before they end up where they belong: in the amorous embrace moviegoers seem to crave. *The Emperor's Candlesticks*, based on the book by Baroness Orczy, is directed by George Fitzmaurice, whose career included numerous silent films.

Let's not forget the plotline required to bring the would-be lovers together. The son of the Russian tsar, Grand Duke Peter (Robert Young), is kidnapped by a band of Polish nationalists demanding the release of Polish patriot Thaddeus Orlich, who is scheduled to be executed by the Russians in fifteen days. It's Orlich in exchange for the grand duke. But of course nothing works that easily. For their own reasons, both governments, Polish and Russian, want to find the grand duke before he is murdered, and so each assigns a top agent to the caper—handsome Polish baron Stephan Wolensky (William Powell) for the Poles and Countess Olga Mironova for Russia.

The action centers on finding a pair of trick candlesticks and the secret messages concealed in their hidden compartments. The hunt begins in Saint Petersburg, depicted in the film as "perfectly enchanting with snow falling in great, soft, Tchekovian flakes."[46] But the two competing agents have little time to appreciate the city. There is a grand duke to be rescued. Soon it is spy versus spy in a dash across Europe in search of the candlesticks and their secret message. The pursuit of the candlesticks takes the two through a series of farcical encounters in Budapest, Paris, and finally London, where out of necessity they agree to pool their resources to buy the all-important candlesticks at an auction.

Of course, they end up not only with the candlesticks but with one another as well. Affairs of state take a backseat—the rumble seat—to romance, and all ends amorously. Grand Duke Peter is released unharmed, Orlich (remember Orlich?) is pardoned by a grateful tsar, the spies find one another, and everyone miraculously avoids the looming disasters that earlier seemed inevitable.

The change of heart that transforms enemies into lovers is similar to the leitmotif of personal transformation in two other films with

Russian characters. Both are morality plays in which good conquers evil. Paramount's *We Live Again* (1934) was directed by Russian-born Rouben Mamoulian, an innovative though erratic talent who once confided to critic Andrew Sarris that "rhythm and poetic stylization" were his constant objectives.[47] Mamoulian was nearly born into the theater. His mother was president of the Armenian Theater during his childhood in Tiflis. He attended school in Paris, went to Moscow University and then on to London, embarking on a directing career shortly after the Russian Revolution. He is best remembered in Hollywood for helping break the sound barrier in early films like *Applause* (1929) and *Love Me Tonight* (1932), and later for the first feature film in Technicolor. *We Live Again* fails to match his more memorable efforts.

Set in pre-Revolutionary nineteenth-century Russia, *We Live Again* depicts sensitive and honorable Russian people living under an oppressive and hierarchical tsarist system. Enter the two protagonists, Russian prince Dmitrii Nekhlyudov (Frederic March) and the beautiful peasant girl Katusha Maslova. Right on cue, the leading characters fall deeply in love. But in Russia the love of nobleman for commoner is forbidden fruit. Can it survive? The initial prognosis seems poor, even to prince Dmitrii, despite his deep feelings for the lovely Katusha, played by golden-haired Russian-born actress Anna Sten.

At first everything is idyllic as the two share youthful summers at prince Dmitrii's family summer residence. However, the lovers are separated when the prince heeds duty's call, marching off to military service. Dmitrii's family wants nothing to do with the commoner. To seal the lovers' separation, the family conceals Katusha's pregnancy from Dmitrii. Time passes, and Dmitrii next sees Katusha years later. He is preparing for a judgeship in a court where Katusha is being tried for a theft and a murder that she did not commit.

When the system treats Katusha unjustly, the socially privileged Dmitrii Nekhlyudov is racked by doubt, a role for which Frederic March was well suited. One film historian writes of March that "as a portrayer of tortured and distressed men, he has no equal."[48] Dmitrii emerges from his introspection an idealistic reformer. Of course, this is not an entirely new Dmitrii, but a reborn Dmitrii. Early in *We Live Again*, hints of Dmitrii's clear vision and progressive-style consciousness surface. At one point he observes, "Russia is in pretty rotten condition. We're going to have a revolution if we don't look out." In another instance he declares, "All the people are equal and the land should belong to everybody."

If not sufficiently pained by the insensitivity to social justice shown by his own class, the prince suffers further during Katusha's trial, which forces him to confront dark personal demons. He discovers not only that his former lover is wrongly accused of a crime but also that he is responsible for making her a social outcast by unknowingly leaving her pregnant. When Katusha is found guilty and sentenced to five years in Siberia, Dmitrii must resolve his crisis of conscience. He renounces his position and wealth to join her in Siberian exile. Here the two can "live again," free of title and pretension. "Dear Heavenly Father," Dmitrii prays, "give me courage—I have so much to do—so many wrongs to make right, give me courage not to fail! Help me, Dear God, to live—again!"

The plaintive Russian folk music that is beautifully woven into the drama prevents any eye from remaining dry. One reviewer, though overstating the case, describes this tearjerker as "capturing the mystic socialism and Christ-like abasement which lay so close to the heart and mind of the later Tolstoy," upon whose novel *Resurrection* the film is based.[49] It's all rather schmaltzy, perhaps, but film historian Richard Koszarski claims that the quest for psychological meaning characterized Rouben Mamoulian's work; *We Live Again* fits that like a wet leather glove.[50]

Much less noteworthy is another metamorphosis film, *Espionage* (1937), a sixty-seven minute B movie from M-G-M. Directed by Kurt Neumann, *Espionage* is a light farce centering around the moral conversion of a wealthy and powerful Russian munitions magnate named Anton Kronsky (Paul Lukas). The film opens with a blizzard of cables, phone calls, and coded messages alerting an array of international spies and news reporters that the mysterious Russian arms maker, Kronsky, has secretly boarded his private car on the Paris-Istanbul Express. A newspaper editor's excitement sums up the overreaction to Kronsky's movements. "Sneak tonight onto the Transcontinental Express," the editor tells a reporter. "Now you get on that train, find out where he is going. It may mean war!"

But who is this Kronsky that he should command such attention? Talking about their Kronsky over drinks in a bar, two of his employees capture the film's ambivalence toward the Russian. "Gold, greed, avarice, intrigue! All makers of munitions are monsters. The world will be a better place without them," says one. The other disagrees. "Why, the boss is a sweet guy behind his armor and I know you'd like him, if you knew him." It seems they are both right. Kronsky is a torn man; while intensely interested in music, his position as an arms dealer forces him to repress this softer side of his personality. One critic commented wryly of Kronsky's inner turmoil that he seemed "equally interested in aesthetics and ordnance."[51] Where Kronsky goes can war be far behind?

Eventually it emerges that Kronsky has not embarked on any secret arms deal. Just the opposite. Kronsky's tender side has asserted itself. He has boarded the train to marry a charming young innocent, Sonia Yalonoff (Ketti Gallian). Incredible as it may seem, Kronsky is so smitten by the sensitive and beautiful Sonia that—as a wedding gift to her—he will turn swords into plowshares, abandoning his lucrative munitions works for more socially useful production.

While love finally frees Kronsky of inner conflict, *I Stand Condemned* (1935) portrays the Russian people as rent by social conflict and by the forces of good and evil. Directed by Anthony Asquith, *I Stand Condemned* is set in the Russia of World War I, where a Russian kulak and grain merchant, Peter Petrovich Briukov, has moved beyond his peasant roots to become a man of wealth and power in war-torn Russia. However, Briukov (Harry Baur) cannot leave his peasant ways in the field. A good man, he possesses none of the charm, confidence, or social graces expected of a man of substance. And he hates himself for his social inadequacies. At one point Briukov acknowledges the obvious, "I was born a peasant, I've been a peasant all my life, and I'm still a peasant."

When Briukov falls in love with the beautiful and cultured volunteer war nurse, Natasha Kovrin (Penelope Dudley Ward), he fails to win her. Natasha finds him crude and uninspiring. But what Briukov lacks in charm, he makes up in rubles. Natasha finds herself forced into an engagement with the grain merchant by her impoverished family—hardly a match made in heaven. It turns out that Natasha really loves a dashing army captain, Ignatoff, played by a young Laurence Olivier in one of his first film roles. Recently wounded in battle, Ignatoff is convalescing in Natasha's hospital. He has an impressive war record, as well as military bearing. At first, his views seem compatible with Natasha's. The brash Ignatoff dismisses Briukov as "the biggest and dirtiest profiteer of the lot" and tells Briukov to his face, "I hear you're making fifty-thousand rubles a day; that's about twenty rubles for every man who's killed." Despair over Natasha's dutiful resignation to marrying the elderly and unattractive Briukov fuels Ignatoff's self-righteous bitterness.

But wartime situations can change suddenly. Captain Ignatoff faces his own moral crisis when he loses eighty-thousand rubles in an impulsive gambling competition with the affluent Briukov. Unable to repay Briukov within the traditional three days, facing disgrace, Captain Ignatoff contemplates the suicide expected of a Russian officer and gentleman. Fortunately, he can't bring himself to do it; unfortunately, he is unaware that Natasha has secretly convinced Briukov to cancel the debt. Instead, Ignatoff borrows the money from an aged and nefarious spy, Madame Sabline (Athene Seyler). Sabline intends to use the debt to force Ignatoff into providing military intelligence for Russia's wartime enemy. Before she can put her scheme into action, the espionage squad unexpectedly raids Madame Sabline's home. She commits suicide, leaving the naive Ignatoff wrongly accused of treason. The captain bravely pleads not guilty, but he faces a death sentence if convicted. In an ironic twist, Peter Briukov alone possesses the information that can save Ignatoff. The merchant of humble origins decides to "do the right thing," winning Ignatoff's acquittal and a happy ending for Ignatoff and Natasha, who are now free to marry. Briukov may have lost the girl, but he demonstrates noble bearing beyond shallow measures of birth or superficial manners.

Do not look for such soul-searching moral issues to be played out in *Charge of the Light Brigade* (1936). This classic adventure, rounding out the treatment of middling 1930s films about Russians, was directed for Warner Brothers by Michael Curtiz. It might even appear misplaced in our filmography. Although the story concerns events of the Crimean War (1853–1856), in which Russia was a major belligerent, Hollywood's version of the story has almost no Russian presence. Precisely because Hollywood expunged Russians from their own historical narrative, *Charge of the Light Brigade* warrants attention.

It might have been hoped that at least one of the four Warner brothers knew or cared a whit about the actual war. In the real-world Crimean War, religious tensions coupled with Russian expansionism triggered a sad and costly war between Russia and Turkey, which was supported by the British and French. Under Tsar Nicholas I, Russia claimed exclusive protection of Orthodox Christians in the Turkish empire. With Turkish control over Russian access to the Mediterranean potentially at stake, Turkey rejected the Russian claim and resisted Nicholas's efforts to stir revolt among Balkan Christians. When war ensued, Russia found itself in an unfavorable strategic position. Under Prince Menshikov's weak military leadership, the Russians suffered a significant military blow to their status and fell from the major European powers. The British and French played only support roles.

Historical accuracy is often the first casualty in Tinseltown's war films. But if Michael Curtiz's *Charge of the Light Brigade* feels no debt to historical fact, it does pay homage to Alfred, Lord Tennyson's famous poem. *Charge of the Light Brigade* invents a mythical Persian villain—Surat Khan of Suristan—as the film's scamp. Where are the Russians? To the extent that the British were actually involved in the Crimean War, they did not fight any Persians. They fought against Russians.

So where does the filmic Surat Khan fit in? It turns out that earlier Surat Khan had barbarously massacred women and children at the battle of Chukoti, a British outpost far removed from Russia, Turkey, and the Mediterranean. The British 27th Lancers are determined to avenge the massacre; when Surat Kahn becomes an active ally of the Russians in the Crimea, the British Lancers have their chance. All this is an elaborate set-up for the filming of the charge of the Light Brigade against Surat Khan's Persians at Balaclava. The exciting attack scene, led by British Major Geoffrey Vickers (Errol Flynn), employs the formulas of Hollywood westerns, and helped elevate Flynn to Hollywood superstardom. His performance in the saddle is described as having been "badgered, terrorized and coaxed" out of the inexperienced actor by director Michael Curtiz.[52]

Light Brigade was intended to mimic Paramount's action-adventure hit, *Lives of a Bengal Lancer* (1935). *Light Brigade* drew moderately favorable reviews and did well financially for Warners. Jack Sullivan won an Oscar for best assistant director; Max Steiner was nominated for music. According to one critic, "the Freres Warner, bless 'em, may not give a hang for history, but they do know how to turn out a smashing and spectacular adventure film."[53] Animal rights activists would surely disagree, since many horses were sacrificed to achieve the spectacular falls recorded in the famous charge scene. One remains hard put to decide which was more shot full of holes—history or the horses.

A Few Favorable Movies

The *Charge of the Light Brigade* makes Russians bit players in their own war. Two of the era's other Russian-genre films break with Hollywood's overall indifference to spin an unambiguously favorable Russian tapestry, and none weaves so bright a fabric as does *The Soldier and the Lady* (1937). Both the Russian people and the tsarist order, supposedly threatened by an 1871 Tatar uprising in Siberia, are handled delicately by director George Nichols Jr.

The Soldier and the Lady, adapted from Jules Verne's novel *Michael Strogoff* for RKO Radio, shares some of the swashbuckling qualities of *Charge of the Light Brigade*. It starts with barbaric Tatars, under the command of a renegade named Ogareff (Akim Tamiroff), brutally leveling peaceful Slavic villages in Siberia. While Ogareff terrorizes the countryside, the reform-minded Tsar Alexander II (Paul Harvey) is busy emancipating Russia's serfs in a move akin to the abolition of slavery in the United States. If not quite a Slavic Lincoln, the tsar is presented as honorable and thoughtful. When Ogareff lays siege to the tsar's brother and his troops and cuts telegraph lines to the Siberian interior, Tsar Alexander II dispatches a personal courier from Saint

Petersburg with a crucial letter to his supporters detailing plans to send reinforcements. The letter must get through.

The dangerous mission is entrusted to captain of the guards and native of Omsk, Siberia, Michael Strogoff. This most perfect hero, played and overplayed by Anton Walbrook, begins his adventure with the tsar's words ringing in his ears: "Captain Strogoff, the fate of Siberia and the life of my brother are in your hands. Go, Michael Strogoff, for God, for Russia, and for the tsar!" And "go" he does, but not without company. As Strogoff travels east across Russia by train he encounters the mysterious and sultry Zangarra (Margot Grahame) who "accidentally" sits next to him and who, the audience later discovers, is actually a spy and the mistress of the unscrupulous rebel leader, Ogareff.

On the same train is the beautiful Nadia Pedrova (Elizabeth Allen), en route to visit her sick father in Strogoff's home town of Omsk. When Nadia encounters visa problems in Irkutsk, Captain Strogoff intervenes in her behalf. The lovely Nadia and the noble Strogoff proceed onward together. Zangarra—ordered by Ogareff to either steal Strogoff's secret orders or kill him—follows Strogoff and Nadia aboard a boat headed for Omsk.

The evening's entertainment on board the boat includes a dancing bear that breaks free of its chains and charges the audience, heading straight for the terrified Zangarra. At the last second, she is rescued by none other than Michael Strogoff—who leaps to her defense and dispatches the bear with a small knife. Such incredible heroism begets conversion. One dead bear and Zangarra begins switching her loyalty from the evil Ogareff to the virtuous Strogoff.

While Zangarra is shifting alliances, Strogoff discovers the many charms of the innocent Nadia, who understands celluloid symmetry and falls in love with Strogoff. The love-struck couple becomes separated during a savage Tatar raid in which Strogoff gets captured. Doing battle with the bear is nothing compared to the pain inflicted by Tatar torturers. Brave and loyal, Strogoff endures, refusing to divulge the tsar's secret orders. Ogareff, less than pleased, declares that "Allah is all-powerful!" and sentences Strogoff to have his eyes put out. But all is not lost. Zangarra rescues Strogoff, his eyes now bandaged over, and reunites him with Nadia. Zangarra pays the ultimate price for disloyalty: execution at the hands of Ogareff.

Meanwhile, Michael and Nadia make their way to the tsar's brother, Grand Duke Vladimir. In a bizarre twist, miraculously, Michael does not lose his sight, unlike the Strogoff of Jules Verne's original novel. Hollywood's version does not even require glasses. His vision now perfect, Michael leads the valiant Slavic counteroffensive that defeats

Ogareff and his Tatars. Strogoff then marries Nadia, is promoted to colonel, and receives Russia's highest honor, the Order of St. George. The swashbuckling hero Strogoff, the virtuous Nadia, the converted heroine Zangarra, and the newly liberated Slavic peasants of Siberia stand in stark contrast to the swarthy, rebellious, and murderous Islamic Tatars of *The Soldier and the Lady*. Such unambiguous sympathy for Russians is unique in the American cinema of the 1930s.

The only other movie favorable to the Russians is *Balalaika* (1939), an M-G-M musical romance lean on plot but robust with chivalry, directed by Reinhold Schunzel. Set near Saint Petersburg on the eve of World War I, *Balalaika* depicts the same mixture of appealing noblemen and commoners noted in *We Live Again*. Baritone Eddy Arnold plays an officer, Prince Peter Karagin, who passes prewar evenings incognito in the cafe "Balalaika" masquerading as Cossack singer Peter Taranda. There the prince meets a comely young cabaret singer, Lydia Pavlovna Marakova, "so blonde and so lovely even the Union Leaguers will forgive her for being identified with the Bolshevik Revolution." Lydia is played by Ilona Massey, a Hungarian actress in her Hollywood debut.[54]

Balalaika follows the unconvincing musical love affair between nobleman Peter and commoner Lydia. The film depicts all Russians positively, irrespective of politics. But politics prove problematic for Lydia, as she finds herself torn between two seemingly incompatible groups of friends: Bolshevik revolutionaries and Cossack soldiers. The Cossack officers are noble and loyal, and the Bolshevik revolutionaries principled and unselfish.

All have good voices, so even if they fail to see eye to eye politically, they still make good music together, which in *Balalaika* counts for more than anything except sentimentality. Off in the trenches of World War I on Christmas Eve and lonesome for his love, Lydia, Peter Karagin sings "Silent Night," only to have it sung back at him from across enemy lines in the Austrian trenches. Neither war nor revolution can keep Hollywood lovers separated, especially lovers with good voices. Lydia and her prince finally reunite in an upside down postwar Parisian world of exiles, where former servants have become entrepreneurs and ex-royalty are mere citizens, but all sing in tune!

Era-Ending Criticism

The flip side to these warm images of Russians materializes in one unabashedly critical film, Paramount's Alaskan sea epic *Spawn of the North* (1938). A darkly realistic tale of the northern waters, directed by Henry Hathaway, it received an Academy Award for special effects. *Spawn of the North* boasts a first-rate cast. Akim Tamiroff, once again a villainous character (he played Ogareff in *Soldier and the Lady*), portrays Russian pirate fisherman Red Skain. Henry Fonda and George Raft join together as all-American heroes, continuing a tradition of paired buddies in Henry Hathaway pictures. John Barrymore and his love interest, Dorothy Lamour, add to the star quality of the players.

Born into a stage family in California, Henry Hathaway started acting a as a child, became a protégé of the prolific director Allan Dwan, served in World War I, and made his movie debut as a feature film director in 1932. The northern frontier offers a rugged setting for this tale of raw power and greed. The conflict sparks over international fishing rights to salmon spawning grounds. It also seems a perfect setting for director Hathaway to demonstrate his specialty: adventure movies shot in exotic locations.

As Russian captain of the *Viluska*, sea brigand Red Skain delights in poaching the fishing traps of his American competitors. Totally devoid of conscience, Skain not only lies and steals but also takes particular pleasure in boasting about his misdeeds to the Americans from whom he pilfers. With a "catch me if you can" attitude, the black-clothed Russian paints the battle over fish with a jingoistic brush, exclaiming to the Americans, "That's the one thing you Yankees couldn't steal from my country. You got everything else, but you can't get all the fish!"

But Skain is less driven by nationalism than by the delight he takes in evil. He knows no sympathy. Skain abuses his crew like a slave driver. In need of a quick escape, he abandons his simple-minded but loyal assistant, Dimitri, on an American fish trap from which the captain is stealing. When caught by the owners, Dimitri is shot. As the film ends, Red Skain finally gets his. He dies as cinematic villains usually do, at the hands of the morally virtuous, in this case the American fishing boat captain Tyler (Henry Fonda).

Two other American films, released after the August 1939 Molotov-Von Ribbentrop Pact, but before Operation Barbarossa (22 June 1941), also took critical aim at the Russians. The script of Warner Brothers' *Confessions of a Nazi Spy* (1939) blasted the Soviet invasion of Finland as aggression paving the way for Nazi expansion eastward. But timing is everything. No sooner was *Confessions of a Nazi Spy* released than it was withdrawn. The film was reedited and rereleased in 1941, when the international climate had changed dramatically, and the Soviet Union had become an ally. Not surprisingly, the picture's anti-Soviet line had been excised.

In *Comrade X* (1940), directed by King Vidor for M-G-M, Clark Gable is at his best playing an American reporter named McKinley B.

Thompson who covers the notorious purge trials in Moscow. Gable was a rough-and-tumble actor from the coal mining town of Cadiz, Ohio, who loved hunting and fishing. Gable also liked to carve out his own personal space. As McKinley Thompson, he enjoyed no such luxury in Stalin's Moscow. Denied freedom of the press, Thompson cleverly conceals his true identity by posing as a drunken playboy. While pretending to be swimming in a bottle, Thompson writes articles under the pseudonym "Comrade X" and smuggles his hard-hitting exposé of Communist injustice past Soviet censors.

Most of the screenplay was written by Ben Hecht, whom critic Otis Ferguson says "has always tasted bile at the thought of the Comrades."[55] Director King Vidor, relatively independent-minded for the times, grew up in rural Texas with a nervous affliction that turned him toward Christian Science. He later cut his cinematic teeth studying the techniques of D.W. Griffith during the filming of *Intolerance* (1916), and went on to make films carrying a "message to humanity."[56] Vidor considered *Comrade X* to be one of his message films. The film's prologue, however, gets it wrong when it proclaims, "Russia—the never never land of steppes, samovars, and spies. Beards, bears, bombs and borscht—where almost anything can happen, and usually does." Such a characterization might better apply to Vidor's Hollywood.

With the purge big news back home in the United States, reporter Thompson effectively scoops up the top stories. Enraging the Russians, he covertly exposes the purge as an exercise in gross injustice, in one case reporting on the execution of more than one hundred peasants on trumped-up espionage charges. Thompson is discovered by a desperate employee of his hotel who threatens to turn him in to the authorities unless Thompson does as he says. The porter-turned-blackmailer does not want money. He wants McKinley Thompson to smuggle his daughter Theodore (Hedy Lamarr) out of the Soviet Union. As a loyal but opinionated Communist, Theodore's father fears she will end up as a purge victim. Theodore turns out to be an attractive and strong-willed streetcar driver who accepts Thompson's offer to go to America only because she hopes to convert the American working class. The unlikely pair undertake a marriage of convenience to permit Theodore to leave the Soviet Union with Thompson.

Meanwhile, the secret police headed by Commissar Vasiliev (Oscar Homolka), a screaming fanatic who announces that "all reporters will be treated like enemies of the Soviet state until Comrade X is caught," are busy hunting Comrade X. Before Theodore and Thompson can depart, Thompson is arrested by the secret police on suspicion of being Comrade X. Theodore and her father, as Thompson's accomplices, also hear the dreaded knock in the night. Unlikely as it may seem, all three arc imprisoned together. Nothing like hard time to clarify one's politics and priorities. Theodore soon sees through the wicked hypocrisy of Communism and falls in love with Thompson. Previously tough and cynical, Thompson is also smitten.

The only ones not included in the circle of love are Soviet commissars and government officials. In a confusing but convenient plot twist, Vasiliev is ousted by the two-faced Comrade Bastakov (Vladimir Sokoloff), of whom Theodore's father remarks, in a curious syllogism on Soviet justice, "Everybody loves Bastakov; Bastakov kills everybody—everything balances!" As unbelievable as it is necessary for a happy ending, Thompson, Theodore, and her father out-fox Bastakov and the secret police. Out of prison, they make a dash for the Rumanian border at the Dniester River in a stolen tank, crossing the frontier to freedom just ahead of their Soviet pursuers. Before anyone can ask, Whatever happened to the restrictive American immigration laws of the 1930s?, Theodore and her father are in the United States with Thompson, hot dogs in hand, cheering on the home team at a Brooklyn Dodgers' baseball game.

Comrade X, like *Ninotchka*, features a once loyal communist woman finding love and rebirth in the arms of a westerner, but its anticommunism has far more bite than *Ninotchka*. At one point, McKinley Thompson's media colleague, Jane Wilson (Eve Arden), sums up *Comrade X*'s view of the Kremlin: "Same old rat-trap—full of stuffed shirts double-crossing the masses. Some day the people are going to get wise and take it apart brick by brick."

Comrade X is contemptuous of the Soviet citizenry, as well as of the Soviet system. At one point McKinley Thompson growls at his secretary, "I haven't seen a Russian yet who wasn't suspicious. It's pathetic!" Like *Spawn of the North*, *Comrade X* also ran afoul of changing political realities. A revised version of *Comrade X*, released shortly after Hitler's invasion of Russia, tries to downplay its anti-Soviet message, opening with an "introductory trailer explaining that the film was just harmless fun between two good friends, two superpowers, who were now allies in a war for survival."[57]

Cinematic Themes

With the exception of *Ninotchka* and *Charge of the Light Brigade*, few thirties films have lasted in memory. They do, however, reflect the Hollywood of their day. Several themes leap out of this period, especially love and marriage. In most Russian-genre movies, huge obstacles crumble before the power of love between two seemingly ill-matched characters. Just as love finds a way to bridge differences, marriage brings happiness. These films also tend to draw clear distinctions between the Russian people and the Soviet government. If Americans appear at one with their government, Russians generally are not. But with few exceptions, political systems are treated as little more than plot props. Where the Soviet system gets portrayed as inefficient, even nearly dysfunctional, it is not so much condemned as teased in a jocular, ribbing way. Russian people are generally likable and mostly apolitical characters preoccupied by love relationships.

But the communist versus noncommunist backdrop in some films cannot be ignored. A half-dozen movies have communist characters. Only a few are portrayed as truly evil. Even when the communist system is gently chided, Russian people rarely are. At worst, most seem naive and open to "conversion." The worst villains of the era (Red Skain in *Spawn of the North* and Ogareff in *The Soldier and the Lady*) have nothing to do with communism.

Male and female protagonists balance one another quite evenly in 1930s films. All villains are male characters, while women are generally seen as pure, loyal, and beautiful. There are also a number of high-profile roles for women leads. But if women at first are loyal to the Soviet system, their loyalty usually crumbles as they succumb to the charms of a handsome western male.

Was Hollywood's vision out of step with that of American society? No. American films of the 1930s ultimately follow the flag, but for much of the decade the flag's direction was uncertain. Hollywood's Russians and Washington's Russians aroused many of the same feelings—suspicion, muted criticism, and a sense of ambivalence struggling against deteriorating relations from 1933 through 1940. In an era when domestic economic issues topped the American agenda, few felt anxious to give the Soviet Union or its people much serious thought. Pearl Harbor would change all that.

Chapter Two

1941–1945: Accommodative War Alliance

The day is 22 June 1941, and the morning quiet yields to the roar of countless Nazi bombers flying eastward. Operation Barbarossa, the German invasion of the Soviet Union, has begun. As conjured up by Hollywood, among the first victims of the Nazi onslaught is the small and peaceful Russian collective farm of North Star.

Without warning or military purpose the village gets brutally bombed. The peasants are stunned, but soon rally. The injured must be tended, and the dead must be buried. But another imperative exists—resistance. Even as the village smolders, Boris Simonov organizes North Star's survivors to confront the oncoming Nazi army. With every villager gathered in the town square, the village elder implores his neighbors to unite in defense of the fatherland:

> Comrades, we have good reason to know that our country is at war. In our small village 30 people have been injured; eleven people have been killed. But this is not a time for mourning; this is a time for *revenge*! We will divide into two groups, each to do its duty from this day until death. The able-bodied men are to come forward to the right of this building. We will go to the hills and take our position as guerrillas.
>
> I will go immediately to Comrade Petrov's garrison to get the guns. The second group has the hardest job. They must stay behind. As guerrillas we must have aid and information. As villagers you must, before the entrance of the Germans, destroy everything.
>
> *Everything* Comrades! The houses you have built, the crops you have sown with your hands, the cattle you have raised. The Germans are not

more than fifty miles away—yours is the dangerous job. For this job you will volunteer. It is you who may have to live with the—the *Germans!* [*With disgust in his voice*]

Inspired, the town's residents join in resonant chorus, proclaiming their loyalty through the guerrilla oath: "I, who am about to become a guerrilla fighter of the Soviet Union, take this solemn oath. I will not lay down these arms until the last fascist is driven from our land. I am willing to give my life, to die in battle to keep my people from fascist slavery. *We Swear!*"

In *The North Star* (1943), director Lewis Milestone uses this small *kollektiv*, and one village family in particular, to celebrate the noble heroism of the Soviet people's struggle against Nazism, a struggle of Russians marching in lockstep with the American people. The sacrifices of the Simonov family—one after the other—symbolize the burden of suffering shouldered by all Russia's people.

Village leader Boris Simonov becomes the first brave resistance fighter to give his life for the cause. Returning to North Star with munitions for the resistance, a German stuka bomber attacks his truck. Thrown from the vehicle, the old man collapses while throwing sand on the burning wreck. As Boris gasps his final breath, his two sons, Kolya and Damian, arrive on the scene to help their father:

Boris. [*Barely able to speak*] Damian: Get the guns out, save the guns.
Kolya. [*Frantically*] Get them out!
[*The two sons work feverishly to save the guns*]
Boris. Did you do it?
Kolya. Yes, Father, they're safe now.
Boris. They're for our men. Take them to them. Do you hear me?
Damian. Yes, Father. We'll take them back.
Boris. Say hello to your mother for me. [*He dies*]
[*Kolya and Damian bury their father and promise at his gravesite to "do their best"*]

They prove as good as their word. Their brother Kolya Simonov serves his people as a bombardier flying mission after successful mission. Bravery notwithstanding, his luck eventually runs out. To save precious bombs, Kolya's pilot attempts a low-level strafe of a German convoy. The pilot is wounded during this dangerous maneuver, and Kolya climbs forward to assume control of the damaged airplane. He yells encouragement to the pilot, now lying behind him and dying faster than Kolya realizes.

Kolya. Hold on! I'll let go of what we've got left and I'll have you on the ground in ten minutes. We're badly clipped in the back; it's worse than I thought. You crawl in back, I'll let you know when to bail out.

All right, crawl in back now! If you can't get the hatch, I'll do it for you. This plane's too bad to land; I'm going to try something else. It doesn't take more than one man to do it. Now, don't argue with me and sound brave and be a nuisance! I can do it alone; get ready to jump.

[*To himself*] Well, get ready for it! This is going to be for my father, me and my village and people I've not seen. Those are big words, I guess I'll have to stand by them now.

[*To the German convoy below*] I'm coming down, and I'm coming down just where I want to, and it is going to *hurt you*, because I was a good bombardier and a good pilot too!

[*His plane explodes in the center of the convoy*]

Kolya's younger brother Damian, no less committed to the common struggle, sets aside childhood dreams to embrace manhood as a resourceful guerrilla fighter with but one thought in mind: killing Nazis. Like all partisans from North Star, Damian knows that guerrillas live on borrowed time. They live life fully, since most will not live for long.

But Damian learns there are worse things than dying in battle. As the partisans ambush a German supply convoy, an exploding grenade leaves Damian blind. But Damian is not one to wallow in self-pity. When he gains consciousness, his concern is not for himself but for a comrade, the young partisan girl who fell fighting beside him. Bereft of sight, Damian pledges to fight on against the Nazis.

In this unrelentingly heroic depiction of the Simonov family at war, *The North Star* typifies Hollywood's World War II Russian-genre films. While *The North Star* tends to overdo it, the film expresses an American psychic need to find shared values with its wartime Soviet ally. These are Russians, but at heart they are just like Americans, meaning they will fight for what is right. And if this desire to bond with comrades in arms dictates an ideological suspension of disbelief, then so be it.

Suddenly Allies

Bonding appeared uppermost in the thoughts of the American administration as well. No sooner had Hitler launched his 1941 surprise attack against the Soviet Union than the pendulum of American-Soviet relations abruptly swung back. United in battle, Washington and Moscow pledged themselves to defeat a common Nazi enemy in Germany.

Even long-time anticommunists like publisher Henry Luce joined the patriotic parade. A special issue of *Life* magazine devoted to the Soviet Union paid the Russian people the supreme compliment. According to one article in *Life*, Russians were just plain folks—"one hell of a people [who] to a remarkable degree look like Americans, dress like Americans and think like Americans."[1] Russophoria may have known no higher point than when *Time* magazine gave its Man of the Year award in 1943 to Josef Vissarionovich Djugashvili—Stalin.

But how far below the surface did the Soviet-American wartime honeymoon penetrate? Clearly the two allies were bound together by a common enemy, not a common philosophy. Differences in ideology were at best papered over. Even before the war, Roosevelt worked to enlist Stalin against Hitler; once war broke out in 1939, and in spite of the Nazi-Soviet treaty, he sought to bring the Soviet Union into the war to defeat Germany. Two years after the Nazis attacked the Soviet Union, the tide of battle began turning in favor of the Allies. From 1943 onward, the president hoped increasingly to lay a collaborative foundation on which postwar peace and security could be built. Roosevelt considered these goals so important that he systematically courted Stalin. And as he wooed Stalin, Hollywood did its part to keep the American public on his side.

Unfortunately for FDR, Stalin did not share the same long-term goals. Stalin harbored a deep suspicion of the Allies. The Generalissimo distrusted western intentions enough to discount repeated American and British intelligence warnings of an imminent Nazi attack, even as Nazi armor was rolling up to the Soviet frontier. When Hitler unleashed his forces, the ill-prepared Soviets suddenly found themselves host to Europe's bloodiest killing field.

American public opinion, then six months shy of Pearl Harbor, remained torn between 1930s isolationism and the president's determination that America remain the arsenal of democracy. The president had already begun his campaign to aid those battling the Nazis by leapfrogging America's neutrality laws and sending lend-lease material to Britain, then bearing the burden of war against Hitler. With the launch of Operation Barbarossa in 1941, bolstered by increasing public sentiment that defeat of the Nazis was in the American interest, FDR extended lend-lease assistance to the Soviets. With Pearl Harbor and formal American entry into the war, any lingering public reservations about aid to the Soviet Union vanished.

Nevertheless, American-Soviet relations early in the European war were strained, especially during the "Black Summer" of 1942. It was only to be expected. The two peoples experienced the war differently. Like the Soviets, the United States had been caught off guard by a surprise attack. But the continental United States was far removed from the brutality of war. In some ways, the country was at peace even as the nation was at war. Not so for the Soviet Union. If the United States was the arsenal of war, the Soviet Union represented its battleground. The Nazi war machine rolled across Soviet territory at terrible cost in Soviet civilian and military lives.

Desperate to respond, Stalin launched a disastrous spring counteroffensive against the counsel of his military advisers. It cost the Soviet Union dearly in both men and materials. The future seemed bleak. As Hitler chalked up success after success on all fronts, it seemed all of Europe might fall to the Nazis before American forces could make a difference. Talk of eventual Allied victory seemed little more than a pipe dream.

Against this backdrop, communications between the Soviet Union and United States through 1942 remained sporadic and guarded. They seemed less allies than cobelligerents, since their leaders had not yet met to thrash out common strategies. American aid to Russia, massive as it was, had a long way to go before it could counterbalance Soviet losses. Comrade Stalin complained bitterly that the Soviet Union was doing the fighting but being shortchanged on supplies. Nevertheless, mutual enmity toward the seemingly invincible Germans, if not shared goals, bound the two countries together as they avoided the great mistake of the Axis Powers, which fought completely separate wars.

In 1943, momentum shifted dramatically. The Soviets won decisive victories at Stalingrad and Kursk. As the British emerged victorious at El Alamein, a new sense of optimism began taking hold. With the Red Army poised to push westward, the Allies slogged their way north through Italy. The long delayed second front involving American, British, and Canadian troops (Operation Overlord), which Stalin wanted so desperately, was approved for 1944.

At the Moscow, Cairo, and Teheran conferences, Churchill, Roosevelt, and Stalin sought to carve out common ground. But the common ground often proved very narrow. Certainly all acknowledged the key strategic role of the Russians in the war effort. But how would such sacrifice be rewarded? Looking forward to victory, Stalin expected payment at the peace table commensurate with his people's sacrifices on the battlefield. For both diplomatic and personal reasons, Roosevelt set aside Churchill's reservations and attempted to pacify Stalin. Diplomat and translator Charles Bohlen argues that Soviet losses created a "guilt complex in [Soviet-American] relations," for which Roosevelt felt compelled to atone.[2] Whether Roosevelt was awash in guilt over Soviet losses remains open to debate. More clear was that the president seemed determined to bring Stalin into the peace as a firm ally.

Placating Stalin

Meeting all of Stalin's demands would prove impossible. Nevertheless, Roosevelt believed that he alone could persuade the Soviet-Georgian to sing the same tune as the rest of the Allied chorus. His determination to mollify Stalin originated with FDR's fear that Moscow, if facing defeat, might attempt to make a separate peace between Russia and Germany, with 1917 and 1939 as ominous historical precedents.

By 1944, the Allies's march toward victory seemed certain, and Roosevelt tried to build the kind of peace he thought America wanted—a peace including the Soviet Union. His tactic? Personal diplomacy. American foreign policy during the war, including its Soviet policy, remained firmly under the personal control of President Roosevelt in a way alien to any American presidency before or since.

But why such personal diplomacy? The answer consists of many parts. It was partially because America was in an all-out war, partially because Roosevelt had been in office for so long, partially because American public opinion had coalesced squarely behind the president, partly because Churchill and Stalin so personified the diplomatic initiatives of their respective states, and, finally, because of his inimitable personal confidence. For all these reasons, Roosevelt played Soviet relations as a one-man band.

FDR's critics point to weaknesses in Roosevelt's personal diplomacy, as when he met virtually alone with Stalin at the 1943 Teheran Conference. Believing the Roosevelt charm could soften up Stalin, the man of steel, one critic claims that FDR "naively hoped that a benign approach would encourage the Soviet leader to moderate his postwar objectives."[3] It failed. Whether the Kremlin leader liked Roosevelt or not did not matter. Stalin knew what he wanted and would not relent, regardless of how much charm the president oozed.

Nor, some argue, was the president as well briefed on the Soviet mindset as he might have been. FDR's continuing distrust of experts, including the State Department's authorities on the Soviet Union, led him to rely on cronies like Joseph Davies for advice. Roosevelt also flew by the seat of his pants sometimes. Neither constituted a wise course in dealing with the wily Georgian. Certainly Davies was a questionable authority. While ambassador to the Soviet Union from 1937 to 1939, and a key Roosevelt confidante on Soviet affairs, Davies so wanted to convince FDR of the wisdom of warm relations with the Soviets that he submitted overly optimistic reports on Soviet intentions. He seemingly believed that "continuous praise of everything Soviet constituted a policy."[4]

When Davies returned to Washington in 1939, he rejected the popular practice of demonizing the Soviet Union. If anything, in his best-selling book *Mission to Moscow*, progenitor to the 1943 film, he erred in the opposite extreme. The book's blindly pro-Stalinist message was so naive that George Kennan contemptuously referred to it as

"Submission to Moscow." Many of Roosevelt's critics also attacked his "I know best" velvet-gloves approach to the future of postwar eastern Europe. They particularly point to the Soviet desire to control postwar Poland, which did not deflect FDR from his accommodative approach.[5]

FDR's Private Logic

Any assessment of Roosevelt's courtship of Stalin requires consideration of FDR's private logic, especially its intellectual and psychological roots. Numerous critics regard President Roosevelt's accommodations to the Soviet dictator as excessive. As one analyst puts it, while historians give FDR credit for contributing to the Allied victory in World War II, most commend him for little else beyond that.[6]

However, given the historical context and FDR's private logic, his attempts to woo Stalin with lend-lease, territorial concessions, and a voice in setting a date for Operation Overlord seem at least internally consistent. Roosevelt knew little of what we now take for granted regarding the horrors of Stalinist Russia—horrors that rival those of Hitler. Not until Teheran did he know that the Soviets would not make a separate peace with Germany. Nor did he know that the atomic bomb would be ready to use against Japan or that Moscow would turn temporary military occupation of eastern Europe into permanent political subjugation.

What was he sure of? Above all, that he needed the Russians to keep on fighting the Germans. Once Soviet participation was assured, he wanted Stalin's pledge to join the Pacific war against Japan as soon as the war in Europe ended. The costly experience of fighting the Pacific war made Roosevelt only too aware that a land invasion of Japan would produce horrific American casualties, should the atomic bomb not work. Finally, with victory in the offing, FDR wanted to convince Stalin to join a postwar peace plan—just possibly creating a lasting world peace.

At the time, hard-nosed realists like George Kennan and Charles Bohlen advised that gestures of goodwill vis-à-vis the Soviets were not only wasted but might even be counterproductive.[7] Such concessions only brought on another series of Soviet demands. Avoiding such advice, Roosevelt clung to the fervent hope that his goals could best be reached by keeping the Kremlin's boss grateful for a cooperative American spirit. Nothing so symbolized that American spirit as lend-lease. Initially hamstrung by 1930s neutrality laws, FDR sought aid for beleaguered states vital to America's national security. Initially encountering opposition from Pentagon officials who feared that aid would hurt American military preparedness, FDR sold the idea directly to the public, using the homey analogy of a length of garden hose needed to put out the fire in a neighbor's home.[8] When the Nazi blitzkrieg began torching tens of thousands of Soviet villages, FDR quickly cranked up the lend-lease hose as high as possible.

Lend-lease provided seventeen million tons of food, roughly one-half pound of concentrated food per day for each soldier in the Red Army.[9] More than ten billion dollars' worth of assistance proved vital to Russia's defending itself against Hitler's invasion. Any criticism of lend-lease to the Soviet Union must acknowledge that it ensured Soviet participation in the war, without which many more thousands of British and American lives would have been lost, making final victory over Nazism far less certain. With twenty-six million wartime deaths, the Soviet Union's human losses were eighty times those of the United States. As an instrument of war used for the strategic purpose of keeping Russia fighting, lend-lease served a valid purpose.

The president's vision of how the American spirit related to the Soviet Union stemmed partly from his own brand of Wilsonianism.[10] As something of a Wilsonian idealist, Roosevelt held fast to a sense of optimism about a better world order, one that might make the world safe for democracy. Such a hope could only be realized if the two nascent superpowers, Washington and Moscow, continued to build on the foundation of goodwill. And he felt he could milk the goodwill out of Stalin.

But Roosevelt's crusade, unlike Wilson's, was balanced by realism.[11] FDR comprehended the mood of the American national psyche, the shrewd politician in him always keeping an "ear close to the grassroots of American public opinion."[12] He sensed an America sharing his vision of the United Nations, not only as a hedge against isolationism but also as a tool for the good of humankind, thus worthy of America's own noble destiny. Victory needed to represent more than an excuse to divide the territorial spoils of war. But could he really bring the Soviet leader to the same conclusion? Roosevelt's defenders believe this was within the power of the subtle and flexible Roosevelt, "a statesman for all seasons."[13] Roosevelt's untimely death, not his failure, they argue, brought on the Cold War.

The More Pragmatic Truman

When President Roosevelt slumped over in his chair, dying of a brain hemorrhage at Warm Springs, Georgia, on 12 April 1945, America's accommodative policy toward the Soviets disappeared as well. Harry S. Truman, a pragmatist sharing few of FDR's foreign policy views, took counsel from experts who fed his native skepticism about continued cooperation with the Russians.

Unlike Roosevelt, Harry Truman was not groomed to be president of the United States or anything else. He was a serious, shy, and honest young man growing up in rural Independence, Missouri, at the turn of the century. His father, John, a small and compact person with a hot temper and good political instincts, was known to "fight like a buzzsaw," especially on election day.[14] Father John taught Harry to "say what you mean, mean what you say, and keep your word." Harry was so old-fashioned that a cousin considered him "at heart a nineteenth-century man." He never learned to dance, play golf or tennis, never joined a country club, and, as far as we know, never wanted to.[15]

Volunteering for active duty in World War I was the turning point in young Truman's life—it got him away from the family farm. He rose to the rank of captain and met people who later aided his political career, like St. Louis Democratic machine politician Jim Pendergast. Out of uniform, Truman most enjoyed local politics, at which he excelled.

Truman was not Roosevelt's first choice as a running mate in 1944. In fact, Truman remarked to Senate colleagues that he was "certain the President didn't like him."[16] Influential party insiders pressed Truman onto Roosevelt in order to nudge the liberal Henry Wallace off the ticket. Roosevelt agreed, but once the election was over, kept Truman at a distance. He did not consult with Truman on foreign policy, or on any other kind of important policy. Kept in the dark about the Manhattan Project, Truman did not learn that the United States was testing an atomic bomb until his sudden swearing-in. Bearing no loyalty to Roosevelt's Soviet strategy, Truman sought out the very experts whom FDR had ignored for so long.

Most critical in shaping Truman's Russian policy was Averill Harriman, the respected American ambassador to Russia since 1943 who had spent more time with Generalissimo Stalin than any other American. It was Harriman's view that the Soviets held dual but contradictory policies: allied cooperation and expansionism into eastern Europe. Harriman advised that Stalin saw American generosity as a "sign of weakness" and that the United States should "stand firm on vital issues."[17]

Truman reflected this view in his harsh reaction to Stalin's 1946 failure to remove Soviet troops from Iran as promised. Even more telling was Truman's curt handling of Soviet foreign minister Vyacheslav Molotov over the question of free elections in Poland. Molotov, Stalin's right-hand man and a tough, experienced professional, had grown accustomed to dealing with courteous and ever diplomatic American officials. However, while Truman had sold many suits as a haberdasher back in Missouri, diplomacy was never one of his strong suits. In their meeting on the Polish question, the president cut off Molotov in midsentence, telling him he was not interested in propaganda and instructing a shocked Molotov to convey Truman's displeasure over Stalin's failure to live up to his agreements.[18]

Truman later remarked that he had given Molotov the "straight one-two to the jaw," and that the Russians were the "most pig-headed people, forever pressing for every advantage." Neither was Truman intimidated by the persona of Joseph Stalin; after meeting at Potsdam, he described the dictator as "a little bit of a squirt."[19] With Truman in the driver's seat and the war over, the wartime alliance disintegrated. Soviet-American relations veered off in quite another direction.

Celluloid Russophoria

World War II represented a great moral crusade. The enemy was clear, and the values for which Americans would fight and die seemed equally clear. The determination of the state and nation to win total victory was matched by Hollywood's sense of duty. Like a bomber or a tank, it represented a weapon of war. Hollywood was a major propaganda arm of the war effort and, as such, embraced the Soviet Union and the Russian people as allies. Any vestige of past ambivalence disappeared. The enemy's enemy became America's best friend on celluloid, just as on the battlefield. The need for films to conform to the narrative parameters of the war meant that pictures varied little in plot, setting, or message.

Not to say that a huge explosion of films about Russians occurred. It didn't. But a number of Russian-genre movies were well financed, technically polished, and vital to the propaganda needs of the day. In some cases, these films were also high-priority business for the studios. Hollywood never strays far from the flag, but during World War II Hollywood had no opportunity to stray. The Office of War Information (OWI), the government's propaganda arm, issued guidelines to studios on aiding the war effort.[20] These prescriptions were hardly necessary, since Hollywood enthusiastically marched off to war with the rest of America. Everyone from Clark Gable to Daffy Duck wore khaki.

The patriotic war films did much to bolster spirits on the home front, even as they sent a message on the rightness of the war. America watched attentively. During World War II, feature films reached more people than books, newspapers, or magazines.[21] Accordingly, it seems only natural that wartime Washington would retain the same kind of vital stake in what the film industry produced as it did in what the steel industry produced.

What did Hollywood produce? During wartime all perceptions become simplified, including the dehumanizion of enemies and lionization of allies.[22] Leaving no room for doubt, filmic images of Russians in World War II remained unrelentingly positive. While Roosevelt courted Stalin, American cinema focused on all the virtues and none of the vices of the Russian people and the Soviet system. Ordinary Russian citizens appeared as outsized heroes, while the depiction of their leaders might have led one to suspect their nomination for beatification. As the Roosevelt administration looked on approvingly, Hollywood even recruited the Soviet embassy in Washington to review and comment on several scripts then in line for production.

The "Message"

The unusual qualities of wartime Russian-genre films appear striking when viewed together fifty years after release. They gush Slavophilism and can be taken seriously only when considered in their original milieu. Whereas 1930s films waffled this way then that way regarding Russians, World War II movies barely wait to finish the credits before bombarding the audience with didactic messages. "Tough, brawny, victorious and apolitical: this was the image of Mother Russia," noted one commentator.[23] Newsreel-like footage, voice-overs, narrative introductions, preachy epilogues, and authoritative text on screen ensured that nobody missed the message.

While superficial plot differences separate one picture from the next, they all seem like the same movie in many ways. The subtext informs audiences that Russians are brave people dying in defense of their homeland; they come from close-knit families and are romantics who fall deeply in love; they also have good leaders who are dependable allies. One film historian concluded that wartime Hollywood wanted Russians to appear as "resistants in a country of resistance," and as people Americans would like.[24] If Russians occasionally talk differently, dance strange dances, wear puffy pants, or prove more emotional than Americans, that's all right. They are, after all, foreigners. Or are they? Under a thin veneer of differences, these on-screen Russians look so much like Americans that they might just as well have been born in Kansas.

Major Productions

Four notable wartime productions enjoyed some popular success. One, *Mission to Moscow* (1943), remains unique. Its overtly political content (even by wartime standards) proved as controversial as the book by Joseph Davies, from which the film was adapted. Both the book and the film whitewash Soviet political oppression. By unabashedly embracing Moscow's leaders in a quasi-documentary motif, the film invited derision from those knowledgeable about the Soviet Union. But for most Americans the cinematic message got through: Soviet leaders, including Stalin, are good men doing fine work in tough times.

The other films convey their messages no more subtly, but at least do so without apologizing for the politics of Stalinist oppression. Stock plots glorify heroic Russian peasants rising up in defense of their nation. Here and there beleaguered lovers die side by side or at least solidify their love on the battlefield.

The North Star (1944) offers up a village full of wholesome and brave peasant patriots. *Song of Russia* (1944) crosses class and national lines as an American composer and a Russian peasant pianist marry and take up arms to defend her village from the Nazis. *Days of Glory* (1944) lionizes a pacifist ballerina turned guerrilla fighting to the death alongside her partisan lover. *Counter Attack* (1945) happened to be released just before V-E Day, making it moot. It follows a psychological battle of wills between a simple but noble Russian paratrooper and the arrogant German officers he takes prisoner, both of whom are trapped in a bombed-out basement for days on end. Falling back on his native intelligence and resourcefulness, the Russian emerges victorious.

A lesser entry is *Action in the North Atlantic* (1944), a cinematic billboard for continued American lend-lease assistance to the Soviet Red Army. In this gritty film, American merchant seamen wax eloquent about how, despite sustaining substantial casualties at the hands of lurking U-boats along the Murmansk run, they must supply Russia with the tools of war: their effort is critical to the survival of the Allied way of life. The few welcoming Russians appearing at the end of *Action in the North Atlantic* vanished in Cold War era prints, but the movie's message about the Russian contribution to the war effort remained favorable. The Russophoric, but lightweight, *Miss V. from Moscow* (1943), involves a clever and beautiful Russian female spy outsmarting German adversaries in Paris.

Bellwether Film: *The North Star*

Atop the list of hindsight bellwether films sits *The North Star* (1943). The genesis of this film occurred in the White House. Hoping to get the pro-Soviet propaganda machine rolling, Roosevelt adviser Harry Hopkins aggressively pursued Lillian Hellman to write a screenplay about the Russian war effort. Hellman seemed a natural choice as screenwriter, since she was regarded by many as friendly toward the Soviet Union.[25] If some historians describe Hellman as too soft on communism, others see her as a "moral exemplar" for defying the House Un-American Activities Committee (HUAC) in the early 1950s.[26] All agree on one thing: Hellman's embarrassment concerning *The North Star*'s overzealousness.

She later remarked that, if handled differently, it might have made "a good picture instead of the big-time, sentimental, badly directed, badly acted mess it turned out to be."[27] In any event, what Hellman originally envisioned as a simple story about ordinary people became exaggerative when producer Samuel Goldwyn turned her simple story into a "lavish production number."[28] Even though he once quipped that "messages are for Western Union," not movies, Goldwyn's fingerprints appear all over the saccharine message about heroic Russians in *The North Star*.

Consequently, the romanticism, musicality, idealization, and Americanization—so characteristic of the era's films about Russians—are particularly acute in *The North Star*. What *Porgy and Bess* (1959, also produced by Sam Goldwyn) does for the tragic African-American experience, this film attempts for the wartime Soviets. Aaron Copeland orchestrates a stirring musical score, for which he received an Academy Award nomination, as did screenwriter Lillian Hellman and cinematographer James Wong Howe. David Lachine's ethnic choreography, while impressive, seems equally tangential to this story as his later work in *Song of Russia* (1944).

Director Lewis Milestone, known for portraying strong heroines, powerful relationships, and social movements, lays it on with a trowel. Milestone already had one World War II film to his credit, *Our Russian Front* (1942), which used Russian newsreel footage to chronicle the struggle against Nazi invaders in 1941. A year after *The North Star* he would also direct *Edge of Darkness*, an equally melodramatic war movie.[29]

The studio so hoped *The North Star* would succeed that it enjoyed the rare honor of simultaneous openings at two Broadway theaters. Both filled to capacity on opening night. Through the first reel the audience met relaxed and happy peasants in the Ukrainian collective farm village, North Star.

Forget about ethnic particularism. For Hollywood, Russians and Ukrainians blend together. Tinseltown's only distinctions between Ukrainians and Russians boil down to little more than the design of stitching on their peasant blouses. Close-knit families, smiling faces, and ebullient singing and dancing might even leave the American audience thinking it was watching a Slavic *Oklahoma*.[30] According to Hollywood, balalaikas accompanied by exuberant, deep-throated male voices told everything worth saying about village life—at least when peasants were not killing Nazis, which they frequently were.

The star-studded cast of *The North Star* includes such matinee idols as Anne Baxter, Dana Andrews, Walter Brennan, Farley Granger, Ann Harding, Walter Huston, and Dean Jagger. Together they represent salt-of-the-earth peasants on a collective farm—and what a collective farm! Ignore that real living conditions in Stalin's collective farms, during war or peace, were never even decent, since he stripped the peasantry to feed his crash industrialization. Samuel Goldwyn and Lewis Milestone create a pastoral paradise on the eve of Thanksgiving Day in the village of North Star. The place has such a wholesome Kansas feel about it that Dorothy and Toto would have seemed right at home.

The North Star's early musical operetta is abruptly crushed by an onslaught of Nazi tanks and bombers. All over Ukraine, villagers retreat from the onrushing Nazi army in traditional scorched-earth style. But not for long. Once peaceful peasants, these men, women, and children rally by taking up arms as patriotic defenders of the motherland. They form guerrilla bands, harassing and challenging the better-equipped Nazis. North Star residents rise as one, at great sacrifice, to oppose the invaders.

Reality, of course, arrived somewhat rougher around the edges than what Tinseltown served up. Many Ukrainians, like their Byelorussian Slavic counterparts, did not resist. Indeed, many at first greeted the invading Germans as liberators from Moscow's imperial grasp, showering the Germans with the traditional Russian gifts of bread, salt, and flowers. Why did this happen? Ukrainians harbored three hundred years of grievances against the Russians and a particular hatred for Stalin. In the 1920s, Ukrainian nationalists supported the dream of an independent Ukraine. Their dream was violently snuffed out by Joseph Stalin, the commissar of nationalities. Furthermore, in Stalin's obsessive industrialization during the 1930s, he broke the backs of the peasants who made up the bulk of Ukraine's population.

Since prosperous peasants known as *kulaks* were most resistant to Stalin's drive to collectivize agriculture in the rich Ukrainian breadbasket, they fared the worst. Stalin's rival, Leon Trotsky, had once equated the illogic of collectivization with trying to combine a group of small boats into an ocean liner.[31] Kulaks were targeted for punishment, if not wholesale murder. The most appalling aspect of Stalin's campaign against the kulaks was the Great Famine.[32] From 1932 to 1934, Stalin starved 7.5 million Ukrainian peasants to death while

shipping Ukrainian grain abroad for hard currency to fuel his industrialization program. He denied reports of the famine and refused
assistance offered by western relief agencies.

Thus many Ukrainians at first saw the Nazis as liberators, hoping
the Germans would support an independent Ukrainian state. Because
they were regarded by many as saviors, the speed of the Nazi conquest
in their southern (Ukrainian) offensive, in terms of territory and prisoners, far exceeded that of the central or northern fronts. They took
Kiev in the south easily, but not Leningrad in the north or Moscow in
the center. Only after the Nazis and their collaborators had murdered
the Jews and Gypsies of the Ukraine did many Ukrainians see the
Germans as being worse than the Russians. Their hopes of an independent Ukrainian state were dashed.

But none of this for Hollywood's lens. Although *The North Star*'s
director, Lewis Milestone, had been born in Odessa (Ukrainian Russia)
in 1895, his life experience removed him from the Nazi onslaught in
1941. Milestone moved with his middle-class Jewish family to
Kishinev (Bessarabian Russia) at age five. While studying engineering
in Germany, he impulsively left for the United States in 1913, four
years before the Russian Revolution. He found a job as a photographer's assistant and worked for the Army Signal Corps in World War I,
eventually producing military training films. Milestone slowly graduated into feature films. His big break came in 1930 with the successful
adaptation of Erich Maria Remarque's antiwar novel *All Quiet on the
Western Front*.

Milestone became an important contributor to the Hollywood studio
period, directing thirty-eight feature films during his thirty-five-year
career. But he was forever the prisoner of his literary sources: when
adapting first-rate material like Remarque's classic novel, his work
stood tall; when saddled with a lesser work, the results generally deteriorated accordingly. His biographer concludes that "clearly not an
auteur," Milestone had a career that exemplified the ups and downs of
the studio system's committee approach.[33]

The North Star is so packed with pretty faces as to demand attention.
Damian Simonov (Farley Granger) and Marina (Anne Baxter), innocent, love-struck high schoolers, see their world torn apart by war.
Class valedictorian Damian plans to attend Kiev University on scholar-
ship. The supportive Marina could not be any more sensitive or
responsible. Both come from large, fun-loving, and close-knit families
who seem to spend as much time singing and dancing as tending their
fields.

A perfect couple in a seemingly perfect world, the young lovers celebrate their graduation with a joyous outing to Kiev. En route, the sky

falls on them in the form of bombs raining down from attacking German planes. Forced to grow up overnight, Damian becomes a hero of the resistance only to be blinded leading a guerrilla attack. Marina lovingly cares for her wounded Damian and also musters the courage to smuggle a much-needed cache of guns across enemy lines to eager partisans.

The leader of the ill-fated trip to Kiev is Damian's older brother, Kolya (Dana Andrews), an air force bombardier home on leave. The surprise Nazi air attack barely ended, the normally jovial Kolya sets upon organizing the group. He later dies heroically, turning his disabled plane into a bomb and steering the flying inferno into a column of German troop carriers.

The other lead is Claudia (Jane Withers), a student and friend of Damian and Marina. With girl-next-door looks, naive and hopelessly romantic, Claudia secretly loves the older and more sophisticated Kolya. Adolescent daydreams disappear with the war's first casualties. Soft edges gone, Claudia surfaces as a strong-willed partisan (a typical Lewis Milestone heroine) who dies with valor in the same guerrilla attack that costs Damian his sight.

Just as youth selflessly dedicate themselves to the defeat of the Nazis, so too the older generation steps forward to take up arms. And if the village youth represent hope and idealism, the three older characters in *The North Star* exude wisdom and principle. One elder, famous retired pathologist Dr. Kurin, is played passionately by the character actor Walter Huston. It might seem unlikely to find a distinguished doctor like Dr. Kurin on an obscure Soviet collective farm, but Huston's character manages to fit right in.

The peace-loving doctor, however, starts to fight. First he fights back depression, then anger, over German maltreatment of local children whom they bleed for plasma to aid Nazi soldiers. Dr. Kurin tries to convince the German doctors—fellow men of science—to abandon the medical abuse of children. But they have subverted their noble calling to the service of evil. After a local boy dies from the bleeding, Dr. Kurin has had enough. Rage explodes as the ethically minded man of science attacks and kills a German doctor, "You are the real filth—men who do the work of Fascists and pretend to themselves they are better than those for whom they work, men who murder while they laugh at those for whom they do it."

Less schooled but equally resourceful is Karp, an old man stranded with the youngsters on their trip to Kiev. The kindly peasant seems immediately recognizable as the "homespun, earthy philosopher who has a counterpart in every American town."[34] Walter Brennan made a career out of playing exactly this kind of lovable old coot and gives

Karp a palpable sincerity. When disaster strikes from the air, Karp ignores personal danger in his effort to save the others. Killed by a German stuka dive-bomber, the group buries him out on the expansive steppe synonymous with his peasant soul.

Comrade Boris Simonov (Carl Benton Reid), father of Damian and Kolya, emerges as a grassroots leader. Delivering a peasant's passionate message of duty, love for one another and the rightness of their cause, he effuses his village with strength and welds together a partisan force ready to confront the oncoming Nazis. Although brave and clever, Boris also proves mortal. He dies early in the war, bravely transporting guns to his fellow guerrillas.

All these cinematic "mirror-image" Russians pander to the American audience's fantasy of the Russians' experience. Despite wearing peasant shirts, the Russians might easily be taken for Americans. They fight the American fight. When rereleased in 1957 under a new title of *Armored Attack*, *The North Star* shed twenty-three minutes of its pro-Soviet baggage. The second time around, the freedom fighters fought communists, not Nazis.[35]

Bellwether II: *Days of Glory*

In *Days of Glory* (1943) yet another band of brave Russian partisans drink deeply of life while battling for a cause even sweeter than life itself. They find time to love as well; in this case, the noble love affair resides closer to the heart of the plot. The Red Army is one of largest armies in the world. Why then do Russian guerrillas play such a dominant role in these pictures? One answer suggests itself. Partisan units allow Hollywood to depict not only heroism but also love under gunfire. It would not ring true for American moviegoers to see women serve as combat soldiers in World War II. They could, however, swell the ranks of partisan fighters, struggling side by side with men and stealing moments of love even as they face death. Partisans opened up a gold mine of plots that can grab an audience and generate sympathy for the Russians.[36]

Not all screenwriters of World War II pro-Soviet films sympathized with leftist philosophies, as did Lillian Hellman. Casey Robinson, who wrote *Days of Glory* for RKO Radio, certainly did not. A conservative married to Russian ballerina Tamara Toumanova, Robinson shared little ideological ground with the Soviet Union, but he knew a potboiler script when he saw one. Tamara Toumanova makes her screen debut as Nina Ivanova, appearing opposite another first-timer: Gregory Peck as a Russian guerrilla leader named Vladimir. These attractive young stars carry *Days of Glory* beyond its melodramatic script and the uninspired direction by Jacques Tourneur, better known for a career built around macabre horror films.

Days of Glory and *The North Star* overlap one another in style and message. As in *The North Star*, the common rural folk in *Days of Glory* perform heroic deeds without reference to either the Soviet system or its bureaucrats in Moscow. Camped in the ruins of a monastery, Vladimir's deep woods collective ventures out at will to stymie the German regulars, often attacking the Nazis with little more than bare hands, pitchforks, and the rightness of their convictions. An American quality of individualism characterizes the partisans in *Days of Glory*. Surrogates for American youth, these Russians act as Americans would if a self-reliant resistance movement was needed in America.[37]

The simple story line of *Days of Glory* revolves around the beautiful, talented, and urbane Nina Ivanova (Tamara Toumanova), star of the Ballet Russe. When accidentally caught behind enemy lines, Nina finds shelter with a peasant band of partisans. Living with these rural commoners, she comes to admire their integrity, courage, and resourcefulness. She also grows to appreciate the singular value of their contribution to the war effort. Yet, as a pacifist, her beliefs soon create a moral dilemma. She first resists—then gradually accepts—the necessity of violence in the face of tyranny. Not a communist, she even wears a cross around her neck. And much like Dr. Kurin in *The North Star*, she ends up fighting the Nazi fire with fire, earning her status as partisan by killing a Nazi soldier.

Several Nazi atrocities witnessed by Nina spark her somewhat implausible conversion from pacifist ballerina to partisan patriot. When the Nazis savagely hang an innocent sixteen-year-old boy, Nina must question her belief in nonviolence. But one must not neglect the catalytic impact of another reality: her blossoming love for the guerrilla leader, Vladimir (Gregory Peck). An engineer before the war, Vladimir no longer builds for tomorrow. He now destroys Nazis to insure the existence of a Russian tomorrow. A serious and dedicated tactician, Vladimir creates endless trouble for the enemy. Though a demanding leader, he is also capable of great warmth and sensitivity, qualities that attract Nina.

The chances of survival for Russian guerrillas? Slim to none. Facing their last battle, Vladimir and Nina pledge their love, knowing they must die fighting German panzers. With her recent conversion to armed resistance, Nina proudly faces her end, reciting the guerrilla oath. As the screen fades to black, a strident voice-over tells the audience to "multiply this little group by countless thousands, multiply the spirit, and this is one good reason the hordes of Hitler fled back, turning their evil faces toward the sun of their defeat!"

Days of Glory also boasts the same stellar cast of supporting types as *The North Star*: like the famous scholar, Oxford-educated Semyon Ivanich (Alan Benton Reid), a well-organized intellectual as important to the resistance as Dr. Kurin in *The North Star*. Young Yelena Kamarova (Maria Palmer) is a modest factory worker-turned-partisan who has a secret crush on Vladimir. Clearly reminiscent of Claudia from *The North Star*, she dies bravely carrying a crucial message through German lines. Sasha (Hugo Haas) is a gregarious gadfly who can be counted on when the chips are down. He dies valiantly in battle, much like the sociable Kolay Simonov. Finally, images of Boris Simonov spring to mind in the person of Petrov (Lowell Gilmore), a resourceful saboteur who sacrifices himself to blow up an enemy tank.

Song of Russia

No major studio could fail to demonstrate support for the war effort. Each had its Russian film, contributing to a reliable flow of assembly-line patriotism pumped out with strong governmental encouragement.[38] Metro's contribution, a typically slick and expensive musical romance, *Song of Russia* (1944), was written by two members of the American Communist Party, Paul Jarrico and Richard Collins, and directed by Gregory Ratoff, another in a long line of Russian-born directors of this genre.

Few surprises here. *Song of Russia* gave audiences another dose of love, armed resistance, and idyllic characters singing it up during the Great Patriotic War. One film critic, obviously taken with the formula, called the *Song of Russia* "really a honey of a topical musical film, full of rare good humor, rich vitality and a proper respect for the Russians' fight in this war."[39]

The usual parade of screen Russians, singing their way from guerrilla raid to guerrilla raid, receives help from an American who also turns out to be no slacker when it comes to making music and killing Nazis. *Song of Russia* follows the adventures of American composer and conductor John Meredith, played by Robert Taylor, whose real-life military service was delayed so he might complete this film judged important to the war effort. While visiting Tchaikovsky's Russian birthplace in 1941, John Meredith meets a pretty young pianist named Nadia Stepanova (Susan Peters). Although of humble peasant stock (as standard in these wartime films), Nadia possesses a folk wisdom that Russians on the silver screen seem to imbibe with their mothers' milk. And Nadia is a gifted musician besides.

One thing leads to another as love of music soon turns into love of one another. Like the United States and Soviet Union, Nadia and John must put aside their foolish stereotypes of one another to make their partnership grow. One evening in a nightclub John exclaims to Nadia that he "can't believe that everyone seems to be having such a good time," because he had assumed "Russians were sad, melancholy people—sitting around brooding about their souls. This is such a surprise." Unable to part, they marry in an Orthodox Church ceremony in her village, and then begin touring Russia, performing beautiful music for appreciative audiences. When war erupts, the couple returns to Nadia's village (Tchaikovskoye). A war must be fought.

Nadia and John join the village in battling the invader. But duty calls on them to serve in another way. They will use Tchaikovsky as their weapon against the Nazis—a musical score to help even the military score. They tour America telling Russia's story musically to an American public hungry to learn about its embattled ally. The music that brought Nadia and John together serves as a bridge linking Americans and Russians in a crusade against a common Nazi enemy. As John Meredith informs an enthusiastic American audience, "we are all soldiers, side by side, in this fight for humanity."

Mission to Moscow

Students of World War II films have focused on *Mission to Moscow* (1943), an easy butt for ridicule, given its embarrassing whitewash of Stalinist horrors. This Warner Brothers film was also unusual in aggrandizing real-world characters in its depiction of Soviet leaders rather than commoners, employing a mock-documentary style that leans heavily on Joseph Davies's nonfiction book, generating controversy uncharacteristic of a patriotic flag waver.

Much the same can be said about Joseph Davies's book when first published in 1941. The purportedly authoritative book promised readers a peek behind the curtain of secrecy that had long shrouded the Kremlin. It became a national best-seller. The American public wanted a comforting image of the Soviet Union and its leaders as the United States and the Soviet Union sidled up to one another in the face of Hitler.

Warner Brothers only did what Hollywood had already proven very good at. It brought fairyland to the screen. Erskine Caldwell did the initial screen adaptation of *Mission to Moscow*, but Howard Koch eventually completed the task. Columbia Law graduate Koch first gained notoriety by writing Orson Welles's radio adaptation of *The War of the Worlds* in 1938. Koch was able to work with his recent collaborator on *Casablanca* (1941), the prolific director Michael Curtiz. Curtiz's career eventually resulted in 165 movies, most of which he directed for Jack Warner. Many were patriotic fare in the mold of his successful *Yankee Doodle Dandy* (1942), starring James Cagney.

However, Joseph Davies retained extensive rights to the story of *Mission to Moscow* and subjected the script to constant scrutiny. At one point, he overruled writer Koch's strong objection to a prologue in which Davies appears in person and assures the viewing public with an imprimatur that the rest of the film renders unnecessary: "While in Russia I came to have a very high respect for the integrity and honesty of the Soviet leaders." His minilecture concludes that "these people are sincerely dedicated to world peace."

Mission to Moscow enjoyed a larger advertising budget than any previous film (including *Gone with the Wind*). Wherever Warners spent the marketing budget, it was not on New York subway billboards, since the city transit authority banned its controversial advertisements.[40] Too political. But four thousand people attended its 1943 gala opening in Washington and President Roosevelt held a private screening at the White House.[41] White House or no White House, the New York Transit Authority knew of what it spoke. Amid the hoopla there was grumbling: even for a wartime film, this one went too far in whitewashing Soviet totalitarianism. The film's leitmotif, and the source of much of the grumbling, is its treatment of the Moscow show trials prosecuted by Andrei Vyshinsky. Hollywood, no stranger to playing hot and heavy with history, gets carried away in its portrayal of the trials.

Forget all the reliable scholarly analysis and eyewitness accounts of the trials. It hardly mattered that roughly one million purge victims were executed—usually by a bullet to the base of the skull that executioners euphemistically referred to as "the nine grams of lead." Or that twelve million others died after suffering in the gulag prisons later grippingly described by novelists like Alexander Solzhenitsyn, Arthur Koestler, Eugenia Ginzburg, and Anatoly Rybakov.

Unbelievably, half of the Soviet urban population appeared on police lists, and one in eight Soviet men, women, and children was actually arrested. By the time Russia entered World War II, Stalin's purges had gutted the Red Army of 90 percent of its generals and 80 percent of its colonels. Forty-three thousand senior officers had been arrested. While the Soviet Union lost six hundred generals during World War II, the paranoid Georgian killed one thousand in the 1930s. Execution had become the "favored solution to every problem, including those caused by previous executions." NKVD officers had quotas similar to the rest of the Stalinist system.[42]

All this counts for nothing in *Mission to Moscow*. Rather than loyal followers-turned-victims to the Kremlin fanatic's terror, we find prosecutor Vyshinsky extracting facile confessions from traitors supposedly conspiring to overthrow Stalin and sell out the Soviet people to Japan and Germany. Vyshinsky describes the plan as the brainchild of Leon Trotsky—Stalin's real-world 1920s rival banished into Turkish exile in 1929 and murdered with an icepick in Mexico ten years later by Soviet henchmen. In *Mission to Moscow*, alleged coconspirator and former secret police director Genrikh Yagoda sings as freely as a nightingale:

> *Vyshinsky.* Citizen Yagoda, you have admitted that these numerous acts of terrorism and sabotage were part of a general plan to weaken the Soviet Union. Did you help to formulate this program?
> *Yagoda.* [*After a moment's pause*] I helped, but in the main, the program was Trotsky's.

Unfortunately for director Curtiz, Trotsky was not one of the defendants. However, no shortage existed of old Bolsheviks ready to confess their sins to Vyshinsky in Mission to Moscow. The real-world Vyshinsky managed to escape Stalin's wide net, later becoming Soviet ambassador to the United Nations, dying of a heart attack well into his seventies while sleeping in his Park Avenue apartment. Even Perry Mason would envy Vyshinsky's acumen in eliciting confessions from loyal Communists like Karl Radek and Nicholas Bukarin.

> [*First Radek*]
> *Vyshinsky.* In the preliminary examination, you also admitted participating in this bloc that was to prepare the way for Trotsky's program. Please tell us what that program was, as you understood it.
> *Radek.* Our eventual aim was to take over the government of the Soviet Union.
> [*Then Bukharin*]
> *Vyshinsky.* So you were working out a deal?
> *Bukharin.* Naturally. Germany and Japan were not going to back us for the sake of Trotsky's beautiful blue eyes.
> *Vyshinsky.* What *were* their conditions?
> *Bukharin.* The partition of our country. Japan was to get our maritime province and our guarantee of Siberian oil in the event of war with the United States.
> *Vyshinsky.* And Germany?
> *Bukharin.* We agreed to open the border for German expansion to Ukraine.

Much of the acting in *Mission to Moscow* was as ham-handed as the story line. But what could you expect when even a fine actor like Walter Huston, portraying Joseph Davies, must utter omniscient lines like, "Based on twenty years' trial practice, I'd be inclined to believe these confessions." Critics suggest that the problem with Davies' twenty years of trial experience is that it occurred in the wrong country.

Torture, sleep deprivation, and threats against family members had been so perfected by Stalin's henchmen that Leonid Zakovsky, head of Moscow's NKVD, once bragged that "he could have made Karl Marx confess to being an agent of Bismarck."[43]

As ambassador to the Soviet Union, Davies made little or no effort to educate himself about the Soviet legal system or much else. The only exception was the Russian art treasures with which he surrounded himself, taking so many valuable ones home after his posting in Moscow that he ended up donating many to the National Gallery in Washington to reduce a hefty duty payment.

The purges were not the only victim of the Davies-Curtiz whitewashing brush. Add the 1939 Russian-German nonaggression pact and the Soviet invasions of Finland and Poland, both of which *Mission to Moscow* ignores. Near the end of the movie Davies meets with Stalin, portrayed by Manart Keppen as a calm, pipe-smoking statesman of great vision. Before taking his leave, Davies toasts Stalin with a confident prediction, "I believe history will record you as a great builder for the benefit of common men." In the end, history, or at least versions other than Stalin's own notrious *Short Course*, have drawn radically different conclusions. And as for *Mission to Moscow*, George Kennan's drubbing of the film as "Submission to Moscow" seems apt.

Mission to Moscow limped out of the fray as a wartime casualty. In spite of costly promotion, it grossed only $1.2 million before leaving theaters, and Warner Brothers made no profit.[44] Generally dismissed as a "case of pamphleteering,"[45] the best the film's producer could say was that it was "an expedient lie for political purposes."[46] Stalin, however, must have been impressed. He screened all foreign films distributed in Russia, and with his imprimatur, *Mission to Moscow* received widespread public suppport within Russia.[47] Stalin apparently repaid Warner Brothers in kind: a year after *Mission to Moscow*, an American hero sporting the name of Jack Warner popped up in a Soviet war film.

The nagging question remains, Why would such an embarrassingly pro-Soviet (as opposed to pro-Russian people) film be necessary? David Culbert's book about *Mission to Moscow* argues that the film was not intended to trumpet the Soviet view on the purges per se, nor even primarily to convince a wary American public that Russia was a deserving ally, since it was already convinced of the second point. Rather, knowing that Stalin was a film fanatic, the hidden agenda aimed to reassure the Generalissimo of America's change of heart and its acceptance of the Soviets.[48] Accommodative expressions of American goodwill appear not only in the film's willful misrepresentation of Stalin's record, but in Roosevelt's allowing himself to be portrayed on film (by Captain Jack Young) this one time only during World War II.

Other Favorable Films

Some less notable Russophoric films, like Producers Release Corporation's seventy-minute B movie, *Miss V. from Moscow* (1943), also hit the movie houses, mostly as the bottom half of a double bill. The original screenplay by Arthur St. Clair and Sherman Lowe, under Albert Herman's direction, follow the conventions of the era's propaganda genre.

Lola Lane's zest as beautiful Russian superspy Vera Marova (Miss V.) provides the film's limited appeal. Vera volunteers for a high-risk assignment: she must infiltrate the ranks of the German SS, posing as Nazi spy Fraulein Greta Hiller. Slipping into both a tight skirt and occupied France, spy Vera Marova uses all of her impressive assets to succeed. She is smart and cool under fire; she also fills the tight skirt beautifully.

Vera manipulates a smitten Nazi SS officer into revealing top-secret information about a pending German naval attack against a major American lend-lease convoy then steaming toward the Soviet Union. Miss V. manages to smuggle the information to Moscow, where authorities immediately relay it to a grateful Washington. The convoy and many American lives are saved, thanks to Miss V.

Soviet-American cooperation takes various forms in *Miss V. from Moscow*, but remains personified in the relationship between the lovely Russian Vera and an American spy named Steve Worth (Howard Banks), who assists Vera in her mission. Atypically, the two characters do not become lovers. Maybe if Miss. V. played a piano like Nadia Stepanova in *Song of Russia* . . . but that was not in the cards. Rather than share a bed, the two spies settle for respecting each other's contributions to the common endeavor.

Counter Attack (1945) similarly enjoyed little commercial success. Released in April 1945, just a few days before the war in Europe ended, *Counter Attack* seemed anti-climactic, and was given a pass in theaters by a war-weary American public. But the war was still raging when Columbia Pictures chose Hungarian-born Zoltan Korda (often associated with the films of his brother Alexander, and best known for sweeping action spectaculars very different from *Counter Attack*) to direct this film.

Zoltan Korda offers up a cinematic psychological mini-war. A resourceful, peasant-stock Russian paratrooper, Alexei Kulkov (Paul Muni), stands guard over high-ranking Nazi officers whom he has taken prisoner under bizarre circumstances. The claustrophobic action, all psychological in character, occurs in a basement sealed off by a bomb blast.

The titular "counter-attack" involves little physical struggle. Rather, it entails psychological warfare between a Russian soldier and the "arrogant tenacity" of his German prisoners.[49] Alexei Kulkov demands information from the officers, who refuse. Already having proved himself a heroic commando, Kulkov's psychological resilience earns the grudging respect of the Nazi officers. Eventually his native resourcefulness wins the day. Kulkov gets the information he wants and gets himself and his prisoners out of what might have become their common tomb.

Thematic Patterns

In an era of Slavophilism, the unblemished Alexei Kulkov represents but one more in a long line of all-American-style Russian heroes. Like the others, he serves to magnify Hollywood's wartime message. Whatever doubt American audiences might shelter about communism or the Soviet system, the good Russian people deserve praise. Only *Mission to Moscow* betrays this formula by canonizing Soviet officials, rather than the people. If that film pleased Stalin, American audiences did not embrace it. They preferred make-believe singing partisans to whitewashed politicians.

And who are these partisans? They all appear as unselfish, clean-cut, wise, and close to the soil. They come from caring families who laugh and sing. The old have chiseled features and a respect for tradition. The young remain open and wholesome. All seem passionate about their land and about one another. Lovers, men and women alike, face death as a natural part of their wartime lives. In sharp contrast to the passive Russian characters populating 1930s films, these heroes could hardly be more dynamic. Musicals scores, built around rousing patriotic melodies, couldn't be more different from the light-hearted prewar fare. Warts, if they exist, do not mar the Russian complexion in any of these films.

Joseph Davies, for example, comes no closer to allowing that life is less than perfect in the Soviet Union than his oblique advice to Americans in *Mission to Moscow* not to look too closely at things they might not understand in the Soviet Union. "How they keep their house is none of our business; all we need to know is if there is a fire, will they be a decent neighbor," essentially echoing FDR's earlier metaphor of Russo-American cooperation.

Suspension of Disbelief

Wartime Hollywood's Russians constituted creations of a war industry as tangible as that which made tanks and bombs. No other period in film history remotely challenges the accommodative war alliance of 1941–45 for consistency of image. To prepare for war psychologically, humans simplify perceptions and remove ambiguities that might get in the way of a singular overarching goal: victory. This process necessitates creating dehumanized mental images of enemies and lionizing images of one's self and one's allies. Once enemy is separated from friend, then weapons get built and are given to soldiers trained to know who to point them at.[50]

For wartime America, this process dictated suspending any sense of disbelief in the virtues of its ally, the Soviet Union. With all ambivalence set aside, the Soviets operated on the side of the angels. Hollywood's Russians were excessive enough to rival the portraits Shadowland painted with silver screen warrior John Wayne, who thought "he won World War II instead of just starring in it," according to one wag.

In the wartime propaganda produced by Hollywood between 1941 and 1945, little room exists for reality checks—witness *Mission to Moscow*. In the postwar world, Tinseltown, as well as Americans generally, would emerge from the sheltered workshop of war propaganda to face a new global situation and a different Soviet Union. The idealized Ivan, marching side by side with G. I. Joe, would vanish as sinister new forces prepared to invade American theaters, and possibly U.S. soil.

Chapter Three

1946–1962: Acute Cold War

With the pound of a gavel and a single question—Are you now or have you ever been a member of the Communist Party?—congressional careers were made. Careers in government, labor unions, and the motion picture industry were shattered. In the case of Hollywood, the House Un-American Activities Committee (HUAC), riding a wave of anticommunist paranoia, served notice: the end of the line had arrived for those not toeing a strict anticommunist line.

Already accustomed to self-censorship under the Hays Office, Shadowland was intent on avoiding external control. To this end, fifty studio executives met in New York late in 1948. Their infamous "Waldorf statement" ushered in a system that eventually blacklisted over 200 artists. As penance for past sins, real or imagined, Hollywood offered up screenwriters like Dashiell Hammett, actors such as Larry Parks, and directors like Abraham Polonsky for public humiliation.

Charles Chaplin moved to Switzerland where he lived until his death in 1977. Chaplin directed and starred in a bitter attack on anticommunist hysteria called *A King in New York* (1957). Howard Koch, screenwriter for *Mission to Moscow* (1943), moved to England where he wrote screenplays under pseudonyms. When asked how he knew his Hollywood career had died, his terse response was that "the phone stopped ringing."[1]

It all happened so fast. America had barely celebrated victory over the Nazi enemy before it sensed a new threat to world peace—communist plots hatched behind the Kremlin's great red walls. Fear of the communist cancer spreading abroad inevitably triggered fear of communist subversion at home. Had America abandoned its vigil during the anti-Nazi crusade? Had basic American institutions already been infiltrated? Had American values been compromised? How deeply had the communist malignancy penetrated the American body politic?

Feeding on public anxiety regarding the condition of the postwar world, HUAC pledged to ferret out enemies of the state, even if it sometimes had to invent them. Shielded from libel laws, publicity-seeking HUAC members let loose a barrage of half-truths and unsubstantiated charges. The burden of proof fell to HUAC's unfortunate victims. Now part of American mythology, the HUAC spectacle operated in the name of information gathering, but these "degradation ceremonies" operated before banks of microphones, popping flash bulbs, and newsreel cameras, crushing many innocents along with the guilty few. But guilt or innocence was often beside the point. For some congressmen, the thrill of publically humiliating well-known figures proved irresistible.

The sixty-four thousand dollar question became, Who would grovel and who would not? A committee feasting on publicity could only salivate at the prospect of banner headlines accompanying subpoenaed Hollywood idols. No shortage of big names existed in Hollywood, as demonstrated by screenwriter Martin Berkeley, who set the standard by naming 155 coworkers. "For every witness from the worlds of labor, science, the armed forces, or education, there were a dozen from the wonderful world of show biz."[2] Before long, a Culver City "who's who" was dragooned by the committee. A third of Hollywood's ninety witnesses provided HUAC with the names of alleged communist sympathizers. Others defied the committee on either First or Fifth Amendment grounds. Those facing the committee included some of the creative lights who so recently had served in America's propaganda war against the Nazis.

Friendly witness Robert Taylor, star of *Song of Russia* (1943), bent with the prevailing political wind, testifying that if he had his way "the Party would be outlawed and they would all be sent back to Russia or some other unpleasant place"; furthermore, that he had made his pro-Soviet wartime film "against my better judgment." However, Taylor proved an uninformed informant, knowing no names useful to the committee.[3]

Lillian Hellman, who wrote *The North Star*, offered to talk about herself, but she would not incriminate others. When the committee rejected her offer, she refused to testify on Fifth Amendment grounds and thus joined Hollywood's blacklist. She was in good company. *Mission to Moscow* screenwriter Howard Koch languished on the blacklist for seven years. Only a threatened lawsuit on Koch's behalf by lawyer Edward Bennett Williams reopened studio doors to him. Although ultimately undone by charges of undemocratic practices and overreaching its mandate, HUAC had already done great damage. The committee left freedom of expression and the self-respect of the film industry among the first American casualties of the Cold War.

How different—this new era—from the one that went before. In the prewar and wartime eras, one man, Franklin D. Roosevelt, forged a working alliance with the Soviet Union and the Russian people. Hollywood helped sell that alliance to the American public. Now Roosevelt and his alliance were dead. The acute Cold War era (1946–62) involved three presidential architects—Harry S. Truman, Dwight D. Eisenhower, and John F. Kennedy. Despite three distinct presidential personalities and two competing political parties, the era's unifying foreign policy theme persists as one of confrontational mistrust between the United States and the Soviet Union.

Two definitive events bracket this period: the end of Soviet-American wartime alliance and the Cuban missile crisis of October 1962. The postwar deterioration in Soviet-American relations cannot be pinned to any one event. Indeed, relations did not so much break down as dissolve. Beginning in early 1946, one tension after another crept into the superpower relationship. By the time the world caught its breath, West confronted East along a fissure that Winston Churchill dubbed the "Iron Curtain." As relations between the Soviet Union and the West worsened in the decade and a half following World War II, management of American foreign policy changed as well. It became less and less the private preserve of the president, and more the domain of an institutionalized, professionalized band of foreign affairs experts. For every administration, however, relations with the Soviet Union continued as the top foreign policy priority.

Cold War Psychology

While the prevailing American view of the Soviets shifted dramatically from that of ally to enemy, in many ways, the psychology of the Cold War paralleled that of World War II. War is war, and an enemy is an enemy. Americans were not shooting at Russians, but many remained convinced that a military showdown, a shoot-out at an international O.K. Corral, might be delayed but not averted. Accordingly, the World War II mental dynamics of simplified thinking and dehumanized enemies was transposed to the new enemy: the Russians were transformed from brave allies into brutal enemies. No room for subtlety. The collective mind at war has no patience for consistency, irony, or paradox—they too become enemies. It is easier to draw a clear line in the sand that separates good from evil. America had such a line during World War II, and it wanted another with the Cold War. The Nazis wore gray; the communists wore green. Both wore heavy jackboots.

If the postwar demonization of the Soviets was simple, conventional wisdom has also characterized the 1950s as "the simple decade."[4] In *Strange Invaders*, a 1983 tongue-in-cheek cinematic retrospective of life in 1958 Centerville, Illinois, the movie opens with a shorthand image of the fifties: "It was a simple time of Eisenhower, twin beds, and Elvis." This popular view of the fifties is obviously exaggerative; yet, it does contain a nugget of truth, particularly when the decade's surface tranquility is contrasted with the more volatile 1960s that followed.

One aspect of 1950s simplicity, perhaps a hangover from the certainties of the war years, consisted of the tendency to see issues in absolute terms: good/bad, black/white, communist/capitalist, American/Soviet. The Cold War brooked no middle ground, and few dared inhabit the wrong side. Nor did it take much to be considered on the wrong side. The Cincinnati "Reds" baseball team changed its name to the "Redlegs," lest anyone impute the wrong connotations. Although the American public felt certain of its enemy, actual confrontation with that enemy occurred only indirectly. The superpowers used every weapon they could muster, short of one-on-one military conflict: no-holds-barred propaganda; sabre rattling with stockpiled conventional and nuclear weapons; open-wallet foreign and military aid schemes to woo nonaligned nations; support for farm-team surrogates in regional armed conflicts; trenchcoat operations by the KGB and the CIA; and toe-to-toe showdowns at the United Nations. All the while the world held its breath.

Defining the American World Role

The term "Cold War" was coined by Herbert Bayard Swope, speechwriter for statesman Bernard Baruch. Columnist Walter Lippman picked it up, and it became a household term. Yet, "Cold War" remains an imprecise expression, and the time frame and stages of it remain open to debate. Nevertheless, the period from 1946 to 1962 is recognized as the "acute Cold War."[5]

This is only clear in hindsight. All that seemed clear at the end of World War II was that, ready or not, the United States had assumed a central role in world affairs—one it felt unaccustomed to. Powers like Japan, Italy, France, Germany, and Britain were in eclipse. Only the Americans and the Soviets exercised a truly global reach in the postwar world. But what was America to do with this newfound status and power? What vision, if any, shaped American foreign policy in the postwar decades?

America's struggle between idealism and realism resurfaced in its foreign policy, the defeat of the Nazis barely realized. Idealists like Henry Wallace and Wendell Wilkie urged that FDR's plan for global postwar cooperation be vigorously pursued. Dean Acheson and George Kennan, as outspoken realists, dismissed Roosevelt's vision as a mere pipe dream. If Truman's instincts told him to get tough with Moscow, his political sense initially forced him to tread with caution. He felt most uneasy stepping into FDR's foreign-policy shoes. In the short time it took to put his own stamp on the presidential office, Truman continued the "cooperative Rooseveltian approach." As a result, policy toward the Soviet Union in the early Cold War years was "much more hesitant and much less self-assured" than previously assumed.[6]

Until Truman found his voice in foreign affairs, America "gyrated" between idealism and realism with "great uncertainty." By early 1947, a newly self-confident Truman settled into a more hard-line, realistic position.[7] As he gained confidence, Truman's new "get-tough" approach became more and more obvious, changing the official perception from "difficult ally to potential foe."[8]

There proved ample opportunity for the United States to demonstrate its new, harder-edged Soviet policy. In the aftermath of war, an exhausted British government cut off military support for the governments in Greece and Turkey, both threatened by left-wing insurgents. Britain, as well as other European allies, prodded an unsure American government to take up the international slack. Fearing communist advances throughout war-ravaged Europe, the Truman administration acted decisively. In March 1947, the United States announced the Truman Doctrine promising anticommunist assistance, military and material, to Greece and Turkey as part of a broader anticommunist commitment. Three months later, the European Recovery Plan, or Marshall Plan, began rebuilding European economies. Militarily, the United States became the moving force behind the NATO alliance. With bold strokes, the United States set itself up as the bulwark against communist expansion in Europe. There was indeed a new line in the sand.

The Containment Policy

This American policy soon acquired a name: containment. In July 1947, diplomat George Kennan published his influential article in *Foreign Affairs*, advocating a policy called "containment." The policy, earlier cabled to Truman in his famous "long telegram" from Moscow, was embraced by the president. It called on the administration to stand firm against any Soviet expansion into noncommunist Europe. And containment had staying power. Although given different spins by the Truman, Eisenhower, and Kennedy administrations, containment became the bedrock of American foreign policy. Before long it was applied globally, serving as the backbone of American policy during all three presidencies of the acute Cold War.

The Cuban missile crisis of 1962, as well as the subsequent Vietnam disaster, eventually weakened the blanket ("we will pay any price, anywhere, to fight any kind of a communist threat") commitment to containment that marked the acute Cold War. Nevertheless, even with American resolve badly shaken, containment continued as the most consistent theme of American foreign policy up to the collapse of the Soviet Union.

Administration "Codes"

One perceptive observer has noted that each new administration organizes its foreign policy around a set of working assumptions, or identifiable "codes."[9] In its first years, the Truman administration's "codes" had to do with skepticism about Soviet trustworthiness, simple images of foreign affairs, belief in American moral superiority, general optimism, and confidence in a long-term American nuclear monopoly. However, the twin shocks of 1949—the "loss" of China to communism and the explosion of a Soviet atomic bomb—destroyed the comforting assumptions of superiority underpinning American policy.

Looking for a comprehensive policy response, Truman authorized a committee headed by Paul H. Nitze to create a document known as NSC-68, which spelled out a confident, expansive, and expensive vision of containment. Sweeping beyond Kennan, who only recommended containment for a selected list of strategic points—with a line in the European sand high on the list—NSC-68 argued that containment must apply to "all points," including those at the margins of American interests.[10]

In hindsight, some regard this expansion as both unwise and unrealistic. One historian remarks that NSC-68 failed to distinguish between "vital and peripheral American interests and transformed international politics into a virtual zero-sum game."[11] If every noncommunist regime was of equal strategic importance, there could be no compromise. Paul Nitze gave far more weight to military solutions than did Kennan, who foresaw economic and political leverage as being equally important. Finally, NSC-68 twisted Keynesian economic theory, arguing that American military expenditures would prime the economic pump and fund further military expenditures. The more bombs, the more butter.

Released in 1950, NSC-68 constituted a game plan in search of a venue. It did not have to search for long, as the Korean War soon put NSC-68 to the test. Did it pass the test? Maybe, maybe not. Korea was a bitter war but a limited one. If it demonstrated American and Western determination to contain communism, it also demonstrated the American public's desire for victory in the all-embracing World War II sense. Stalemate along the 38th parallel hardly looked like victory.

Eisenhower's New Look

With a military man's promise to get tough yet bring the boys home for Christmas, the Republican Party took over the presidency in 1952. As Allied military commander in postwar Europe, Dwight Eisenhower had been responsible for applying Truman's European strategy, and he expressed no "burning sense of dissatisfaction" with his predecessor's approach to containment.[12] Eisenhower promised more of the same, only couched in a more self-righteous tone: "The forces of good and evil are massed and armed and opposed as rarely before in history. Freedom is pitted against slavery, lightness against dark."[13]

Personified by Eisenhower's globe-trotting secretary of state, John Foster Dulles, the "Eisenhower-Dulles orthodoxy" persisted virtually unchanged through two Eisenhower terms in office. The Soviets were "not to be bargained with but converted," and while a real and serious Russian military threat certainly existed, Eisenhower and Dulles "consistently over-reacted to that threat."[14]

Some of this overreaction, of course, was simply for domestic consumption. Eisenhower was particularly sensitive to pressure building in Republican circles to differentiate his foreign policy from Truman's. Underscored in a 1953 document known as "Operation Solarium," the Republican administration laid out its "New Look" approach to containment. The "New Look's" geopolitical codes promised more for less—containment that was more proactive and less costly than Truman's version.[15]

In effect, this translated into more nuclear bang for the military buck. To the conservative Eisenhower administration, fiscal stability and military strength seemed inseparable, and a balanced budget was sacrosanct. The unlimited commitments associated with NSC-68, now considered profligate, gave way to cost containment. Conventional forces were reduced, with less expensive nuclear weapons brought forward to fill the breach. The greatest departure from Truman's containment policy, however, consisted of preaching an "asymmetrical response" in contrast to the "symmetrical response" formulation of

Truman. No more Koreas. If the enemy wants a war, Eisenhower declared, it had better dig in for an atomic one.[16]

"Brinkmanship," going to the precipice of war to get what America wanted, backed up a seeming willingness to push the nuclear button in "massive retaliation," was bold. It also was frightening. Cold War rhetoric, especially electoral rhetoric, did little to spread oil on international waters. Eisenhower referred to Dulles as his "Old Testament prophet." And certainly Dulles seemed as one imagined the prophets of old. The son of a Presbyterian minister, Dulles seldom smiled and "habitually adopted a severe, even censorious posture." He was not to be toyed with, either by the communists or by domestic naysayers.[17] Dulles added a new wrinkle to the anti-communist hype of his day. He spoke not only of containing communism but also of "liberating" those unfortunates behind the Iron Curtain. While this played well to domestic audiences, it played much less well in a Kremlin that was kept guessing about the fine line between bluff and credible intent. Taking no chances, the Soviets continued to feed their nuclear arsenal.

Dulles and Eisenhower had their domestic critics as well. Some dismissed the Eisenhower-Dulles foreign policy as being long on words, short on deeds, and bankrupt of ideas. They particularly attacked the administration as never missing an opportunity to avoid detente. In recent years, however, Eisenhower's overall assessment by historians has improved.[18] On balance, Eisenhower deserves credit for keeping his pledge to end the Korean War (although he did not have the boys home for Christmas) and for keeping a lid on military spending (something hindsight tells us the Soviets did not do). But what about finding common ground with the Soviets? Here not so great. By turning a stony public face toward the Soviets, Eisenhower lost any chance for rapprochement—a failing that he recognized as he left office.[19]

Kennedy's "Flexible Response"

Eisenhower's Democratic successor, John F. Kennedy, hit pay dirt with foreign policy issues in his 1960 electoral victory over Eisenhower's vice president, Richard M. Nixon. And in some ways he out-Republicaned the Republicans. Proving himself an avid cold warrior, Kennedy attacked the Republicans for inertia in their Cuban policy and for tolerating a supposed "missile gap" with the Soviets, a fiction lubricated by the Soviet satellite launch of "Sputnik" in 1957. When then Texas senator Lyndon Johnson heard about Sputnik, his overreaction reached beyond his region and typified the national psyche; gritting his teeth, LBJ uttered, "I will not go to sleep at night by the light of a communist moon."

In a more temperate tone, Kennedy also charged the Republicans with focusing on military spending to the exclusion of political and economic tactics in containing communism. Guns, he warned, might prevent attack from the outside, but they hardly won the hearts and minds of Third-World peoples needing economic and social assistance. To hold back communism, America needed to help people—not merely guard borders. But whether pummeling the Republicans as too slow in military innovation or too narrow in vision, Kennedy's campaign represented a veritable Cold War crusade. His foreign policy attack proved a vote grabber, and in his unusual inaugural address he dealt emotionally and exclusively with international issues.

Kennedy, the second of seven American presidents to see active duty in World War II, accepted the creed of the Munich syndrome—the worst possible foreign-policy mistake was appeasing an aggressor. His Harvard honors thesis, later converted into a book, dissected the lessons of Munich. All this is hardly surprising. He imbibed an anticommunist credo with his mother's milk, growing up in a strong Irish-American, Catholic family that championed individual achievement, competition, and resilience.

But antipathy to communism was one thing. Dealing with the Soviet Union was quite another. If Kennedy was an intelligent and confident politician, his political training included little preparation in foreign affairs. Some historians argue that Kennedy also had an excessive penchant for risk taking. Early in his presidency he took several high-profile and not altogether successful risks over Berlin, Cuba, and Vietnam, all of which strained American-Soviet relations.[20]

It was as if the young and inexperienced Kennedy administration, fearful at any appearance of weakness, over-compensated with a macho style.[21] Somewhat speculatively, one scholar places some of the blame for any excessive "muscularity" in Kennedy's foreign policy responses on the fact that "JFK was a sickly kid, ill much of the time," and in adulthood was racked by carefully concealed illnesses and physical problems.[22] This, he argues, left Kennedy with a need to prove his virility. If this was an administration fueled by testosterone, then what Marilyn Monroe didn't get, apparently the Soviets did.

Kennedy had his own equivalent to Truman's NSC-68 and Eisenhower's Operation Solarium: the Basic National Security Policy. The BNSP contributed the notion of new options for a changing world to the basic containment policy Kennedy inherited from his predecessors. The BNSP also regarded emerging Third-World countries as the new field of superpower competition. To smother any insurgent communist monster in its Third-World crib, JFK promoted prosperity and democracy in the developing world. Where muscle was needed, new counterinsurgency techniques would be unleashed to check communist initiatives. Echoing NSC-68, BNSP also promised the most up-to-date conventional and nuclear forces ready to deal with any eventuality, irrespective of the cost.

Where did Kennedy break with his predecessors? He was convinced of the possibility, if not the necessity, of preventing military intervention by engaging in hands-on political initiatives, such as the Alliance for Progress, Peace Corps, Food for Peace, and a new Agency for International Development. All gave containment's bag of tricks a new "flexible response," hopefully forestalling the need for military force. Yet, despite these innovations, Kennedy's actual foreign policy unfolded more as a "reflection of Cold War orthodoxies than of liberal pronouncements so eloquently enunciated by the President."[23]

Eyeball-to-Eyeball over Cuba

Nothing so exemplified Kennedy's Cold War risk taking, and nothing paid off so well in public adulation for the young president, as the Cuban missile crisis. This high-stakes game of nuclear "chicken" played itself out in the Caribbean, "America's lake." However, it was not proximity alone that made this challenge to American strategic advantage so critical. On the heels of the Bay of Pigs debacle, the failed Vienna summit, and Berlin wall construction, the missile crisis represented JFK's line in the sand of foreign policy. As seen immediately afterwards it also gave Kennedy one apparent victory over Khrushchev before the president's untimely death. And certainly it proved a benchmark event: it forced an end to the acute Cold War, convincing the superpowers that they must edge back from the brink of Armageddon.

It began in late August 1962 when American U-2 spy planes sighted the first Soviet surface-to-air missiles (SAMs) in Cuba. Then Russian medium-range bombers were observed, and in mid-October, the CIA's worst fears materialized: American reconnaisance flights found Soviet ground-to-ground ballistic missiles capable of hitting East Coast cities within a few minutes after launch. While the United States did not know it at the time, by October 1962 twenty-four of the SS-4 launchers carried offensive nuclear warheads, and six tactical nuclear launchers, defensive in nature, had also been delivered to the Cubans by Khrushchev.[24]

Following nearly two weeks of top-secret debate, the Kennedy administration was left with only two alternatives—an air strike against the missile sites (favored by Dean Acheson, General Maxwell Taylor, and the joint chiefs) or a naval blockade, a "quarantine" (supported by Robert McNamara, George Ball, and Robert Kennedy), consisting of American ships ringing the island of Cuba.

The president chose the armed blockade, even as more Soviet nuclear-laden ships steamed toward Cuba. As the threat of nuclear war wratcheted up, humankind held its breath. At the last moment, Soviet ships were ordered home and Khrushchev began removing offensive missiles from Cuba in exchange for an American pledge not to support another invasion of the island. America, it seemed, had won hands down. In forcing the withdrawal of Soviet offensive weapons from Cuba, Kennedy deserves commendation for learning "the danger of uncontested viewpoints" from the Bay of Pigs fiasco and for carefully weighing diverse advice as the crisis unfolded. One can only shudder over what an air strike against the missiles might have precipitated.[25]

But did Kennedy deserve all the accolades of victory that the blockade brought him? Previously classified documentation reveals the extent to which Kennedy and his advisers completely misread Soviet motivations, rejecting out of hand what emerged as the main reason behind Khrushchev's placement of missiles in Cuba. The Americans believed, incorrectly, that Khrushchev sought to challenge the young and inexperienced Kennedy, as he had done at their summit meeting in Vienna. New information reveals that the main Soviet reasons were "to defend the Cuban revolution and deter a U.S. attack." Cuban intelligence sources had penetrated the CIA and produced an Administration memorandum in early 1962 saying that if Fidel Castro could not be gotten rid of by the end of 1962, the U.S. would be forced to take "more drastic action." Nikita Khrushchev apparently interpreted this to mean another covert invasion of Cuba.[26]

The CIA had already attempted to get rid of Castro in some bizarre ways, and Castro was well aware of them. For example, the CIA's Richard Bissell, who was then planning the Bay of Pigs invasion with fellow Groton graduate Terry Barnes, approached mobster Sam Giancana in September of 1960 to commission an assassination of Castro. Journalist Evan Thomas writes that such clumsy efforts fueled Castro's eagerness to accept the missiles touted by Khrushchev as defenders of the Cuban revolution, thus contributing to the escalation culminating in the Cuban missile crisis. The early days of the CIA almost make it too easy to illustrate well-intended, guiltless, and naive excess in the pursuit of American foreign policy.[27]

The president's fear of appearing weak and his need to test his mettle against all comers may well have foreclosed any possibility of finding a direct, negotiated remedy. Did the world need to be brought to the edge of nuclear holocaust before the Soviets would agree to remove the missiles in return for an American pledge to not invade Cuba again? In the end, Khrushchev, by pulling back from the precipice in exchange for what he says he wanted in the first place, a guarantee that the United States would not invade Cuba a second time, seems to have gained a small and belated claim to victory as well.

Irrespective of winners and losers, the world felt fortunate to have escaped nuclear war. The Cuban crisis gave both sides a glimpse at mutual annihilation. Shaken, they began to defuse the acute Cold War, finding ways to coexist in an imperfect world. Perhaps the ultimate winner of the Cuban missile crisis was common sense.

Hard Times in Hollywood

Compared to its Golden Age or to the sense of national mission during World War II, Hollywood experienced hard times in the late 1940s and early 1950s. The motion picture industry seemed to be losing ground in its struggle to overcome a series of challenges, not least of which was the anticommunist temper of the times. Hollywood's glitter became tarnished as exaggerated fears of domestic communism rumbled though Tinseltown. Normally shy of controversy—but fearing outside censorship more—studios over-achieved in an orgy of political self-censorship. Studio bosses wrapped themselves in the American flag, trumpeting their defense of the American way of life and placing scores of writers, directors, and actors on the industry's blacklist. Gone were many of Hollywood's most creative souls, just when they were badly needed.

Perhaps, in part, because they had banished so may bright minds, studios were slow responding to competition from foreign films, especially Italian neorealist imports. Major studios also lost a protracted legal battle with the U.S. Department of Justice over their virtual monopoly of both film production facilities and movie theaters. The landmark 1948 Supreme Court antitrust decision forced the studios to divest themselves of theater ownership. If money was to be made, it would be by producing better films, not selling buttered popcorn.[28]

But American studios were having trouble just getting their former audiences into movie theaters. The most relentless problem Hollywood faced was the popular defection to television. Hollywood felt "equally menaced by Reds and black-and-white."[29] As the 1950s wore on, the box flickering in every American living room set off a free fall in movie attendance. Studio efforts to stop audience hemorrhaging proved futile. By 1958, weekly admission figures hit their lowest point ever.[30] In 1951, fifty-five movie theaters closed in New York City alone. Betting that the little gray tube could not compete with a jazzed-up product, Hollywood threw money after costly technological innovations—wider screens, 3-D, special effects, and spectacular costume epics.

Hollywood Fights Back

Wide-screen CinemaScope, invented in France thirty years earlier and purchased by Fox in the early fifties, debuted in 1953 with *The Robe.* It fared better than competitors like 3-D, VistaVision, Cinerama, and Todd-AO. However, close-ups presented special problems for CinemaScope, and Paramount's VistaVision proved superior in creating natural-looking tight shots, which Paramount used effectively in Cecil B. DeMille's sprawling epic—box-office champ of the 1950s—*The Ten Commandments* (1956).

But where it counted, in the wallet, technology often proved to be more of a problem than a solution. Most technological fixes were just too expensive, and studios quickly abandoned them. Alfred Hitchcock complained that 3-D was a nine-day wonder, and he "came in on the ninth day." Correctly judging that 3-D was on its way out, he resented putting his audiences into two-color glasses so they could get a thrill out of his *Dial M for Murder,* released in 1954. Audiences agreed with him.[31] Other technological panaceas, experiments with sound and even smell, came and went even faster than Hollywood's short-lived flirtation with 3-D.

Hoping that others had answers to the slump in ticket sales, studios began bankrolling independent productions, rather than overseeing the entire filmmaking process. This created exciting opportunities for young and innovative filmmakers to experiment with a few socially daring films. In addition, rather than relying exclusively on Hollywood back lots, by middecade, studios embraced on-location "runaways" that added authenticity and exotica to films while cutting production costs. By the early sixties nearly one-third of all Hollywood films were runaways.[32]

But audiences continued to stay home and watch TV. What did Hollywood fail to do in the fifties that might have brought them back? Reinventing the content of its films would have helped. The decade's pictures seemed schizoid, split between "lowbrow bonanzas on big screens and socially-oriented movies for intellectuals."[33] Hollywood generally seemed to be out of energy and fresh ideas, as if "the creative juices that had made movies in the thirties and forties so promising dried up in the fifties." In spite of Shadowland's technological experimentation, it was television that best catered to popular taste.[34]

Conformity and Mental Health

That is not to say that Hollywood and TV were worlds apart when it came to the intellectual common denominator. Conformism, group-think and antiindividualism pervaded TV and Hollywood fare alike. But there was a difference. Television offered viewers an endless series of guests who visited in their homes for half an hour once a week. Film, on the other hand, seemed considerably less welcoming. Hollywood identified patriotic duty and social responsibility as paramount. Rugged individualism, long revered in the American self-identity, went on holiday, and bland conformity became the litmus test for psychological well-being. Worse than asocial, cinematic loners and rebels suddenly became candidates for analysis.

For the first time, Hollywood served up antisocial behavior, including the standard generation gap, as the product of psychopathology. Hollywood equated the qualities of calmness and conformity with mental health in its characters. Conversely, creative people, intellectually questioning people, loners, and nervous people came across as dangerous. Even worse, they were now depicted as Hollywood's psychologically sick people, warranting compassion and analysis—Mr. Deeds Goes to Therapy.

Sublimated Nuclear Anxiety

Unlike many of the soothing images offered by nightly television, movies of the fifties throb with inordinate, free-floating "dread of the unknown." Nothing seemed more unknown than the maneuvers of America's new enemy—the Soviets—suddenly armed with the bomb.[35] The possibility of nuclear annihilation subtly affected American society, especially its young people. It was they who were asked to swallow the insanity of total destruction as normal. One film historian argues that repressed nuclear anxiety constitutes the underlying reality shaping the era's films.[36]

Nuclear anxiety also helps explain why 1950s American culture exaggerated the potency of Freudianism at the individual level and the threat of Marxism at the societal level—both doctrinaire ideologies purporting to explain human behavior. The American exaggeration of Marxism has been widely analyzed; not so the 1950s embrace of Freudian theory.

Freud's creative synthesis, like that of Marx before him, provided rich explanations of human behavior grounded in humanistic values and intentions. As applied theories, both Freudianism and Marxism have since been overtaken by their competitors. While possessing elegant logic, what seemed plausible in theory did not work in practice, damning both Marx and Freud more and more to a purgatory of impracticality in the world of functioning human beings. But through the 1950s, before this fall from grace, Freud had enormous impact on America, and Hollywood was no exception.

Hollywood's Golden Age of Psychiatry

The acute Cold War years can be described as an era of "psychological primacy." If some aspect of human behavior could not be explained, borrowing on Freud, it was put down to a deep-seated psychological source. During the 1950s, autism, anxiety, depression, hyperactivity, phobia, and schizophrenia were all gathered under the psychosomatic umbrella. In the 1990s, by contrast, biopsychiatry, with its emphasis on genetics, has challenged psychosomatic causation.

But, in its day, psychosomatic explanation swept through Hollywood's screenplays, so much so that psychiatrists and movie buffs Krin and Glen Gabbard regard the period from 1957 to 1962 as the Golden Age of psychiatry in American movies. It reflected the conviction in American culture that "psychiatrists were authoritative voices of reason, adjustment, and well-being." Well-publicized World War II psychoanalytic successes contributed to idealized images of psychiatry, as did the widely accepted writings of Dr. Benjamin Spock on the child rearing of the postwar baby boom children.

Psychoanalysis became increasingly fashionable for affluent professionals, and the mass media touted psychoanalytic panaceas for wideranging social problems. So too in film. While psychiatry had been depicted as little short of quackery in movies of the 1930s and 1940s (and later, in the 1960s), it was glamorized in at least twenty-two Hollywood films between 1956 and 1962. The Gabbards point to Don Siegel's haunting cult classic, *Invasion of the Body Snatchers* (1956), as the harbinger of pictures wallowing in esoteric meaning. In large part, such meaning is bound up with Cold War anxiety.[37]

Two remakes of *Invasion of the Body Snatchers* have failed to capture the sense of dread reeking from Siegel's original. How could they? The times are different and the original remains a product of its time. The 1956 version of *Invasion of the Body Snatchers* uses a "framing device": in a series of flashbacks a distraught and seemingly insane Miles Bennell (Kevin McCarthy), blurts out a bizarre tale to a doctor and a policeman. Miles Bennell, a local doctor, tells of giant seed pods infiltrating the minds and bodies of residents of sleepy Santa Mira, California. Insidiously, citizens look the same as before, but their bodies have been taken over by an alien life force. Miles's beautiful girlfriend Becky (Dana Wynter) discovers that "Uncle Ira isn't Uncle Ira. There's no emotion in him. None. Just the pretense of it." Becky and Miles are unable to convince others of what they know to be true. Only their growing, agitated paranoia—the only alternative to "podlike conformism"—offers them hope of survival and independence. In the end, the FBI comes to the rescue, saving Miles, Becky, and the world.

What makes this film so haunting? Many see *Body Snatchers* as a metaphor for widespread American dread of communist subversion and an imposed conformity. Stuart Samuels also notes that individualism, under siege in the fifties but still resilient in the American mythology, is central to Siegel's *Body Snatchers*.[38]

America's faith in the mythology of individualism contributed to the unprecedented success of another film genre of the fifties, the western. Ideally suited to the beleaguered American psyche of the day, westerns blended escapism, rugged individualism, gun-toting self-determination, and presented them in that most unique of all American settings—the wild west, a land free of moral ambiguity. To an American public believing itself locked into a teutonic struggle of good against evil, freedom against communism, the screen image of the quiet loner squaring off against evil desperadoes or savage Indians struck a responsive chord. Both desperadoes and Indians represented a threatening "other," much like alien seedpods in *Body Snatchers*, and all three made plausible surrogate Russians in the 1950s.

Freudian Analysis

In retrospect, it seems natural that Hollywood would toy with themes of mind capturing. The fifties, heyday of the Freudian psychoanalytic school, also included spin-offs like Jungian analysis, whose notion of "collective subconscious" represents a rare concession in psychology to explanations on the larger social level. Psychoanalysis supplanted the more mechanistic behaviorist psychology of J. B. Watson and B. F. Skinner, popular earlier in the century. Watson and Skinner pointed to environmental conditions as shaping human behavior, a notion that also gained wide acceptance among Soviet researchers. For them, behaviorist conditioning dovetailed nicely with Marxian faith in economic determinism, legitimizing Stalinist efforts to create a new, socially engineered "Soviet man."

But if behaviorism held sway in the Soviet Union, Freud and his heirs mesmerized America with the implications of id, superego, and ego; subconscious desires; Freudian slips; anal retentivism; and unresolved early sexual conflicts. Freudian psychoanalysis held America enthralled through the 1950s, only to give way in the 1960s and 1970s to new "third-force" humanistic and idealistic psychologies, such as the gestalt therapy of Fritz Perls, the client-centered approach of Carl Rogers, the rational-emotive theory of Albert Ellis, and Eric Berne's transactional analysis.[39]

Micro- and Macroperspectives

But what are we to make of this heyday of Freudian thought? What did it say to Americans and the film industry? Like an iceberg revealing only the tip of its mass, it implied that much of what humans refer to as "culture" swirls beneath conscious awareness, even as it influences broad patterns of social behavior. This behavior is a product blended at the multiple contact points between each individual's psychology and the cultural norms of society. Yet individual and society exist in the dynamic tension of a tug-of-war. In the 1950s, and again in the 1970s, America leaned toward the pole of individual psychology on this continuum. The 1960s, conversely, saw the American mind-set shift abruptly toward the societal pole.

Scarce Cinematic Russians

American cinema reflected these polar divisions and, as far as portraits of the Cold War were concerned, it did so in the larger absence of Russians and the Soviet Union. As early as 1949, critics noted that Hollywood's number of British film characters remained constant from the 1930s to World War II and through the postwar period. Russians, however, nearly disappeared from the screen after the war. What would account for such a disparity? Several reasons suggest themselves. During World War II, cinematic Russians and British were portrayed as down-home folks who spoke with an accent. Not so in the Cold War era. If the overlap in Anglo-American cultural values continued, sharp Soviet-American cultural differences led to the near disappearance of Hollywood's soft Russian characters. From 1946 to 1962, Russians rivaled leprosy on the list of what Hollywood preferred not to touch. During that period only sixteen pictures were released with Russian characters—barely one per year.

There was also the perennial profit motive. Loath to deal with controversy and burned by the HUAC proceedings, Hollywood avoided the loaded subject of the Russians lest it be judged soft on them.[40] Given the abuse heaped on studios for their earlier pro-Soviet World War II movies, this Russophobia seems understandable. The fifteen-hundred-member Motion Picture Alliance for the Preservation of American Ideals held sway in Hollywood. Embracing the motto "Co-existence is a myth and neutrality is impossible, anyone not FIGHTING communism is HELPING communism," MPAPAI demanded that Hollywood sign on in defense of Cold War America.[41] Hollywood director Sam Wood, who placed a condition in his will requiring all relatives to swear they had never been a communist, served as president of the MPAPAI. When HUAC decided to hold hearings in Los Angeles, Sam Wood's outfit enthusiastically served as its official host.

Sam Wood had allies. Ayn Rand counted among her anticommunist credits a 1950 pamphlet called *Screen Guide for Americans*, intended as a studio guide in ferreting out collectivist propaganda. She included practical suggestions like "Don't smear industrialists," "Don't Smear Success," and "Don't ever use lines about 'the common man' or 'the little people.' It is not the American idea to be either 'common' or 'little'."[42] With the line at best blurry between what was acceptable and what was not, and no Hollywood studio or producer wanting to be accused of communist sympathies, it was safest to just avoid dealing with Russians.

Nor was it only Hollywood that was frightened. Fear pervaded the American mind-set in the 1950s. The threat of Soviet nuclear intentions constituted a major source of America's anxiety. Recognizing a downer, Hollywood avoided the bomb with the same ardor it devoted to avoiding the Russians. Nevertheless, given the fear of the bomb and the Russians, what could be more natural than for some of those fears to be sublimated, surfacing in melodramatic film venues. One analyst suggests that "displacing forbidden subjects, such as sex or politics, into sanctioned conventions of melodrama" has been a standard Hollywood technique.[43] According to critic Susan Sontag, the technique was worked to death in the science fiction movie, which became a Hollywood mainstay in the 1950s. Sontag argues that the monsters who ran amok across the silver screen in fifty-plus films were a popular culture outcropping of otherwise sublimated Cold War fears.[44]

Surrogates

Two distinct subgenres of science fiction films materialized in the 1950s. In one, America confronted the threat of irradiated nuclear mutant monsters. These large and lethal predators, some glowing in the dark, included threats such as twelve-foot ants in *Them!* (1954), giant mollusks in *The Monster That Challenged the World* (1957), and a mammoth squid-turned-carnivore in *It Came from Beneath the Sea* (1955). The unanticipated by-products of a nuclear age gone wrong, these monsters played on America's fear of the same bomb that Hollywood tried to avoid handling head-on for most of the 1950s.

The second subgenre pits America against malefic alien invaders. These invaders are quite unlike humankind, even if a few manage to disguise their true identity. Evil to their alien cores, they threaten the civilization of humane values. In some movies, like *Invasion of the Body Snatchers* (1956), *Invaders from Mars* (1953), and *I Married a Monster from Outer Space* (1958), alien life forces infiltrate people's bodies and subvert their minds, making it hard to tell "us" from "them." Others like *The Thing* (1951), *War of the Worlds* (1953), or *The Blob* (1958) feature less subtle intruders. In these three movies, the unwelcome invaders try to eat, shoot, and engulf humans respectively.

While some aliens attack America indirectly, infiltrating and subverting, as in *Invasion of the Body Snatchers*, *Invaders from Mars*, and *I Married a Monster from Outer Space*, others take on America in a frontal assault, as in *The Thing, War of the Worlds*, and *The Blob*. But whatever their shape or their powers, all these alien invaders stood in for the dreaded Russians—outsiders threatening America. That both types of science fiction films suddenly disappeared in the early 1960s—about the time when *Dr. Strangelove*'s black humor cut to the bone of America's anticommunist phobia—underscores the sublimation argument.

Real Russians

But if surrogate Russians in the form of alien monsters far outnumbered real Russians, about sixteen of the hundreds of films released in this era depict actual Russians. Half of the films about Russians in the acute Cold War period appeared early in the era, and all dined on crude Russophobia. Later in the decade, half a dozen middling romantic comedies were released. Still later, two oddly favorable films turned the corner into the next era, where they would fit more comfortably. Neither bellwether film, *Prisoner of War*, which demonized the Russians, nor light comedy *Jet Pilot*, rises much above mediocrity.[45]

Prisoner of War

Looking for a villain? Look no further that KGB Colonel Nikita Biroshilov, Soviet "adviser" to North Korean communist underlings in *Prisoner of War* (1954). Played by Oscar Homolka, a Viennese-born character actor remembered for his "strong build, bushy eyebrows, wickedly twinkling eyes and a gravelly voice," Biroshilov relishes teaching prison camp guards new Russian Pavlovian techniques designed to break the spirit of American POWs.[46] If mind control is central to the Biroshilov repertoire, he also delivers torture and deprivation with equal pleasure. A sneering, cynical martinet, Biroshilov gives away his sinister side by smoking his cigarettes while holding them backward, as sure a sign of the evil foreigner as any Hollywood ever devised. But smoke as he please, the Russian colonel is no match for the American spirit, which triumphs in the end.

This M-G-M film was directed by another east European native, Hungarian-born Andrew Marton, who arrived in Hollywood in 1923 with Ernst Lubitsch. Marton spent much of his early Hollywood years working for M-G-M, often as second director. Later he directed from behind a television camera, perhaps explaining why he has received scant attention from film historians. Of course, he likely would not have welcomed too much attention focused on his *Prisoner of War*. It was not one of his cinematic high points. The film opens with a prologue confidently assuring viewers that "the spirit of man can run deep—far beyond the reach of communist torturers." The American spirit award in *Prisoner of War* goes, hands down, to Web Sloane (Ronald Reagan).

One normally expects to find soldiers trying to break out of war camps. Not Web Sloane. He volunteers to parachute behind North Korean enemy lines and break into a prisoner-of-war camp to "see how the enemy is treating our boys." Film historian David Shipman gives Reagan credit for repeatedly pulling off a "screen image of sincerity and boyish honesty," certainly an apt description of Reagan's straight-arrow role as Web Sloane.[47] The plot line is as thin as *Prisoner of War's* premise. After successfully infiltrating the prison camp and gathering evidence of Soviet cruelty to American POWs, Sloane gets captured. But Sloane, all-American boy that he is, does not break, and all ends well. Web Sloane, true and just, escapes Biroshilov's clutches, returning to warn Americans of communism's evil. In a just ending, Colonel Biroshilov is killed by an outraged POW.

The release of *Prisoner of War* drew relatively little critical or public attention. The *New York Times*, however, reported on a controversy over the withdrawal of U.S. Defense Department support for this M-G-M picture. Screenwriter Allen Rivkin revealed that at first the army's psychological warfare branch had been "very enthusiastic about the picture," providing technical adviser Captain Robert H. Wise, a three-year Korean POW, and encouraging interviews with sixty POWs, then the army suddenly withdrew its support. According to Rivkin, the army adjutant general's office forced the reversal because it did not want to draw attention to the pending court-martial of several American POWs who had confessed to germ warfare in Korea.[48]

While Rivkin claimed that *Prisoner of War* accurately depicted the Korean prison camps, the army charged that the film pushed the limits of credibility too far even for propaganda. According to the army, the picture was "just contrary to the facts as we know them." Not looking for fights, and certainly not one with the army, M-G-M ran for cover. It offered "no comment" on the controversy except to say that the studio valued future assistance from the Defense Department.[49]

A Few Bad Russians

The Soviet system, especially the bureaucrats who run it, also took a cinematic beating in *Never Let Me Go* (1953), a virtual remake of King Vidor's *Comrade X*. *Never Let Me Go* was directed by Delmer Daves for M-G-M, which released the film in wide-screen enlargement. This process resulted in some unintended consequences, like cutting the feet off ballet dancers, and one critic bemoaned how proper editing had been sacrificed to screen size.[50] M-G-M's technical experimentation, however, failed to pump life into this flat *Comrade X* remake. More might have been expected from an oddball director such as Daves. He once rode for the Pony Express and had his heel shot out by Ute Indians. A Stanford graduate, he turned his back on careers in civil engineering and law after living several months with Hopi Indians in the Arizona desert. Drawn to Hollywood, Daves wrote, acted, and directed in a series of atypical and unglamorized westerns relatively sympathetic to American Indians.[51] No such hint of authenticity, however, appears in *Never Let Me Go*, one of nine films Daves made in the 1950s.

In this film Clark Gable again plays a hard-boiled newspaperman, this time Philip Sutherland, an American stationed in Moscow. Sutherland's life changes abruptly after he meets the beautiful and talented ballerina dancer, Marya Lamarkina (Gene Tierney). Marya has a long history of abuse at the hands of the cruel Soviet system. As a child of eight, she lost her parents to Stalin's purges. This vulnerable, lovely woman and the tough journalist fall head over heels in love. The two marry in the U.S. Embassy under a portrait of Abraham Lincoln. They hope to leave for America, but Soviet bureaucrats, always under a portrait of Stalin or Lenin, lie, stall, and ultimately refuse Marya an exit visa. Apolitical and wanting only to build a quiet life with her new husband in his homeland, Marya despairs.

The film's dramatic tension ebbs and flows with Sutherland's repeated efforts to win permission for Marya to leave the cold, harsh Soviet Union. Rather than accept failure, he risks all in one daring adventure. Clad in a stolen Russian army uniform, Sutherland steals Marya from a performance of "Swan Lake," commandeers a rowboat, and paddles across the Baltic Sea to freedom.

As the audience celebrates this victory of love over tyranny, its contentment is tempered by knowledge that others in need are left behind in the Soviet Union. Escape, for example, is not available to Red Army translator Svetlana Mikhailovna (Anna Valentina). A friend of Marya and Sutherland, Svetlana dreams of liberation. She encounters the same bureaucratic drones and doctrinaire communists who equate emigration with treason, although she is married to a Briton. She remains behind, having no daring and resourceful American to free her. *Never Let Me Go* won little critical acclaim, but its anticommunist message got through. If nothing else, reviewer Bosley Crowther finds it reassuring that "Clark Gable is one fellow who can still make the Soviet Union's tough guys look like absolute monkeys."[52]

The World in His Arms

Equally hard on Russians who do not fall in love with Americans, *The World in His Arms* (1952) portrays all Russians, save one, as either fools or oppressors. The sole exception, Countess Marina Selanova (Ann Blyth), falls in love with an American. Once again, a Russian woman ends up as a happy American housewife, as the countess finds that true love and freedom go hand in hand.

The movie was directed for Universal-International by Raoul Walsh, whose Hollywood career began in silent films and spanned fifty years. Yet, the "fifties seemed to have passed Walsh by."[53] Addressing the breadth without depth of Walsh's career, film historian Jean-Pierre Coursodon describes rambling story lines, action pictures degenerating into horseplay, and "foreign accents invariably connoting villainy of some sort."[54] He could not have summarized *The World in His Arms* any more cogently had he specifically intended it.

The World in His Arms unfolds against a backdrop of the financial problems of Russia's Alaskan Sea Company in the 1850s, before Russia sold Alaska to the United States. The Russian company's economic decay is put down to its oppression of indigenous Eskimos and the competitive skills of American sealers like captain Jonathan Clark (Gregory Peck). Back in San Francisco after a successful sealing trip to Alaska, Captain Clark receives an unusual offer. The Russian Countess Selanova (Ann Blyth) requests passage to Alaska, hoping to escape an arranged marriage to the Tsar's nephew, Prince Simyon (Carl Esmond). Clark's retort nails down his anti-Russian credentials: "Now listen to this: I have no love for the Russians and even less for the nobility. As for your Countess Selanova, you can tell the old wench she can swim to Alaska for all I care!"

On his next trip to Alaska, however, Jonathan Clark meets the countess but doesn't know it because she is hiding her true identity as a lowly attendant to the countess. Jonathan is entranced by the Russian woman's beauty, sensitivity, and idealism. The two fall in love, and Captain Clark proposes. Bubbling over with hope for her new life, Marina Selanova enthusiastically informs her entourage, "We're going to be Americans; we're going to laugh and sing. We're going to learn to be happy and never to be afraid!"

Not so fast. Prince Simyon is not about to let her go and trails the lovers to San Francisco. The night before their wedding, the lowlife whisks Marina back to Sitka, Alaska, where he intends to force the distraught countess into marriage. After plot twists that would confuse a contortionist, Jonathan finally rescues Marina from Prince Simyon; the two return to America, which Marina now loves as deeply as she loves Jonathan.

If the plot lacks credibility, it does not want for action. Indeed, the plot seems but an excuse for Technicolor on-screen brawling, braggadocio and schooner chases through the churning north Pacific. And at every turn, the Russians are losers (except for the noble lady in love), creating "a great deal of lusty agitation about singeing the tsarist Russians' beards."[55]

Behind the Iron Curtain

A film with dire warnings about Soviet designs on America was *Behind the Iron Curtain* (1948), a heavier-than-lead "faction" account of three Soviet spies in North America. Loosely based on a real-life spy scandal that rocked the Canadian capital, the plot revolves around the defection of a Soviet spy. As the cinematic story opens, the subversives, never far from a portrait of Stalin, use the Soviet embassy in Ottawa to plot their subterfuge. After one of them, code clerk Igor Gouzenko (Dana Andrews), sees the light and defects to freedom, he secretly helps Canadian authorities trap and ultimately convict ten Soviet spies operating in Canada.

Behind the Iron Curtain was directed by William Wellman, formerly of the French Foreign Legion and the Lafayette Flying Squadron, but best known for his classic film about flying, *Wings* (1927). Characterized as a director of "entertaining male-dominated action films" and frequently compared to Henry Hathaway, Wellman addressed issues of survival and, in the case of *Behind the Iron Curtain*, the survival of the free world. Very comfortable within the studio system, Wellman also helped pioneer the 1930s "social problem" film for Warner Brothers.[56] Although Wellman preferred westerns and war films, his filmic politics demonstrated an easy fluidity: clearly liberal in the 1930s, by the late 1940s and early 1950s he was fashionably conservative.

To the chagrin of producer Daryl Zanuck, *Behind the Iron Curtain* failed to make money. Its quasi-documentary style and grainy, cinema noir quality may have suited a film about Cold War intrigue, but it failed to win over audiences. The movie's most distinctive feature remains its haunting musical score, including music by Russian composers Shostakovich, Khatchaturian, and Prokofiev. But the music also haunted Twentieth Century Fox on another score. The studio had neglected to obtain rights to the music and eventually found itself in court facing off against lawyers representing the three Russian composers.

The Red Danube

Cold War intrigue seeps from every frame of *The Red Danube* (1949). This time the Russians prove a particularly reprehensible lot, even by the film standards of this era. Based on Bruce Marshall's book, *Vespers in Vienna, The Red Danube* was directed by George Sidney. Sidney grew up in a consummately showbiz family and made his film debut at ten months of age. His father was a vice president of M-G-M, and his mother was one of the famous singing Mooney Sisters. He spent most of his long career at M-G-M, spinning out musicals and other movies that one historian characterizes as "superficial, attractive to look at, unmeritorious programmers."[57]

The *Red Danube* is something of a change of pace for George Sidney. It opens immediately after World War II with the Soviet government complaining that its wartime allies are harboring anti-Soviet subversives in Vienna. In particular, Stalin wants one émigré repatriated, Volga German prima ballerina Olga Alexandrova (Janet Leigh). An anticommunist, she was exiled to Siberia during the war but managed to escape to Vienna. Known neither for forgiving nor for forgetting, Stalin wants her back. As the plot unfolds, Olga Alexandrova is hiding in a Viennese convent under the protection of the mother superior (Ethel Barrymore), who is aided by a few sympathetic British military officers. No surprise, one of the British officers, Major "Twingo" McPhimister (Peter Lawford), falls in love with Olga. Knowing love is no shield against the Soviets, Olga takes on an assumed identity— Maria Buhlen, an Austrian.

Hoping to persuade the British to turn Olga over to them, Soviet officers repeatedly lie about their true intentions. Olga is a ballerina, the Soviets tell the British. Her artistry is a Soviet national treasure, and she will be warmly welcomed in Moscow. Some British officers see through the Soviets like a pane of glass. They try to protect not only Olga but also other Russians the Soviets are intent on repatriating. Other officers, like General C. M. V. Catlock (Robert Coote), are so concerned with appeasing the Soviets that they willfully turn a blind eye to what the Soviets are really plotting.

If the film depicts the British officials as a mixed lot, so are the Russians. Soviet officialdom is portrayed as pathologically cruel. By contrast, those Russians earmarked for repatriation, such as Professor Sergei Bruloff (Konstantin Shayne), seem intelligent and likable. But they are also desperate. Bruloff commits suicide rather than fall into Stalin's bloody hands. As the Soviets close in on Olga, she too chooses death, jumping from a window of the British military headquarters.

If, in the end, Russian ruthlessness and mendacity are the main villains of *The Red Danube*, the Allied high command is not above reproach. It too takes a cinematic beating for not standing firm in the face of brutal Soviet postwar treatment of displaced persons. It is worth noting, however, that in this film the British, not the Americans, are the weak link in the Allied chain of resistance to the Soviets. American boys would not likely have been so weak in the face of Soviet shenanigans.

The Manchurian Candidate

In the early years of the 1960s, Hollywood released *The Manchurian Candidate* (1962), regarded by many today as a classic thriller. The film was the product of John Frankenheimer, one of a new generation of directors who cut his professional teeth in television's golden era of live broadcasting in the 1950s. He directed fifty plays, mostly for the CBS series *Playhouse 90*, and received Television Academy of Arts best director nominations five years running. Moving from televison to film, Frankenheimer brought intensity and freshness with him.

If *The Manchurian Candidate* is now lauded for its suspenseful plot twists, when it was released the taut story line spoke darkly to movie audiences schooled by years of domestic cold warriorism. If the film made a single point, it was that some would stop at nothing—not even the murder of a president—to further political ends. The story swirls around experimentation by scientists from Moscow's Pavlov Institute to program the minds of American POWs, as well as around Soviet co-optation of America's radical right into a conspiracy to overthrow American democracy with one bullet. Savagely ironic and cynical, this thriller about the unholy mix of science and politics warns humanity to be wary of both. Science is not neutral, but rather a weapon to those who master it for their own political ends.[58]

Foreshadowing a 1960s loosening of the iron grip that Cold War vigilantes had exercised on Hollywood, Frankenheimer's film also indicts domestic extremism and demagoguery in the United States, epitomized in the film by a McCarthy-like right wing senator willfully operating in league with global communism. It's hard for the viewer not to be drawn in. A bizarre surrealism pervades both the brainwashing and the conspiracy sequences, providing Frankenheimer with cinematic space to stretch the envelope of Hollywood's psychopolitical discourse.

The Manchurian Candidate boasts an outstanding cast, including Frank Sinatra, Laurence Harvey, Janet Leigh, Angela Lansbury, and Henry Silva. Lansbury was nominated by the Academy for best actress. Richard Condon's popular novel provided grist for George Axelrod's screenplay. But United Artists almost did not release this thriller produced by Howard Koch. On the thirtieth anniversary of its release, director Frankenheimer, writer Axelrod, and star Sinatra taped an interview tagged onto the video release of *The Manchurian Candidate*. In it, they contend that UA executives did not want to release the film on the eve of a summit between President Kennedy and Secretary Khrushchev scheduled for Geneva. Fearing the film might pollute the rarefied air before a superpower meeting, the nervous studio intended to smother the film. According to Sinatra, he informed studio executives of his recent visit to Hyannis Port and of Kennedy's fondness for the novel and his interest—even enthusiasm—for the pending film version. JFK particularly wanted to know who played Mrs. Iselin. It was this anecdote, Sinatra claims, that saved the film.

The film, however, fell victim to the flow of history. In November 1962, shortly after the film was released, President Kennedy was shot to death in Dallas. Life echoed fiction. Although the film was a critical success, its story line involving assassination collided with political sensibilities. In the face of public grief, *The Manchurian Candidate* quietly slipped from view.

Less Notable Russophobia

A much less lugubrious Cold War overachiever, *Red Planet Mars* (1952), was directed for United Artists by Harry Horner. The Czech-born architect and art director had only seven low-budget films to his directing credit, but he had won a 1949 Oscar for art direction. The plot of *Red Planet Mars* has American scientist Dr. Chris Cronyn (Peter Graves) using the blueprints of an old Nazi scientist, Dr. Franz Calder (Herbert Berghof), to create a "hydrogen valve" enabling him to send radio messages to Mars. To Dr. Cronyn's delight, responses to his messages start returning from the red planet, at first suggesting a highly advanced civilization. Before long, however, the Martian messages set off world-wide panic. We soon discover that, not Martians, but a bitter Dr. Franz Calder, conspiring with the Soviets, is sending the panic-mongering messages to Dr. Cronyn.

With civil order about to collapse, the deity intervenes, not through a burning bush or tablets from Mount Sinai. The movie audience witnesses a miracle of technological showbiz. To save the democracies from Soviet deception, the deity takes to the airways (Voice of America, no less). All the world's peoples are suddenly huddled in front of their radios listening to the sacred message, a cross between Sunday-school treacle and a Fourth of July barn burner, all in their own languages. And now the revolutionary shoe is on the other foot. The inspirational word inspires Russian peasants to resurrect long hidden icons, overthrow the communist government, and replace it with an Orthodox theocracy. Amidst the transition, a voice-over informs viewers that this is "a nation finding its soul." Amen.

There is plenty of celluloid soul to go around in Hollywood. In another cinematic purveyor of Cold War values, *California Conquest* (1952), audiences are treated to a thinly veiled Cold War allegory set in the California territory from 1825 to 1841. Directed by Lew Landers for Columbia, *California Conquest* spins a bizarre tale of Mexican-American competition over the California territory. The lack of any nod in the direction of historical accuracy did not escape a disbelieving *New York Times* reviewer who took obvious delight in picking apart the "preposterous nature" of producer Sam Katzman's role in shaping the plot. Most preposterous in this California oater, however, is that "believe it or not, the real culprits are the Russians."[59]

No Russians actually appear in the first seventy-five minutes of the film, but moviegoers soon learn that Russians are feverishly at work behind the scenes, manipulating their Mexican puppets. Thus, what looks at first like a Mexican-American territorial struggle runs much deeper; in the shadows hides a power-hungry Russian autocracy hoping to manipulate its Mexican lackeys in a bid to take over California.

They do not go unchallenged. The hero, Don Arturo Bordega (Cornel Wilde), and heroine, Julia Lawrence (Teresa Wright), are lovers fighting for American annexation of California in the face of a threatened Russian invasion force. Of all the evil Russians, the worst is haughty aristocrat Princess Elena (Lisa Ferraday), a formidable adversary who skillfully manipulates the Mexicans. In the end, however, the Russians are unable to hide behind the faltering Mexicans. The Russians invade. Bordega and Julia Lawrence lead the battling pro-American Unionists. The Russians are beaten back and, as the lovers embrace, California is free to join the United States.

Ninotchka Clones

Amid all the tales of evil Russians and the pernicious Soviet system, a trio of 1957 middling films deviate from the hard-line theme. All three are light romantic comedies baked in the mould of *Ninotchka*. They share a common plot line built around a dour and ideologically committed Russian female who is humanized by love for an irresistible western male. In the end, each defects to stand side by side with her one true love.

The first in the series, originally produced in 1950 by RKO Radio owner Howard Hughes, *Jet Pilot* (1957) is the bellwether of the group. However, it was withheld from release for seven years, perhaps out of fear the comic plot might be seen as too soft on communism. Certainly Hughes was no softy when it came to battling the left. His anticommunist zeal won praise from Richard Nixon and other HUAC members and, at one point, Hughes closed RKO film studios briefly to clean house of communists.[60] Hughes sold RKO in 1955, then purchased back *Jet Pilot*, releasing it independently.

Jet Pilot's director, Joseph von Sternberg, was master of a visually poetic style. He orchestrated some breathtaking airborne footage into the film's original print, but it had become dated in the seven years the film sat in the can, and much of it ended up on the cutting-room floor in reediting.

While *Jet Pilot* is cast in the *Ninotchka* style, a little espionage gets tossed in for added pizzazz. But in spite of the spy-chasing-spy subtext, the film hardly rises above a silly and convoluted plot. It opens with female Soviet fighter pilot Lieutenant Anna Marladovna (Janet Leigh in another Russian role) easing her Yak-12 onto an American airfield in Alaska and requesting asylum. She claims to have disobeyed an order and now fears being shot by Soviet authorities. Although she wants to defect, she is no traitor and refuses to provide information to American intelligence. Enter premier American pilot Colonel Jim Shannon (John Wayne). The Duke's character has been assigned to "soften her up."

Exactly who is softening up whom becomes confused as the plot unfolds. Even as the two clash over politics, their libidinal thermometers rise with every encounter. What will win out—politics or passion? They struggle against it, but in the end, the two can no longer deny their love for one another. In a confession of her deep feelings, Anna confides in Jim, "So, I'm attractive to you in every way except politically." In the curt reply that became a John Wayne trademark, Jim replies, "That's about it!" Anna reads a lot into these three words: "I feel exactly the same way about you; one minute I want to kill you, and the next minute I want to kiss you, and kiss you." It's a toss-up as to which the audience would have preferred.

When Jim learns that the air force intends to deport Anna back to the Soviet Union, he flies her to Arizona and they get married. Upon returning to the base, Anna is amazed that Jim receives nothing more than a mild reprimand for an act that would have brought a far worse punishment in her homeland. "That's wonderful!" she exclaims. "Boy, this is an amazing country. Do you know what they would do to you in Russia? Why, they'd either shoot you or ship you out to the uranium mines!"

But all is not so well. When the air force suggests that Anna may be sentenced to an American prison as a spy, Jim *pretends* to defect with her to the Soviet Union, all the while knowing he will later be traded for five Soviet spies held in the United States. But once again things do not go as planned. Neither of the lovers knows that, once in Soviet hands, Jim will be interrogated with a new mind-bending drug that will destroy his memory. Discovering what awaits Jim, Anna must now choose between loyalty to the Soviet Union and love of Jim and the United States. Alaska, here we come. Snatching Jim from his Soviet guards, Anna defects *back* to American territory in a daring jet fighter escape that stretches credibility even by Hollywood standards. During their getaway Anna proves her political and emotional change of heart by shooting down a Russian MiG. Back on American soil, Jim and Anna are finally safe and together.

The whole plot is so improbable that those in the audience who are not left airsick might join reviewer Bosley Crowther as he wrote, "We blush to tell you what is its story."[61] Despite *Jet Pilot*'s silly and convoluted plot, John Wayne and Janet Leigh are effectively cast, blend well, and make up in style what the film lacks in content.

There is even less to redeem the other two Cold War romantic comedies. In spite of its stars, *The Iron Petticoat* (1957) was both a critical and popular disaster. Bob Hope, neither funny nor believable, is another American air force pilot who falls in love with a Russian woman, this time played by a sadly miscast Katharine Hepburn, who never appeared more uncomfortable on screen. Billed as a comedy, Hepburn's unconvincing Russian accent provides the film's only humor. As to the protagonists' immiscibility, Bosley Crowther moans that "the notion of these two characters falling rapturously in love is virtually revolting."[62]

Briton Ralph Thomas, who began his career as a journalist after serving in the British Ninth Lancers in World War II, directed *The Iron Petticoat*, which was released in VistaVision and distributed by M-G-M. Smelling a real stinker, screenwriter Ben Hecht coyly removed his name from the credits. The pablum plot parallels that of *Jet Pilot*. We find yet another female jet fighter pilot, Vinka Kovelenko (Katharine Hepburn), defecting to the West for love of Bob Hope's character and perhaps for a chance to visit the local shopping mall.

Whatever its problems, *The Iron Petticoat* did not fail because it milked the *Ninotchka* motif. Indeed, the same year as *The Iron Petticoat* bombed, Hollywood successfully repackaged *Ninotchka* again in the critically acclaimed *Silk Stockings* (1957). Chosen by the *New York Times* as one of the Ten Best Films of the Year, *Silk Stockings* was the last film directed by Russian-born stage director Rouben Mamoulian, one of the most innovative directors to emerge from the Paramount studio system.

Cole Porter's score provides reason enough for the pleasure audiences took in this musical *Ninotchka*. Equally enchanting is the dancing of Fred Astaire and Cyd Charisse. As in the other *Ninotchka* clones, romantic interludes and bourgeois indulgences contribute to transforming the female Russian character in *Silk Stockings* into a love stuck woman. The light-footed dancing and romancing of Fred Astaire's character leads this *Ninotchka* clone to replace her dark and heavy Soviet stockings with luxurious silk Parisian ones. We know her conversion to the West is complete when she symbolically turns a portrait of Lenin face down.

Complete character metamorphosis, reminiscent of 1930s films, also occurs in *Anastasia* (1956), set in Paris of the 1920s. The film was directed by Russian-born Anatole Litvak, who once again tackled a Russian-genre picture. The screenplay for this well-received and successful film, written by Arthur Laurents, was based on a French play about a mystery woman claiming to be Anastasia, and living in 1920s Paris.

The plot line, which owes much to Pygmalion, begins with rumors that Anastasia, youngest daughter of Tsar Nicholas II, escaped from the July 1918 Bolshevik execution of the Romanov royal family. Picking up on these rumors, an ambitious group of émigrés looks for "a reasonable facsimile" of the grand duchess to train and then present to the world as the "real" Anastasia. More interested in larceny than ideology, their goal is to get their hands on ten million pounds held in a London bank under Anastasia's name.

The sophisticated leader of the plot is the former general and aide-de-camp to the tsar, Sergei Pavlovich Bulyin (Yul Brynner). The woman chosen for the conspirators' plan (Ingrid Bergman) is a disturbed soul on the verge of a suicidal plunge into the Seine River. But what is fake and what is real? Previously held in an asylum, the physically and emotionally ill girl told a nun that she is the Grand Duchess

Anastasia. In the hands of the conspirators, who train her, she becomes more and more confused as to her real identity. Reprogrammed by General Bulyin, the girl remains haunted by nightmares about her past and desperately yearns to find her own identity. But who is she? She remains half-convinced that she is the real Anastasia, and perhaps she is; the film deliberately leaves this question open.

Unable to convince the entire Parisian émigré community of her authenticity, the conspirators seek the endorsement of the Mother Dowager (Helen Hayes), Anastasia's grandmother. Although skeptical at first, the mother dowager is finally convinced by the girl's nervous cough, which she identifies as her granddaughter's. Sweet irony then reigns supreme. Amid triumph, assured of ten million pounds, Bulyin and Anastasia disappear together. However, like Dr. Higgins in *My Fair Lady* (1964), Bulyin has fallen in love with his creation. Hello romance; good-bye ten million pounds.

Back in Tinseltown after years of exile in Europe amid rumors of "immoral behavior," Ingrid Bergman won an Oscar for best actress in *Anastasia*. Alfred Newman received an Oscar nomination for music. But the film's success owed little to the actual history of the era it purports to depict. Although set in Paris a decade after the Bolshevik Revolution, with nearly every character a White Russian émigré, there is no hint of the lost struggle that created the real White Russian émigré community and held together its Russian core. They seem lost in time and space. Although the cinematic émigrés are obviously Russians, it was as if there was no Bolshevik Revolution, except as a necessary pretext for the arrival of Anastasia on the scene.

Harbingers

Three films about Russians, best understood as epitaphs to the shrill Cold War films of the era, appeared toward the end of this era and served to preview coming attractions. In a film that would have been unthinkable at the beginning of the period, *Romanoff and Juliet* (1961) treats the Cold War as a diplomatic joke. *Romanoff and Juliet* is the creation of writer, director, producer, and star Peter Ustinov, the British-born son of Russian-émigré parents. In it, Ustinov plays the president of Concordia—a European microstate whose United Nations vote the Americans and Soviets are both courting.

Cold War tensions dissolve into farce as the American and Soviet ambassadors shower Concordia with aid, only to have their efforts complicated by an unexpected love affair between the son of the Soviet ambassador and the daughter of the American ambassador. The Soviet ambassador, portrayed by Akim Tamiroff, so adept at overplaying

Russian characters, amused reviewer Bosley Crowther as a "stubborn, snorting, high-handed and generally simple-minded Slav."[63] But, rather than deriding Russians, Ustinov's picture seeks to expose the insanity of Cold War competition itself. The wedding between the two young lovers serves as his metaphor of Cold War exaggerativeness. And unlike the *Ninotchka* clones, love is not portrayed as politics by another name. The two lovers consider themselves above the politics of their parents' generation, and they wrap themselves in one another, not the stars and stripes.

Just as *Romanoff and Juliet* bore the nonconformist stamp of Peter Ustinov from A to Zed, *The Mouse That Roared* (1959) similarly provided a venue for one of Peter Sellers's multiple-role tours de force. The world's prototypical microstate, Grand Fenwick, seeks to improve its balance of payments by declaring perfunctory war on the United States and then, surrendering, reap the benefits of generous American reconstruction. The bomb serves as the real culprit in this Cold War spoof, which finds the Russians and Americans in roughly the same straits. *The Mouse That Roared* feigns satire, but never really rises above its mission to feed Peter Sellers's ego. It was a case of too little too early, and it never generated much attention from audiences or critics.

Like *Romanoff and Juliet* and *The Mouse That Roared*, a third film at the tailend of the era challenges the era's singular demonization of loyal Russians. *Taras Bulba* (1962), a United Artists ode to Cossack bravado, features Yul Brynner as the titular character. Cossack plainsmen, glamorized as noble freedom fighters, fight off sixteenth-century Polish aggressors. Possessing limitless emotional and physical range, it's a wonder the Cossack heroes don't suffer whiplash as they are jolted from religious family men to fun-loving, hard-drinking free spirits to violent warriors. And fighting off invading Polish aggressors (played by eight-thousand Argentinian horsemen) requires great sacrifice, even from Andrei Bulba (Tony Curtis), the brave (though Brooklyn accented) son of Taras Bulba. Of course, the scenes of battlefield violence are sanitized in the form of "comic book wildness."[64]

Both *Taras Bulba* and *Romanoff and Juliet* were markedly different from the era's other films portraying Russians or the Soviet system. In *Taras Bulba* the Russians—or their sixteenth century Cossack brothers—were the heroes, unthinkable in other films of the era. Equally remarkable, in *Romanoff and Juliet*, the Soviet and American characters are equally balanced, character for character. The two ambassadors are interchangeable as programmed stooges of their respective governments and the young lovers are, as young lovers should be, floating above politics, with not a defecting Soviet jet on the lot. In

their even-handed depiction of Russians and their rejection of Cold
War rhetoric, these films serve as weather vanes indicating shifting
winds about to sweep across Culver City, California's Russian horizon.

Bad System, Bad People

These later films of the era aside, the resilient theme of the era's few
films depicting Russians was that they are devious subversives. This is
light years away from the lively sarcasm of thirties films. The 1930s'
distinction between the Russian people and the Soviet system has disappeared in the 1950s. Russians are now inseparable from the Soviet
system. As a rule, Soviet ideologues populate the screen. There are few
if any passive Russians. This allows Hollywood icons like John Wayne
(*Jet Pilot*) and Gregory Peck (*The World in Her Arms*) to proclaim their
distaste for anything that smells Slavic.

Although furtive, these Russians have no cinematic link with
American communists, who stake out a different film genre. In films
like *Behind the Iron Curtain* (1948), *Never Let Me Go* (1953), and *Red
Planet Mars* (1953), communism is evil incarnate; the West cannot
expect to do business with such miscreants. There is no cinematic
room for a meeting of the minds between the humane Western spirit
and heartless communist materialism. But communism is vulnerable.
In several cases, religion is offered as an antidote to communism's poi-
son. But as a rule Hollywood knows there is nothing like love and marriage, inseparably fused in the 1950s, to defang the communist
ideologue or at least the female of the breed. All that is needed is an
older and wiser Western male. Those few Russians who are not among
the party faithful can only dream of escaping to freedom, since Soviet
officials deny them legal departure. In the meantime America is best
served by keeping up its military guard.

The *Ninotchka* clone films appear in the second half of the decade
and offer a first hint of cinematic change toward Russians and the
Soviet Union. If the Cold War is still a backdrop to this mixed bag of
light comedies, negative deadpan depiction of evil Russians no longer
proves an ideological imperative. At the end of the period, a few in the
mold of *Romanoff and Juliet* even dare to mock Cold War competition.
The times they are a-changin'.

Homegrown Communists

One American film genre of the era deserves special mention: domestic communists. Fear of subversion was widespread. HUAC and other
investigators needed to "link the menace without to the menace

within" to justify their activities. Even President Truman "oversold the Communist menace at home" to gain support for the Truman Doctrine when he issued Executive Order 9835 creating a loyalty program for federal employees and updating the old list of subversive organizations.[65]

But American domestic communists constituted a threat somehow separate from Russians in Hollywood's Cold War consciousness, which kept these topics apart in the fifties. No domestic communists darken the doorways of films about Russians, and Russian characters make little more than cameo appearances in movies about American communists. Nevertheless, films built around the activities of home-grown communists could not help but have a spillover effect on attitudes toward Russians.

More than thirty-five movies about domestic communism, mostly low budget B movies, popped up on the screen from the late forties to the middle fifties, peaking in 1952, when twelve were released. None succeeded financially.[66] But moneymakers or not, this more than doubled the number of films with Russian or Soviet themes. Nora Sayre's visual profile of American communists in these films both entertains and informs:

> Most are apt to be exceptionally haggard or disgracefully pudgy. Occasionally they're effeminate; a man who wears gloves shouldn't be trusted. . . . But you can sometimes spot a Communist because his shadow looms larger and blacker than his adversary's. Also, movie-Communists walk on a forward slant, revealing their dedication to their cause. Now and then they're elegantly dressed, equipped with canes and stick-pins—which prove them hypocrites. But most are scruffy.[67]

Among the genre's best-known pictures, *The Red Menace* (1949) made the most of its low budget. The producers saved money by hiring a cast of complete unknowns, and the no-name cast lent an authentic feel to the film. The story involves domestic communists playing on the anxieties of a discontented war veteran in the hope of converting him into a pro-Soviet subversive. In the case of M-G-M's *Conspirator* (1950), a young soldier sucked into communism works so well as a spy that even his wife does not know what he is really up to.

Many of these communist-under-the-bed films employed a grainy black and white, quasi-documentary style. None was better in this respect than *I Was a Communist for the FBI* (1951), which depicts Pittsburgh steelworker Matt Cvetic operating undercover to identify blue-collar reds for the FBI. A little different was Edward Ludwig's film, *Big Jim McLain* (1952). Set in Hawaii, it offers nice scenery and big stars, including John Wayne, who plays a HUAC special agent exposing communist subversives. Also noteworthy is Paramount's *My Son John* (1952). Talk about a dysfunctional family! This film explores the trials of a family two of whose sons are devout Catholics, football stars, and Korean War heroes. The third son, the bad seed, turns out to be a two-time loser: both an atheist and a communist. Director Leo McCarey received an Academy award nomination for his original story.

Fear versus Anxiety

The key to understanding American culture in the 1950s lies in the distinction between fear and anxiety. Fear consists of the feeling of concern appropriate to an actual threat. Anxiety is an exaggerative and debilitating worry about a perceived threat. Both American foreign policy and Hollywood films made in the shadow of that policy exhibit anxiety-ridden overreaction to perceived threats. America began with a profound misunderstanding of Stalin's postwar intentions as ideologically motivated and bent on world conquest. This was fed by a crucial misreading of Stalin's February 1946 speech on the Marxist concept of inevitability of war (in which Stalin was actually referring to war between capitalist countries). This in turn fueled a gross exaggeration of the real but limited Soviet military threat.[68] Convinced that containment, enforced by American military might, was the last best hope against Soviet expansionism, it was imperative to keep American military superiority out front.

An itchy finger on the button gave American military superiority its credibility. In at least six instances the United States employed nuclear blackmail in the face of a real but exaggerated Soviet military threats. It was precisely the fear of that finger that forced Khrushchev to back down from the 1962 crisis he created in Cuba. But there were costs to this strategy on both sides of the Cold War. American anxiety, well founded or not, meant continued investment in maintaining American military advantage and in sweeping military commitments at the expense of domestic social spending. Some argue this course led America into the rice paddies of Vietnam and the race riots of its inner cities. The bills for the Cold War are still coming in.

The Soviets also paid a price. Driven by their own mirror-image fears of American intentions, the Soviets attempted to play high-tech catch up. By the 1970s the Soviets under Leonid Brezhnev achieved parity in nuclear terror. If the threat of mutual annihilation eventually forced both sides to step back from the brink, all this spending exacted a high price. It led to terminal decay in the Soviet economy and a consequent disintegration of the Soviet state. One can only hope that what emerges in its wake will not be worse than what went before.

In the end, America reacted to acute Cold War anxiety, as might any individual, with militant, overreactive defensiveness coupled with avoidance of the source of anxiety whenever possible. If all this found expression in a Golden Age of psychiatry in American culture generally, it also found expression in Hollywood films. The acute Cold War came to a close with the Cuban missile crisis, forcing a change in American thinking. Hollywood again kept pace. New Russians and a different Soviet Union were about to light up the silver screen.

Chapter Four

1963–1971: Liberal Backlash
and Transition

Norman Jewison must have had a finger on the national pulse when crafting his gentle comedy, *The Russians Are Coming, The Russians Are Coming* (1966). No film of the era so sharply depicts tension between deep-seated American anticommunism and a yearning for accommodation with the Soviet Union—which just might provide a respite from fears of nuclear war. But how could America reject communism, compete against it, yet live at peace with the Soviet Union? And was the other side of the Iron Curtain ready for such a rapprochement?

Many Americans wanted to believe in affirmative answers to such vexing questions. They wanted to believe that deep down the other side was also run by human beings. Feeding this hope, Jewison served up a filmic vision of Americans and Russians transcending Cold War mania. As to whether people of good will might get along or even cooperate in spite of differences separating them, Jewison responded yes, a thousands times yes.

The first ninety minutes of *The Russians Are Coming* exudes humorous satire, mostly at the expense of knee-jerk Cold War reflexes. The movie begins as a Soviet submarine runs aground near Gloucester Island, a Nantucket clone. A landing party is sent ashore to commandeer a powerboat to pull the submarine free. As misadventure trips over misadventure, the submarine eventually works its way free. The film moves toward its climax when the vessel steams into the local harbor, guns trained on the villagers. The captain (Theodore Bikel) demands the return of his landing party, but a standoff develops. Scores of locals—a self-styled militia—stand shoulder to shoulder at water's edge, rifles aimed at the Soviet submarine. All are holding their breath, anticipating an inevitable exchange of fire, when a young boy slips from his perch atop the church steeple. His pants become caught on a nail and he dangles precariously, high above the ground.

A child's desperate cry and his mother's panic touch Russian and American hearts alike. Forgetting the threat they represent to one another, townsfolk and Soviet crew members instinctively cast aside their weapons and rush headlong to save the child. Forming a human chain, men who were prepared a moment earlier to shoot one another rescue the child in an act of human bonding. As the Soviet shore party heads back to its ship, all suddenly realize that U.S. Air Force jets are on their way. Now the Soviet sailors hang by the seat of their pants while the townspeople rush to their rescue. With American warplanes overhead, the local community forms a flotilla of small craft to escort the Soviet submarine safely to deep water.

Viewed only a few years after the traumatic 1962 Cuban missile crisis, the climactic standoff in *The Russians Are Coming* held special meaning. This potent scene in the United Artists's film captured a new day's spirit, one warning against infantile overreaction: humanity must come to its senses and cooperate in order to survive and flourish. In the celluloid standoff at Gloucester Island's tiny port—like the real nuclear standoff in the Caribbean—both Americans and Russians become hostage to their weapons. For deadly confrontation to be avoided, America needs to recognize that its most serious enemy is not the Soviet Union, but the nuclear brinkmanship threatening human extinction.

Brinkmanship—no better word describes the rush to mutual annihilation so palpable during the showdown known as the Cuban missile crisis. America basked in silent victory in this round of the Cold War, demonstrating that it was not to be toyed with in its own hemisphere. But nothing clears the mind like a brush with nuclear war. Before long, the first flush of triumph gave way to sober second thoughts. Shaken by narrowly avoided annihilation, both sides edged back from the precipice, not to avoid conflict—that would have been too much to expect—but to seek alternatives to total destruction. Mutual psychological receptivity emerging from the Cuban missile crisis held fast until the SALT I Treaty in 1972, despite serious challenges from the Vietnam War and the Soviet invasion of Czechoslovakia.

What did this mean? The Soviet system, still an enemy, had given way to a greater enemy—total war. If the Soviet Union epitomized a social order rejected by America, nuclear overkill threatened an end to any social order, and possibly to humankind. Forced to find a new modus operandi, the two superpowers acknowledged the limits of power, especially unleashed nuclear power. Not that America lacked for a renegade state needing to be reigned in. In the 1960s, China more and more crystallized in the popular mind as the most irresponsible source of communist "adventurism." The Soviets, by comparison, appeared relatively conservative. As America felt its way through the 1960s, the anti-Soviet legacy of the 1950s faded to the margins like some past indiscretion better forgotten.

A Looser Containment Policy

Despite the shock of the Cuban missile crisis, the containment policy served as the analytical framework for American foreign policy throughout the sixties. It was, however, a different type of containment. The aggressive nuclear sabre rattling of Truman and Eisenhower was gradually abandoned. In its place a psychic "fire-break" appeared. It more and more separated the notion of limited conventional conflict, still strategically discussable, from total nuclear war—now a genuine taboo.

The superpowers did not fall into each other's arms, but the climate of American-Soviet relations improved measurably if, initially, only from bad to mediocre. As such, the 1960s represent a transitional bridge from a toe-to-toe standoff during the acute Cold War to full-fledged detente in the 1970s. The greatest single obstacle to better relations was the seemingly interminable Vietnam War. While it would not prove necessary for the war to end completely for detente to blossom, it was necessary to rachet down the war. The shift from "escalation" to a gradual "winding down" did not happen until the early 1970s, and not without terrible human cost.

A strange irony pervaded American foreign policy during the period from 1963 to 1971. Intent on improving relations with Russia and beginning to make overtures toward China, the United States slipped deeper into a brutal war in Indochina fought ostensibly to curb the spread of Russian and Chinese influence in Asia.[1] Like flies capturing the flypaper, successive administrations found themselves stuck. Their every move only left them more stuck. To the American people, the war became a bottomless pit into which America threw its youth, resources, and military self-confidence.

The Sino-Soviet Rift

In spite of all the tension that Vietnam generated between the United States and the Soviet Union, the Soviets had their own reasons for improving relations with the United States from 1963 to 1971. The Sino-Soviet split forced the Soviets to court the West, if only to lessen military pressure in Europe and thus enable them to concentrate resources on the Chinese border in the east. In 1949, when communists emerged victorious in the Chinese civil war, a Sino-Soviet honeymoon ensued. But the communist alliance was built on a quicksand of territorial, racial, historical, ideological, and strategic animosities.

By the mid-1950s, the relationship was showing strains, but most in the West failed to see them. Blinded by belief in a monolithic communist threat, American observers downplayed the gravity of the Russo-Chinese rift. But by the late 1960s the Moscow-Beijing chasm had become so wide that even myopic cold warriors could recognize it. The Soviet Union massed one million troops along its border with China. In the spring of 1969, clashes along the Ussuri River and in the Dzungarian Gates region between Kazakhstan and Xinjiang Province left hundreds of military casualties. Deteriorating relations between communist rivals, along with America's desire to extricate itself from the Vietnam quagmire, set the stage for a new look at Soviet-American relations.[2]

The United States shares no border with China, yet the buffer of distance was insufficent to produce good relations. American hostility toward Beijing was returned in kind. Indeed, the Chinese list of Soviet sins was headed by the view that the Soviet Union was too soft on the West. Once the Soviets had launched Sputnik in 1957, and increasingly during the 1960s, Mao Tse-tung declared that the "East wind prevails over the West wind." Mao urged Moscow to press the supposed communist advantage by aggressive confrontation with the West. But memories of the Cuban crisis were still fresh, and the Soviets were in no mood to play Russian roulette with the West. They branded Mao's hawkish agenda as dangerous "adventurism." The Chinese, in turn, accused the Soviets of "capitulationism" for their timidity. Before long China seemed more contemptuous of Moscow than of Washington.

Ruptured Sino-Soviet relations forced the Soviet Union to seek normalized intercourse with the West, a process accelerated by the 1964 ouster of Nikita S. Khrushchev. The triumvirate replacing Khrushchev hoped for sustained international calm, free from foreign adventures, in order to consolidate power at home. Soviet signals for improved relations were well received, since the American mood desired no unnecessary conflict with the Soviets. With spasms of domestic unrest shaking a nation badly divided over Vietnam, with American cities a tinderbox of racial tension and the economy unsteady, American policy makers had enough trouble on their hands without a superpower confrontation. Any defrosting of the Cold War, if only by a few degrees, was welcome in Washington.

Johnson's Psychological Profile

Washington could well understand settling-in problems facing Moscow's new leadership, since it was going through its own administrative shake-up following the assassination of President Kennedy on 22 November 1963 and Lyndon B. Johnson's ascension to power. Like Truman before him, LBJ assumed the presidency following the sudden death of a popular leader and having American troops committed overseas. But if Truman successfully mastered the job he inherited, LBJ ultimately proved a tragic figure, destroyed both by his own rigid character and by events beyond his control.[3]

Rising above his humble origins yet fundamentally insecure about himself, Johnson was a classic overachiever. Unlike Kennedy, this self-made Texan was known as a consensus seeker with a command of domestic issues. His great misfortune? That foreign policy—not domestic affairs—dominated his administration. Unlike Truman, he did not take over at the end of a popular war, but in the midst of a conflict dividing America. Although Johnson needed to hear from and listen to dissident voices, he consistently failed to do so. Most debilitating was his emotional inability "to admit any error or misjudgment." Defeat of any kind represented "unbearable humiliation" to LBJ, and he trucked no disloyalty or serious criticism. He inherited Kennedy's advisers but kept most of them at a distance. His own inner sanctum, top heavy with hawkish yes men, offered emotional support, but little sage counsel.[4] One who articulated the "Vietnam is winnable" message was fellow southerner Dean Rusk, Johnson's secretary of state.

Guns and Butter

While fighting the war in Vietnam, Johnson forged ahead with an expensive agenda of domestic activism, believing that the American economy could expand to meet both obligations. But if his heart pulled toward domestic policy, his energies were tapped by the war that refused to go America's way. More a "true believer" than Kennedy about Vietnam, Johnson was more willing to commit American combat troops there. Either unaware or unimpressed that Kennedy's final days found him expressing doubts over the wisdom of American Vietnam policy, LBJ pressed on. Two days after Kennedy's death he instructed American ambassador to Saigon, Henry Cabot Lodge, to "tell those generals that Lyndon Johnson intends to stand by our word," and "our word" demanded staying the course. Not willing to be seen as a quitter who failed the test, LBJ saw Vietnam as a test of

America's capacity to deal with Third World wars of liberation supported by Khrushchev.

Having little foreign policy background, Johnson readily bought into his predecessors' foreign policy codes, especially the domino theory. He wasn't able to think of Vietnam as a "local struggle between Vietnamese."[5] Nor would he consider ignoring the lesson of Munich: aggressors cannot be appeased, only defeated. His Texas machismo bleeding through, Johnson feared being considered a "Chamberlain umbrella man," causing him to confuse compromise with appeasement.[6] Johnson could accept no scenario short of victory. But there would be no victory, and like Woodrow Wilson, LBJ placed his unshakable faith in a failed policy. Both represent "active-negative" presidents for whom "surrender is suicide, an admission of guilt and weakness."[7] Years would be wasted, resources squandered, and many thousands of lives lost before Johnson acknowledged the inevitable.

Ironically, Johnson's injunction against retreat in Vietnam contributed to improved relations with the Soviet Union. In 1967–68, with American military strategy bogged down and domestic resistance to the war flaring up, Johnson approached the Soviets as honest broker, hoping they would influence the North Vietnamese to agree to a cease-fire or a military cutback. Soviet feelers to North Vietnam failed, but the United States and the Soviet Union ended up signing a nuclear non-proliferation treaty, and relations improved in several other venues: Johnson lobbied Congress to pass legislation widening East-West trade relations; he met with Premier Alexei Kosygin in a Glassboro, New Jersey, summit to discuss slowing down the arms race; and open communications were maintained during the 1967 Arab-Israeli War and the 1968 Soviet invasion of Czechoslovakia, against which Johnson offered only half-hearted protest.

Even as Soviet-American relations improved, the American war effort stalled while public disenchantment with the war spread like the common cold. Everything came to a head for LBJ with the Tet Offensive on 30 January 1968. Not so much a military as a psychological defeat, Tet incinerated the belief that victory was possible, let alone close at hand. With it, the president's political career went up in smoke. LBJ announced he would not seek reelection. With a lame duck in the Oval Office and the war still grinding on in Southeast Asia, America awaited the hand of a new leader.

"Nixingerism": Realpolitik and Secrecy

The hopes of the Democratic Party to rekindle memories of Camelot and to end the war in Vietnam were pinned on Robert F. Kennedy. But his assassination and the ill-fated 1968 Democratic National Convention in Chicago sent the Democrats into free fall, while the nation elected Richard M. Nixon. Clearly a man of deeply divided personality, Nixon is likely the most psychoanalyzed of all American presidents. The policy manifestations of his troubled and segmented self have fascinated observers of foreign affairs, which Nixon saw as his specialty.

Having cut his political teeth on the red-baiting of the 1950s, Nixon was known as a hard-liner on Soviet relations. But instead of steering the ship of state on a collision course with the Soviet Union, even with the war in Vietnam dragging on, Nixon's White House chose the calmer waters of accommodation. Nixon's anticommunist credentials afforded him license to bridge the "minimalist detente" of the 1960s to a "maximalist detente" in the 1970s. Unlike a liberal president, Nixon could deliver a chorus of anticommunist voices to the cause of detente—not only with the Soviet Union but also later, with China.

During his first three years in office, however, Nixon's foreign policy differed little from the Kennedy-Johnson era, either with respect to Vietnam or to relations with the Russians. Transferring the lessons his generation learned at Munich to Vietnam, Nixon catastrophized the consequences of an America pullout, arguing in a 1970 televised address to the nation that "if the world's most powerful nation acts like a pitiful, helpless giant, the forces of totalitarianism and anarchy will threaten free nations and free institutions throughout the world."[8]

But the winds of change were blowing. What most shaped the change in Nixon's foreign policy were his administration's geopolitical codes—"Nixingerism."[9] Nixingerism was the brainchild of the other half of the Nixon foreign policy team, Harvard professor Henry Kissinger, first appointed national security adviser and later secretary of state. The two shared broad-based conceptual approaches to world affairs and realpolitik values about the behavior of nations.

They also concentrated power in their own hands, concealing much of what they were doing from the State Department, from Congress, and from the public. It was no coincidence that Nixon appointed passive team players to secretary of state (William Rogers) and secretary of defense (Melvin Laird). This centralized approach, with its passion for secrecy and fear of leaks, alienated bypassed bureaucracies, outraged critics, and exacerbated the presidency's isolation, which, down the road, would lead to Watergate and Nixon's resignation. Kissinger later justified their mania for secrecy as necessary to leapfrogging cumbersome and stale bureaucracies. Others see the problem as less that of bureaucratic inefficiency than Henry Kissinger's personal style.

Considering himself the "Picasso of American foreign policy," he liked to play his diplomatic cards close to the vest, and improving relations with the Soviets was one of his top goals.[10]

New Geopolitical Codes

The geopolitical codes associated with "Nixingerism" have been described as the pair's "grand design," an intentionally vague concept of peace and stability achieved through a nineteenth-century-like pentagonal balance of power between the United States, Soviet Union, China, Japan, and Western Europe. While the Soviets were seen as partners in the system, the emphasis was not on any one national component but on the larger picture of systemic stability. Like a juggler, Kissinger sought to keep all the national balls moving at one time.

This, Kissinger argued, required "greater conceptual coherence" in foreign policy and less concern for the narrow crisis-management style so central to the Kennedy-Johnson advisers. To bring the Soviet Union and China into the system, he also felt that American policy needed to be further deideologized. And if narrow ideological blinkers kept other states from seeing the larger picture, a regimen of rewards and sanctions reminiscent of behavior modification would bring them around. If everything fell into place, Nixon and Kissinger would have themselves a new world order with the United States the first among equals.[11]

Continuity in U.S. Actions

But how to bridge the gap between theory and practice? Other than secret talks begun in 1969–71, the actual policies of the Nixon administration toward the Soviets initially did not differ from Johnson's. Gradually, Kissinger combined his linkage theory with a "diplomacy of ambiguity" in parallel talks with the Soviets and the Chinese. But always there was the ongoing war in Vietnam gumming up the works. Although relations with the Soviets were improving, and even relations with the Chinese showed promise, there would be no giant leap forward so long as the United States remained mired in the rice paddies of Vietnam.

An Emboldened Hollywood in the Sixties

Hollywood of the 1960s mirrored America's experience that change was desirable, but often difficult. Weekly film attendance figures seemed ominous in 1960, hovering around forty million. A nadir of 154

Hollywood films crept out of the studios in 1960. By the end of the decade attendance figures had plummeted by fifty percent to twenty million. As a result, old structures and economic arrangements needed to be discarded for new ones. Creative competition from television accelerated the demise of old studio empires and corporate conglomerates moved in to pick up the pieces.

Gone was the single voice of the studio superboss who imposed conformity. In his absence, unprecedented autonomy fell to Hollywood directors. By the mid-sixties, probing realism—Hollywood style—was in. To attract a late-teens and twenties audience with coin in their pockets and dissent on their minds, more and more filmmakers attacked the dominant values of their society.[12] One film historian goes so far as to characterize the decade's films as wallowing in nihilism.[13] Certainly, many directors cast aside the timidity typical of the 1950s, introducing the advent of the "auteur" in American film.[14]

Comfortable fifties values, like conformity and collective responsibility, failed to weather the storm of rebellious sixties movies. Mental health, earlier equated with acceptance of societal norms, now demanded the assertion of the self. Movies depicted an American society mired in middle-class neuroses—summed up for many moviegoers in one word, "plastics." Only rebellion against social hypocrisy could possibly liberate the protagonist. The day of the rebellious antihero had arrived. But even for the antihero, peace of mind was hard to come by. In many 1960s films futility rated equal billing with rebellion. The easy rider was never truly at ease. In an era when social values and institutions were held up to derision, even the military establishment, long revered by Hollywood's dutiful executives, was not immune. Look out John Wayne![15]

Post-Cuban Crisis Russians

In the wake of the Cuban missile crisis, Hollywood released several important films involving Russians. Most treated them favorably or at least as being equally victims of the Cold War. But if the Soviets and their system were not the source of all evil, what was? Hollywood fingered nuclear weapons, the military-industrial complex, and lust for power as the real enemies. A number of films produced in the early part of the 1963–71 period depict Russians less as the enemy and more as the pawn of American domestic political maneuvering.

In John Frankenheimer's *Seven Days in May* (1964), homegrown right-wing generals, incensed by a president who trusts the Russians to honor a disarmament agreement, plot a military coup. Building on his other journey into psychopolitical fear, *The Manchurian Candidate*

(1962), Frankenheimer explores how lingering 1950s-style anticommunist militarism continues to provide powerful cold warriors a forum for political scheming and, in this case, a venue for subversion.

However, the American system prevails, as order and civil democracy are affirmed. The generals are discredited and their plot is foiled. Screenwriter Rod Serling, who rose to prominence with his *Twilight Zone* television series, provides the hero of *Seven Days in May*, Colonel "Jigs" Casey (Burt Lancaster), with the dialogue that makes sense of the military's bizarre overreaction. Near the end of *Seven Days in May* Colonel Casey sums it all up by explaining that "the enemy's an age—a nuclear age. In this situation we look for a champion in red, white, and blue."

A cinematic step beyond portraying the Soviets as pawns on the chessboard of American domestic politics consists of depicting them as partners with the West in maintaining world order. Enter 007. American producers Albert Broccoli and Harry Saltzman purchased the film rights to Ian Fleming's best-selling James Bond spy novels, which included President Kennedy among its legion of fans. The first Fleming novel to be adapted for the screen was *Dr. No* (1962). An instant hit, this stylish spy adventure, packed with sexual and technological high jinks, grossed almost $6 million in one year, against an investment of only one-quarter that amount. A moneymaking formula—a little skin, some suggestive talk, a few deadly space-age gadgets, lively escapes, the villain and his minions ultimately getting their comeuppance without obvious in-your-face messages—produced film after successful film.

But the series was notable for more than its commercial success; it also broke with the convention of depicting Soviet agents as amoral evildoers serving aggressive Soviet ends.[16] Instead, Bond films often allied Western and Soviet governments—unthinkable before the Cuban crisis—in a common effort to save the world from third-party megalomaniacs such as Dr. No, Auric Goldfinger, Carl Stromberg, or SPECTRE chief Ernst Stavro: characters bearing no allegiance to nation or people, only to naked power.

Television, feeding off the Bond phenomenon, went one step further by denationalizing the spy business. In the hit series, *The Man from Uncle*, two superagents, one American and one Russian, team up weekly under the umbrella of UNCLE, an international agency dedicated to fighting evil as embodied by the machinations of THRUSH, a criminal network bent on world domination. Compared to a sexual Olympian like James Bond, the UNCLE team seems akin to plucked capons. But they too fight the good fight against money and power, rather than ideology or national interest.

Russo-American Filmic Empathy

In some Hollywood films, like *Seven Days in May*, the Soviet Union serves not as the cause of action, but as an excuse for it. In these films, Russians are presented either in a favorable light or as being no worse than Americans. The favorable films often feature a thread of Soviet-American cooperation running through the fiber of their plots. Like 1950s Cold War pictures, they also depict a clear and present danger to America, except that the Russians are not it.

In both *The Bedford Incident* (1965) and *The Billion Dollar Brain* (1967), the American military constitutes the threat. In *Fail Safe* (1964), humanity is threatened by overreliance on nuclear technology. Both *Dr. Strangelove* (1964) and *Seven Days in May* (1964) identify the military mind and its itchy finger on the nuclear button as the source of crisis. *The Russians Are Coming, The Russians Are Coming* (1966) draws laughs from the well of American Cold War paranoia, while *The Shoes of the Fisherman* (1968) and *The Chairman* (1969) shift the locus of state villainy eastward from the Soviet Union to the People's Republic of China. Hardly a Soviet cad in the bunch. As if to underscore the seriousness of issues addressed, many of these films were shot in black and white.

Bellwether I: *Dr. Strangelove*

Two black-and-white films released the same year, *Dr. Strangelove* (1964) and *Fail Safe* (1964), share a similar plot premise: without warning or presidential authorization, a nuclear attack is launched against the Soviet Union. Both films shatter Hollywood's previous reluctance to tackle the nuclear threat to human survival. As antiwar films, they attack the deterrence logic of the suicide pact known as mutually assured destruction (MAD). In these films Russians and Americans are equal hostages to the balance of terror. But if they convey similar subtexts, the two pictures offer up their nuclear sermons in sharply contrasting tones—one through gallows humor and the other via nail-biting suspense.

Stanley Kubrick's intimate, emotional, and spontaneous *Dr. Strangelove*, and Sidney Lumet's coolly rational *Fail Safe*, provide the yin and yang of antinuclear parables. The characters of *Dr. Strangelove* are exaggerative and out of control; those in *Fail Safe* are understated and cautious. *Dr. Strangelove*'s protagonists—the elites of government, the military, and the scientific community—turn craziness and sanity on their heads. Kubrick portrays the government and military as not only responsible for the problem but also as the problem itself.

Fail Safe expresses the liberal credo somewhat differently. While politicians and soldiers may be partly responsible, technological exoticism—the machine disobeying its maker—constitutes the real problem. *Dr. Strangelove* ends in a musical Armageddon, while *Fail Safe* delivers the siren of limited nuclear war as a wake-up call to humanity. For all these differences, the noir feeling that permeates both films has a similarly bonechilling quality.

Fail Safe was adapted from a successful novel by Eugene Burkick and Harvey Wheeler, with the screenplay by once blacklisted writer Walter Bernstein. Prolific American director Sidney Lumet crafts the film for Max Youngstein and Columbia Pictures. Lumet's forty films include hits like *12 Angry Men* (1957), *The Pawnbroker* (1965), *Serpico* (1973), and *Network* (1976). Like many innovative directors emerging in the sixties, Lumet learned his trade in the creative milieu of 1950s television. One film historian describes Lumet as at his best when "dealing with claustrophobic situations and characters at their breaking points." *Fail Safe* works perfectly as a vehicle for these skills.[17]

The story line pits humankind against the technical wizardry it creates, but equally importantly, asks why machines of nuclear destructiveness need be created in the first place. The technoglitch occurs when a mechanical failure at Omaha's Strategic Air Command sends the wrong message to a wing of bombers, ordering them to drop two twenty-kiloton (Hiroshima-size) bombs on Moscow. No longer recallable, the bombers cross the fail-safe point and assume the attack mode.

The American president (Henry Fonda) uses the hotline, all the sincerity he can muster, and secret information on the American military's decoy system to assist the Soviets in defending their territory against the invading B-52s. In this upside down nuclear nightmare, air force officers at S.A.C. headquarters embarrassingly catch themselves cheering for Soviet attack jets sent to destroy the onrushing American bombers. But one resourceful American pilot slithers through Soviet defenses to obliterate Moscow, verified by a whistle on the president's hotline caused by the American ambassador's melting phone.

Avoiding Soviet nuclear retaliation, and proving to the Soviets that the American attack was not premeditated, the American president makes the only decision he sees open to him in so tragic a situation. He orders the ultimate quid pro quo by sending an air force bomber with two twenty-kiloton bombs over New York City to even the nuclear score, despite his wife's being in New York.

Much of Sidney Lumet's film probes the paradox of thinking the unthinkable, but the message is clear—humanity must come to its senses and resolve its problems by putting its faith in communication and arms control. As in *Seven Days in May* (1964), reasonable people act to contain the crisis, providing the species (except those in Moscow and New York, of course) with a chance to see at least one more sunrise. Film critic Bosley Crowther crowed that the film "packs a melodramatic wallop that will rattle a lot of chattering teeth" and found its rational overtones preferable to the parody of *Dr. Strangelove*.[18] In the end, however, *Fail Safe* is an establishment film. It reassures that a "balance of terror may extract an enormous cost, but fundamentally it works."[19]

Kubrick has stated repeatedly that he set out to make a straightforward film decrying nuclear weapons, but it just kept coming out satirically. Viewers might find it hard to conceive of *Dr. Strangelove* as humor by default. Only a masterful mind could deliver gallows humor that works so well at a variety of different levels. Immediately mesmerizing critics and big-city audiences alike, *Dr. Strangelove* was generally rejected in small-town America, where patriotism (sometimes the love-it-or-leave-it variety) and faith in America's military ran deep. But money could be made pleasing urban youth audiences, and *Dr. Strangelove* did make money. It finished as the fourteenth leading box office earner of 1964, right behind the Beatles' *Hard Day's Night*, a seemingly impossible record for a picture pulling its laughs from two previously taboo subjects. It makes light of a hopeless Armageddon and ridicules the American civil and military establishments as a collection of madmen. Of course, the incineration of humankind is hardly a Hollywood staple, and certainly not one played for laughs, but Kubrick cleverly buries the forbidden subject under mounds of unrelenting sardonic humor.

The star of the film, with three important roles, is Peter Sellers. Shot in England because of Sellers's divorce proceedings, the film established that if his wife no longer loved him, audiences did. He also impressed the Academy, which gave him an Oscar nomination for his work. For all its genius in casting, *Dr. Strangelove* lives as a tribute to Stanley Kubrick's uncompromising style of filmmaking. Kubrick grew up in an upper-middle-class Bronx family with a prominent physician for a father. He developed interests in chess and photography early in his life, and at eighteen, began his professional career as a photographer for *Look* magazine. Shifting to film, Kubrick satirized social violence and hypocrisy with "a combination of humor and pathos—laughter leading to thought."[20] His moral mantra repeated the message that humanity has "no way out."[21] Kubrick invariably exposed fatal human flaws; those obsessive weaknesses that produce disaster.[22]

Dr. Strangelove was based on Peter George's novel *Red Alert*, brought to Kubrick's attention by Alistair Buchan of the Institute for Strategic

Studies. Whether as writer, director, or producer, Kubrick always brings destructive aspects of sex and war to the screen. In *Dr. Strangelove*, he projects these interests in a protest against the "dominant cultural paradigm," namely, the Ideology of Consensus: that American society is sound but communism is a clear danger to its survival.[23] It is this boil of self-righteous surety and exaggerative anticommunism that Kubrick sought to lance. *Dr. Strangelove* expunges the anxiety and paranoia of the fifties and contributes to a new mind-set for the world of the 1960s.

The two Russian characters in *Dr. Strangelove* are no worse than the Americans, nor are they any better. The same biting satire savages everyone. Even the characters' names smack of sex or violence. As *Dr. Strangelove* opens, renegade U.S. Air Force general Jack D. Ripper has ordered an attack against the Soviet Union. When American president Merten Muffley (Peter Sellers) reaches Soviet premier Kissof on the hotline, hoping to warn him of the attack, the premier is preoccupied—dallying with his mistress. The premier, never actually seen on camera, voices upset at this diplomatic coitus interruptus; but the Russian ambassador, Alexei de Sadesky (Peter Bull), begs the understanding of the American president. After all, the premier is "a man of the people, but, a man nevertheless."

Wall-to-wall absurdity characterizes the hotline argument between President Muffley and Premier Kissof as to who feels worse over the impending tragedy. The exchange ends with the premier revealing just how ill-timed the attack really is, not just for him and his lady friend, but for all humankind. The Soviet Union has recently completed a "doomsday machine." If the Soviets get flattened in a nuclear confrontation, a series of automatically triggered nuclear explosions will wipe out all of humanity. One for all and all for one. When Dr. Strangelove (Peter Sellers), the film's presidential adviser whom Kubrick concocted from a composite of Henry Kissinger, Edward Teller, and Wernher Von Braun, demands to know why the Soviets have not informed the world of the device, since the "doomsday machine" is pointless unless the enemy knows it exists, the ambassador responds futilely that "Premier Kissof loves surprises." It seems he intended to announce the defense system at the party congress "this coming Monday."

The only Russian appearing on camera, Soviet Ambassador de Sadesky, a repulsive toady, provides no help during the crisis. As inveterate a cold warrior as any of the Americans, the ridiculous de Sadesky secretly takes photos in the Pentagon war room. Absurdity follows absurdity with a regularity that generates its own logic. When General Buck Turgidson catches the Russian ambassador taking photos and wrestles him to the ground, the U.S. president yells in protest, "You can't fight in here, this is the war room!" And the room is an imposing presence in itself. Described by one critic as "an immense tent-shaped chamber with concrete walls, glassy silicone floors and immense illuminated strategic maps on the walls," it dwarfs the men who, until very recently, had viewed all this military hardware as little more than a playground.[24] But *Dr. Strangelove* demands that the real threats to humanity's future are the public complacency and the military mindset treating human existence as a negotiable commodity.

Four bizarre American figures represent the macho military mentality, and each is central to the unfolding plot. There is Sterling Hayden's brilliant portrayal of General Jack D. Ripper, who unleashes his squadron of nuclear bombers. A paranoic, he drinks only vodka, never water, because he believes in a communist plot to "sap our precious bodily fluids" through fluoridation, a contention that the John Birch Society continues to advance thirty years after the release of *Dr. Strangelove.*

Equally off the wall, General Buck Turgidson (George C. Scott) of the Joint Chiefs of Staff, sees the accidental war as a golden opportunity to devastate Russia at minimal cost to the United States. "I'm not saying we wouldn't get our hair mussed—maybe ten to twenty million, tops!" Keenan Wynn portrays the officious Colonel Bat Guano, who refuses to fire on a Coke machine to retrieve a coin for a telephone call to the president that might prevent the war, fearing that the destruction of a Coke machine violates "private property." And perhaps no image is so indelibly etched into the film audience's mind as that of Slim Pickens as Major T. J. "King" Kong, riding a glistening missile to earth like a rodeo cowboy, even as he ignites global holocaust. The film's parade of fanatics "continued to function as though they were not about to die: faced with extinction, few had the wit to worry."[25]

Bosley Crowther, never more clearly the voice of the American establishment, churned out three reviews of the film, all labeling *Dr. Strangelove* as excessive and showing poor taste. He may have been partly right; but that it was *meant* to be so seemed to elude him. Most reviewers responded positively and one even went so far as to label it the "most courageous film ever made." If *Dr. Strangelove* warranted such accolades, it did so by establishing that no matter how excessive, it could not even approximate the horror of nuclear devastation contemplated by the superpowers.[26]

Other reviewers declared *Dr. Strangelove* the "first break in the catatonic cold war trance that has so long held our country in its rigid grip,"[27] calling it "relentlessly perceptive of human beings to the point of inhumanity."[28] Loudon Wainwright's piece in *Life* dismissed the film's detractors, noting that "the half-life of not getting the point is forever."[29]

Dr. Strangelove received Oscar nominations for best picture, best actor, best director, and best screenplay. The *New York Times* included it in its "ten best" list, and Kubrick was selected as best director by the New York Film Critics. It is worth noting that in Peter George's novel, from which the film is adapted, a soft landing is provided. At the end of the novel the bomb is dropped, but it turns out to be a dud and does not explode. Humanity gains a reprieve. Kubrick's audiences are spared nothing, as he carries his convictions to their logical, destructive conclusion, resulting in audiences applauding Armageddon.

Bellwether II: *The Russians Are Coming,* *The Russians Are Coming*

Oscar Wilde once observed that "laughter is not at all a bad beginning for a friendship," an apropos insight into the motivation of Canadian-born filmmaker Norman Jewison's direction and production of his light satire, *The Russians Are Coming, The Russians Are Coming!* (1966).[30] William Rose's screenplay humanizes the Russians; it also personalizes Cold War stereotypes, rendering them absurd in a context of comedic geniuses like Ben Blue, Carl Reiner, Jonathan Winters, and Theodore Bikel. No other film of the time so elegantly and benignly deflates the puffed up anticommunism of the 1950s, in the process receiving Oscar nominations for best actor (Alan Arkin), best picture, and best writing.

The plot has a curious Soviet submarine commander running his vessel aground on New England's Gloucester Island. A succession of zany, often slapstick encounters spring from this simple premise as Russian crew members are sent ashore to steal a boat that can free their helpless vessel. Their task is complicated by local Yankee residents. These parochial locals are suspicious of American mainlanders, not to mention Soviet sailors. In a microcosm of the Cold War, every encounter between frightened Russian sailors and insular islanders, no matter how harmless, expands the circle of misunderstanding.

The Soviet sailors attempting to steal a powerboat to use in freeing the submarine are led by an affable, inept officer, Rozanov (Alan Arkin's first film role). Audiences find no difficulty identifying with the frustrated Rozanov as bizarre events cascade out of control. Equally likable and sincere is his impulsive captain (Theodore Bikel). Bikel plays the role enthusiastically and completely in Russian, with his impossible predicament making him even more endearing. The other main Russian character, whose personality is the opposite of his Captain's, is Alexei Kolchin (John Philip Law), a handsome young sailor in Rozanov's disorganized landing party. Kolchin meets a lovely young

American girl named Alison Palmer, who provides the film's love interest. Kolchin's pleasant and gentle demeanor proves irresistible to Alison Palmer. In the critical denouement scene, it is Kolchin who helps rescue the endangered young boy, and, according to one critic, personifies the idea that Russians and Americans "share basic human qualities."[31]

Other Russo-Exonerators

Lacking the gentility of *The Russians Are Coming*, *The Bedford Incident* (1965) and *The Billion Dollar Brain* (1967) launch more aggressive frontal assaults on military values. *The Bedford Incident*, a Cold War suspense thriller, sends the overzealous commander of a U.S. Naval destroyer, Commander Eric Finlander, chasing after a Soviet adversary in the North Atlantic. The obsessive Finlander (Richard Widmark, playing the kind of role he does best) takes "inordinate risks" in pursuit of his elusive Soviet quarry.[32] He also suffers from what one historian refers to as "an ideological tic: he *hates* communism." No surprise. Richard Widmark based his portrayal of Captain Finlander on the idiosyncracies and statements of Barry Goldwater's 1964 presidential campaign.[33]

Finlander's ideological pathology, played like a deadly serious Jack D. Ripper, leads to a nuclear confrontation when Finlander's weapons officer misinterprets a frenzied order from the commander and fires at the Soviet submarine. The Soviets retaliate and chaos ensues. *The Bedford Incident* argues that deranged Cold War zeal can only lead to disaster. By not playing the Cold War spirit for laughs, this film comes from the other direction, but it joins *The Russians Are Coming* in imploring America to "lighten up."

Not everyone seemed ready for this twin message. The U.S. military, not surprisingly, refused to provide technical support to Columbia and producer/director James B. Harris for *The Bedford Incident*. Harris, best known for his work with Stanley Kubrick, also finds inspiration elsewhere. In addition to *Dr. Strangelove*, he seems heavily influenced by *The Caine Mutiny*. In *The Bedford Incident* he benefits from James Poe's screenplay, which remained faithful to the original novel by Mark Rascovitch.

Director Ken Russell's *Billion Dollar Brain* (1967) is rooted in quite different soil. Russell's career parallels that of John Schlesinger: both men tried photography and acting before taking on directing. Russell made thirty-five documentaries for BBC-TV before he slid into feature films. Many of Russell's films employ historical themes as backdrops to contemporary dramas about "romantic idealists struggling against their own personalities."[34]

In 1967, producer Harry Saltzman hired Russell because Saltzman was convinced that Russell's documentary experience suited a biographical film capturing the life of Russian dancer Vaslav Nijinsky. The project collapsed when dancer Rudolf Nureyev pulled out of the lead role. Rather than let Russell go, Saltzman somehow convinced him to direct a change-of-pace spy movie, *The Billion Dollar Brain*, an obscure backlash piece for United Artists.[35] It did provide a ready vehicle for what a film historian calls Russell's "flights of dramatic fancy."[36] Although the plot line of *The Billion Dollar Brain* wobbles outside the boundaries of reality, it joins the list of films portraying the Soviet Union as nonthreatening, and maybe even cooperative. Not everyone appreciated the message. One critic warned his readers that *The Billion Dollar Brain* tilted too far the other way and was "anti-American and pro-Soviet by virtue of a chuckling, sympathetic performance of a Soviet counter agent by Oscar Homolka," in yet another Russian-genre role.[37]

Built on the premise that Soviet and Western intelligence agencies need join forces to defeat those who would lead the world to war, this film relies on the appeal of actor Michael Caine, who plays British agent Harry Palmer. But the role provides little for actor Caine to work with. Unlike James Bond, who relishes his job as a spy, Harry Palmer hates his, staying with it only because he has no choice—it's either spying or the military prison from which he was plucked by British intelligence. Nor does Harry Palmer share Bond's stylish, fast-paced, and libidinous lifestyle. He is, instead, an irreverent and street-smart loner kept on a short string and a miserly salary by British officials. While Bond can be seen as patriotic, Palmer is a pragmatist with survival on his mind; most of the time Palmer wonders whether his own government is not his worst enemy.

In *The Billion Dollar Brain* one thing is certain: the Soviets are Palmer's key ally in a battle of wits with fanatical anticommunist Texas oil tycoon, General Midwinter (Ed Begley). General Midwinter has secretly built a personal army to liberate Latvia from the Soviet Union and ultimately to dismantle the Soviet system. This mad scheme, if it gets off the ground, could soon escalate out of control.

Echoing *The Manchurian Candidate* (1962) and *Seven Days in May* (1964), *The Billion Dollar Brain* paints a picture of anticommunist vigilantism ready to destroy the world rather than accept coexistence. Only Harry Palmer, the reluctant spy, and a lovable old Soviet spymaster, played by Oscar Homolka, thwart General Midwinter's plan to overthrow the Soviet Union. The general's weapon is not an assassin's bullet or a military coup, but a massive computer clicking away, the titular billion-dollar brain, which is programmed for a lightning quick invasion of Latvia. But no computer playing video games with world peace is going to outsmart Harry Palmer and his Soviet partner. As the general's heavily armed invading force tries to dash across the winter ice toward Latvia, Soviet bombers crack the ice, sending the general's army to a watery grave.

As Soviet-American relations slowly improved, Hollywood's search for villains reached beyond right-wing crazies. Several films, echoing the headlines, cast China as the devil incarnate. And why not? There was China's support of North Vietnam, development of nuclear weapons, refusal to sign the partial test ban treaty, and Mao Tse-tung's violent purge known as the Great Proletarian Cultural Revolution, to complain about. Both *The Shoes of the Fisherman* (1968) and *The Chairman* (1969) roasted the Chinese as global miscreants.

Anthony Quinn stars in M-G-M's ponderous, overlong yawner, *The Shoes of the Fisherman*, which preaches the gospel of humanitarianism. Quinn plays Kiril Pavlovich Lakota, a pious Catholic priest who rises to the position of Archbishop of Lvov. No friend of godless communism, the archbishop spends twenty years as political prisoner 103592R in a Soviet gulag, where he loses neither faith nor hope.

Archbishop Lakota's piety is rewarded when he suddenly finds himself whisked out of prison and into the office of his former interrogator, Piotr Kamenev, recently elevated to the position of Soviet premier. Strangely enough, Premier Kamenev (Laurence Olivier) has arranged for Archbishop Lakota to transfer to the Vatican, where he soon becomes a cardinal. When the Pope dies and seven deadlocked ballots fail to elect a successor, a reluctant Lakota is selected as Pope Kiril I.[38]

Election of the principled Lakota as Pope proves serendipitous not only for the Catholic Church, but also for all humanity. Political chaos and economic collapse in China have created massive starvation. The desperate Chinese, under a militant new dictator, threaten expansion into the Soviet Union in an attempt to ease their desperate circumstances. Nuclear war appears imminent until the creative negotiator, Pope Kiril I, guides humanity away from catastrophe. To convince the Chinese of his sincerity and to buy time to rebuild the Chinese economy, the pope pledges much of the Church's wealth to feed the starving Chinese masses. Good-bye Cistine Chapel. The Chinese are placated, and humankind is spared a Chinese-initiated rendezvous with Armageddon.

While China was convinced not to bomb the Soviet Union, *The Shoes of the Fisherman* bombed in American theaters. Reviewers were also less than generous in their comments. After wading through this wall-to-wall fluff, they may have felt bloated with hot air. Pauline Kael crucified it as the "worst big picture of the year," and held British director Michael Anderson (son of actor Lawrence Anderson) responsible, albeit only indirectly. The real culprits were the demise of the studio system and the 1950s blacklist, which wiped out a critical generation of directors. Kael lamented that few British directors brought in by Hollywood to fill the void proved capable of delivering the goods.[39]

The Shoes of the Fisherman was no exception, although it did receive an Oscar nomination for Alex North's music, and it probably deserved nominations for cinematography and costume. But its stylized, skin-deep visuals could not conceal that the body of the film remained dead from the neck up. *Shoes of the Fisherman* is noteworthy on one level only. It celebrates two Russian heroes—Anthony Quinn as the saintly and heroic pope and Laurence Olivier as the perceptive and flexible Premier Kamenev. The Chinese, as willing catalysts of thermonuclear destruction, played the bad guys.

The other late-1960s picture identifying the Chinese as new international villains was *The Chairman* (1969). Here the Russians work hand in hand with the Americans, although the Russians play the greater role in saving the world from the scheming Chinese. Again the plot represents a stretch. Under Chairman Mao, the Chinese have developed a new "enzyme" that enables them to grow food almost anywhere, providing enormous leverage with poverty-stricken countries. Too bad the Chinese did not have this "enzyme" in time for *The Shoes of the Fisherman*. The Church could have kept its riches.

In *The Chairman*, American scientist and spy, Dr. John Hathaway (Gregory Peck), is summoned by China to provide technical assistance on this vital project. The Chinese discoverer of the new enzyme had been Hathaway's former professor. Before leaving for China, the CIA implants a listening device in Dr. Hathaway's scalp—a chip in the old block. What Hathaway does not know, however, might blow his mind: the CIA can detonate the transmitter as a bomb, which is what they intend to do if he gets close to Chairman Mao. Forced to run for it, Dr. Hathaway flees north to the Soviet border, where Russian agents rush in just in time to save him from Chinese border guards.

No comparable miracle rescues the plot, which shifts away from Dr. Hathaway to Russian KGB agent Alexander Sertov, who joins forces with the CIA against the Chinese. Except for his accent, Sertov is indistinguishable from his American counterparts, belying a real brotherhood of trenchcoats. He fits in so comfortably that nobody seems to blink an eye when this Soviet intelligence agent pops up more often than a box of Kleenex™ in secret American installations like Omaha's NORAD headquarters. Fortunately, close Soviet-American cooperation succeeds at the expense of the Chinese. Ben Maddow's screenplay was DOA, and director J. Lee Thompson failed to breathe the kind of life into it that he brought to his work in *Battle for the Planet of the Apes* (1973) and *Conquest of the Planet of the Apes* (1972).

Middling Films

While most of this transitional era's films treat Russians and the Soviet Union quite favorably, a few darker entries dot the landscape. None has a more campy gallery of Russians than the James Bond series. Near the top of the list rests the second in the Bond series, *From Russia with Love* (1963). The film made just under $10 million during 1964, placing it among the top five pictures for the year. British director Terence Young, whose career peaked in the 1960s, brought smiles to the faces of executives at United Artists.

Among the things that drew audiences into movie theaters to watch *From Russia with Love* was the odd pair of Russian nasties taking on Bond. But if these Russians are villains, the Soviet Union is not. The film treats the Soviet Union gently. Like the United States, it is a potential victim of dastardly plots by SPECTRE, something of a free-enterprise cross between NASA and the Mafia, but intent on world rule. And just in case the audience misses the point, Bond's love interest here is Russian. This beautiful KGB spy is no fool. After hitting the sack with 007, she defects. Oh, the power of love!

The plot opens where *Ninotchka* ended, in Istanbul, as the seductive KGB operative Tatiana Romanova (Daniela Bianchi), a tool of the Cold War, attempts to lure James Bond (Sean Connery) into a death trap. The ploy: 007 is sent off to retrieve Tatiana, who is pretending to defect to the West (prior to bedding down with the British agent), bringing along a top-secret coding machine (lekter) as a sweetener. Instead of killing Bond, Tatiana melts in his arms, and together they defeat the picture's real malefactor—SPECTRE.

Tatiana is not the only KGB agent to defect. Unfortunately for Bond, however, the other two KGB agents do not defect to the West. They sell out to SPECTRE. Colonel Rosa Klebb (Lotte Lenya), KGB head of operations and one of Hollywood's most dastardly Russian creations, is a SPECTRE double agent. And how does the moviegoer know that the cruel Klebb is beyond redemption? Because, among other things, she remains impervious to Bond's charms, single-mindedly wanting him dead. Although a first-class villain, as a killing machine she falls down on the job. Her high-tech efforts to finish off Mr. Bond misfire, like trying to jab him with poison-tipped blades that snap out of her shoes. In no way can moviegoers confuse Klebb with Mother Teresa, but Klebb's lines of dialogue don't help her cause either. "The Cold War in Istanbul," she warns at one point, "will not remain cold very much longer." Such lines demand a horrible end for her, which arrives at the hands of Tatiana, proving her new loyalty to James and the West by shooting the repulsive double agent.

The other Soviet scamp, KGB Colonel Kronsteen, a world-class chess player as well as villain, couldn't be more cunning or egotistical. SPECTRE signs his real paycheck, as it does Klebb's. He is the brain behind SPECTRE's plot to steal the top-secret lekter and achieve world domination. He also issues the order to kill Bond. Kronsteen stakes his life on the success of his plans. Foiled by Bond, Kronsteen must pay the price. Unlike the obnoxious Klebb, who is dispatched by Tatiana, SPECTRE deals with Kronsteen's failure. In the push-button age of spying, it takes only the flick of a switch by the unforgiving Number One, the head of SPECTRE, to zap Kronsteen.

Dr. Zhivago

If one Russian-genre film towers over all others, it can only be *Dr. Zhivago* (1965), ranking ninth on Joel Finler's top box-office hits through 1980. No other Russian-genre film cracks Finler's top ten decade-by-decade list of box-office hits.[40] Second in earnings for 1965 at more than $47 million, *Dr. Zhivago* trailed only the megahit, *The Sound of Music*, at almost $80 million.[41] *Dr. Zhivago*'s total income of approximately $61 million places it second among all films of the 1960s.[42] A major cinematic achievement, *Dr. Zhivago*, based on Boris Pasternak's long and introspective Russian novel, walked away with five Academy Awards, for musical score, cinematography, screenplay, costumes, and art direction/set direction. Movie producers had discovered by the 1960s that recordings of the musical score and theme of a film could both sell movies and make money on their own. Of all Russian-genre films, none benefited more aesthetically and commercially in this way than *Dr. Zhivago*. The film was nominated for best picture, and David Lean received a nomination for best director.

The nomination was well deserved. *Dr. Zhivago* reveals Lean's fingerprints in every department. Born in Croydon, England, and raised as a Quaker, as a boy he was forbidden to see movies. Once on his own, Lean compensated for his earlier impoverishment. He first stuck his foot into a studio door as a teenager, serving tea during shooting breaks. By twenty he was an assistant editor and quickly moved up the editing ladder. His big break came when the legendary Noel Coward asked Lean to codirect *In Which We Serve* (1942), for which Coward had written the original script.

Between 1957 and 1965, Lean went on to direct a trilogy of films focusing on strong men in struggle: *Bridge on the River Kwai* (1957), *Lawrence of Arabia* (1962), and *Dr. Zhivago* (1965). Deserving of the label "auteur" (fashionable in the sixties), Lean receives ample praise for his professionalism, flexibility, and discipline.[43] After his first two macho epics, Lean remarked, "I'm rather sick of having men. I want to get back to the ladies."[44] With the beautiful Julie Christie playing Lara, Lean well realized that ambition in *Dr. Zhivago*. Lean sought full artistic control and battled with M-G-M executives to shoot the film completely in Europe. The once-proud lion no longer roared as in the studio's Golden Age and Lean prevailed in nearly every dispute.

Only vaguely typical of the era, *Dr. Zhivago* constitutes an unusual bellwether film. Boldly sweeping across three decades, from 1905 to the mid-1930s, *Dr. Zhivago* chronicles the human journey of one man through a labyrinth of monumental events that included the Russian Revolution of 1905, World War I, the 1917 Bolshevik Revolution, and the Russian Civil War of 1918–21. Against such social and political forces, *Dr. Zhivago* illustrates how strong characters constantly find themselves separated and overwhelmed, underscoring what one critic calls "the puniness of man when he measures himself against this scale."[45]

A major struggle emerged over the production parameters of *Dr. Zhivago*: the auteur Lean versus the M-G-M brass. While the lion emitted its familiar roar, people no longer shuddered. The studio was in terminal decline, and David Lean ended up calling most of the shots, including where the film would be shot, in Europe. With its haunting musical score, brilliant visual touches, and emotive story, the film represents a sensual feast—a *Gone with the Wind* with snow. Director Lean well knows how to use contrasting colors to emphasize certain dramatic moments. To get just the right effect, some scenes were blown down with a spray gun to neutralize normal color to grays, whites, and blacks, thus highlighting well-chosen scenes of bright color.[46]

Most of all, it is hard to avoid being swept up in the narrative, which is what Lean wanted. A perceptive film historian points out that Lean's work is crafted around a desire to "immerse his audience in the environment of the story he is telling." The plot line follows the life of Yuri Zhivago (Omar Sharif), an orphan raised by a warm aristocratic family, the Gromykos. In its nurturing bosom, Yuri develops into a principled and honorable physician; his real obsession, however, is writing poetry. The family's daughter, Tonya Gromyko (Geraldine Chaplin), a fine and cultured young woman about Yuri's age, seems a perfect match for Yuri; they marry just as their country explodes, first into the bloodletting of war, and soon thereafter into the chaos of revolution.

Pleasant days are few as the young lovers become separated when Yuri is called to service in the Russian medical corps during World War I. Under harsh and depressing conditions, Yuri works side by side with the other tragic figure of *Dr. Zhivago*—the beautiful and sensitive

Lara (Julie Christie). As a young doctor in Moscow, Yuri had two previous and brief professional encounters with Lara. Lara, only seventeen, was then caught in a steamy affair as mistress to an amoral opportunist, Victor Komarovsky (Rod Steiger). Perfectly cast as Komarovsky, Yuri Zhivago's spiritual opposite, Komarovsky comes to personify expediency and cynicism.

Wartime tragedy calls for heroic sacrifice. At the front Yuri and Lara daily witness death, suffering, and sacrifice. In the face of such pain the two bond. While their relationship remains Platonic, they know that their feelings for one another run deeper than they dare confess. (Boris Pasternak's real-life mistress, who served as the inspiration for Lara, served eight years in Soviet prisons for her relationship with the outcast writer.) Yuri returns to his wife Tonya at war's end, but the audience knows that Lara remains very much in his thoughts. War's end brings no peace. Torn by revolution, conditions in Moscow deteriorate as the Gromyko family moves to its country home in the Urals. What about Yuri's life with Tonya? Although warm and caring, it lacks the passionate fire demanded by Yuri's poetic soul. And passion soon overwhelms Yuri, when, by implausible circumstance, he encounters Lara in a nearby village. Their carefully controlled Platonic love explodes into full-blown passion. Typical of the film, however, history crashes in on the lovers. The Red Army kidnaps Yuri, forcing him to serve as a medic in their civil war against the Whites.

Director David Lean once described himself as "drawn to the person who refuses to face defeat," and few of his characters exemplify this trait more than Yuri Zhivago.[47] Yuri's family flees to the safety of Paris; he will never see them again. Yuri, drowning in the misery around him, eventually pulls himself free of the Bolsheviks and the horrific civil war. Clinging to life, he makes his way back to Lara, who nurtures him back to health. But Zhivago's happiness is short lived. Her long-estranged husband Pasha (Oscar nominee Tom Courtenay), a revolutionary who has fallen-out with the Bolsheviks, has been branded a political pariah. As Pasha's wife, Lara is also in danger. Safety is only possible at the hands of the unsavory Komarovsky. Lara's final emotional separation from Yuri extinguishes the flicker of hope that managed to light this dark-edged film. Epic in its reflection on human suffering, *Dr. Zhivago* allows no space for a relationship to grow naturally: events always trample dreams.

What message does *Dr. Zhivago* deliver about Russians and the Soviet Union? From the very first dialogue in this three-hour epic, Russia is difficult for the audience to comprehend. It seems as much an experience as a place. The film's narrator, General Yevgraf (Alec Guinness), half-brother of Yuri Zhivago, speaks with a young female

engineer (who may be the love-child of Zhivago and Lara) at a model
Soviet hydroelectric dam in the mid-1930s:

> "Don't be too impatient Comrade Engineer, we've come very far very
> fast!"
> "Yes, I know that Comrade General."
> "Yes, but do you know what it cost? There were children who lived off
> human flesh in those days [civil war], did you know that?"

Not exactly a "love/hate" relationship, *Dr. Zhivago* has more of a
"love/fear" relationship with Russia. Little room exists for neutrality
about Russia's mix of peoples, good and bad, or its culture of heroic
passion. And always present is the vastness of the place, which engulfs
those who struggle to survive within it.[48] But the message is anything
but monolithic. Russians are thrust, unprepared, into a world of
change. It is a world that cries out for order, but defies human control.
Russian culture appears as a kaleidoscope of contrasting appetites.
The Russian people, subject to complex and competing moods,
become overwhelmed by out-sized physical and social environments.
In the end, it leaves few unambiguous images. Strong mixed messages
render Russia a land of mystery, which, inadvertently, may bring *Dr.
Zhivago* closer to reality than even David Lean realized.

Films Critical of Russia

Hollywood's Russian-genre apogee arrived with the generally
accepting *Dr. Strangelove* and *The Russians Are Coming*, as well as
the heavier, more ambivalent *Dr. Zhivago*. But two other critical
films joined *Dr. Zhivago* as Oscar winners. *Fiddler on the Roof*
(1971), a hit Broadway musical brought to the screen, celebrates
Jewish tradition rather than its Russian setting; the key characters
are Russian Jews who are resident outsiders who never quite
become a part of Russia.

If the tiny Jewish village of Anatefka is a place of the imagination, the
world of official and unofficial anti-Semitism is a long and dark Russian
historical reality. Government-sanctioned pogroms of 1905 form the
backdrop for this story, loosely based on characters drawn from Shalom
Alechem's stories. The film's central figure is the proud but simple
dairyman, Tevye, played with sympathetic understanding by the Israeli
actor Topol. Pauline Kael describes Tevye as a character of "Old
Testament size brought down by the circumstances of oppression."[49]

On one level, Tevye wrestles with repeated ethical dilemmas relating
to his five unmarried daughters, who one by one challenge him to

question the boundaries of Jewish tradition through their marital intentions. On another level, Tevye's struggle extends beyond his family. As he battles to hold his daughters within the homegrown truths of village and family, the larger world of change, which once bypassed Anatefka, now intrudes and exacts a heavy price. But Tevye's primary concern remains with his family.

First, Tzeitel (Rosalind Harris) requests permission to marry the poor tailor Motel rather than accept an arranged marriage with the wealthy widower, town butcher Lazar Wolf. Tevye reluctantly agrees. Then Hodel (Michele Marsh) announces she will marry the secular free-thinking radical, Perchik, with or without her father's blessing. Tevye, stretched to the limit, again concedes. But when daughter Chava (Neva Small) confesses that she has secretly married a Russian Gentile, Tevye finally snaps and disowns her.

Tevye's defense of a traditional world may have been threatened by the life choices of his daughters, but it was ultimately destroyed by another tradition—Russian anti-Semitism. Flayed about in an effort to consolidate support for its decaying legitimacy, the creaking Tsarist regime deflected hostility onto the Jews. Officially sanctioned attacks on Jews followed. In fictional Anatefka, as for tens of thousands of actual Russian Jews, state-sponsored terror inflicted death, destruction of property, rupture of families and, for many, exile from all that they had ever known.

For Tevye, the shadow of Russian anti-Semitism gradually fell across his family's path. The audience is initially made aware only of Tevye's cautious unease with Gentiles, as he is surrounded by a group of Russian men drinking together in a village inn. The threat proves hollow this time, but not the next. Hodel follows her husband Perchik into Siberian exile for his "political crimes." Tzeitel's wedding is violently ended when anonymous Russian horsemen attack the defenseless Jewish villagers.

Finally, the villagers are cast out to face an unknown future. The town constable, a Russian, gets along well with Anatefka's residents and has a soft spot for Tevye. But he neither protects the villagers from attack nor hesitates to carry out the government's eviction order. *Fiddler on the Roof* concludes with the end of Anatefka and the beginning of the villagers' trek westward to the New World. Similar flight offered the sole recourse for many thousands of nineteenth- and early twentieth-century Russian Jews, some of whose descendants would later help shape the emerging Hollywood studio system.

Fiddler on the Roof provided a major critical and commercial success for United Artists. Joseph Stein's screenplay, based on his own Broadway musical, includes production and direction by Norman

Jewison in this three-hour film. Oswald Morris won an Academy Award for photography, as did John Williams for musical direction. Nominations went to Norman Jewison for direction, Topol for best actor, and Leonard Frey for supporting actor. *Fiddler* also received an Oscar nomination for best picture.

Another beautifully staged, yet critical, Russian-genre film appeared with the release of Columbia Films's *Nicholas and Alexandra* (1971). Working with a screenplay by James Goldman, director Franklin J. Schaffner made *Nicholas and Alexandra* into another of the era's lengthy panoramic films. Schaffner's efforts were rewarded with two Academy Awards: one for costume design and another for art direction/set direction. *Nicholas and Alexandra* also received nominations for best picture and best actress (Janet Suzman). But praise for the film was far from unanimous. Several respected critics of the day regarded the film as overblown, lacking either the breadth of *Dr. Zhivago* or the endearing qualities of *Fiddler on the Roof*.

Nicholas and Alexandra bears one heavy burden. In spite of its visual beauty, like a montage of photographs in an expensive coffee-table collection, it portrays the royal pair as so vacuous and unlikable that moviegoers must work at mustering any concern or sympathy for their fate. Schaffner's *Nicholas and Alexandra* represents a feast of visual bites as barren of insight as contemporary media sound bites. In this historical autumn of the Romanov dynasty's rotting grandeur, one cannot fault audiences' cheering for winter.

One critic, blaming Michael Jayston's lifeless acting for the film's problems, claims that "for emotion, he widens his tiny eyes from time to time."[50] But this is too simplistic. More problematically, *Nicholas and Alexandra* eviscerates history and fails to ring true. Audiences are parceled out only the narrowest of portraits, flat images without a frame. Of course, Tsar Nicholas II never achieved greatness as a ruler. He made a series of ill-timed, disastrous decisions. Against the advice of counselors, he jumped into a catastrophic war with Japan, prematurely committed his ill-trained and ill-equipped forces to World War I, and, despite scant knowledge of military affairs, assumed personal command at the front while leaving the unpopular Alexandra to rule in Saint Petersburg.

But Nicholas II was not as hopeless as *Nicholas and Alexandra* portrays him—a narrow-minded bigot, unrealistic dreamer, extreme reactionary, excessively proud, vindictive, and completely blind to reality. He was also part and parcel of explosive times—times about which the audience is provided little sense. Director Franklin Shaffner magnifies Nicholas's failings to imply that, like one man turning back the hands on a clock, had the tsar acted sooner and more wisely, he could have prevented the revolution. Nicholas II was more than just the wrong man for the job. He was also tsar of all the Russians. To comprehend events tearing down a tsar and a dynasty, filmgoers need to grasp something of Russia, not merely its royal drawingroom.[51]

The film's Tsaritsa Alexandra (Janet Suzman) comes off little better than her husband, even if allowed humanistic motivations, such as the health of her hemophiliac son. But like Michael Jayston's Nicholas II, Janet Susman's Alexandra is hardly a personality anyone would wish to call a friend. Her nagging, controlling ways and superstitious ideas make her every bit as disagreeable as the tsar. Making things even worse, she has fallen under the spell of the hedonistic, unordained monk Grigorii Rasputin, whose very name means debauchery. Her image is not helped by the fact that she came to her royal wedding as the daughter of a Lutheran German royal family. In Orthodox Russia, at war with Germany, the rumor mill is abuzz with suggestions that she is a German spy.

The royal couple, not the only objects of derision, are joined by their court, whom critic Pauline Kael dismisses as "a family of dullards." She also laments the movie's failure to capitalize on its lone interesting character—Rasputin.[52] Another critic cites the film's "fictional inventions of a sometimes ludicrous order" when comparing it to Robert Massie's book. The celluloid *Nicholas and Alexandra* tries to "cram too big a picture into too small a frame," resulting in narrowly drawn protagonists who act like "cartoon characters."[53]

Mixed Cinematic Themes

Reversing the previous decade's Russophobia, the majority of transitional Russian-theme films are either neutral or positive, even though many use the Cold War as a backdrop. Most also presuppose that bilateral cooperation is not only acceptable, but desirable. With the Kremlin no longer providing Hollywood the villains it requires, Hollywood need only look either right or left to find them elsewhere. Overzealous domestic anticommunists or new communist adventurers abroad, the Chinese, offer Hollywood ample plot variations. Neither would constitute a cinematic threat, however, without new technology, particularly in the guise of nuclear blackmail.

One repetitive theme makes excessive militarism responsible for the nuclear standoff holding both superpowers hostage. Finding a way back from the brink becomes more important than scoring Cold War points. This doesn't make Soviet communism any more agreeable to Americans, but it does reinforce Armageddon as the option to living with Soviet-American differences. Hollywood also resurrects the thirties' distinction between an evil system governing some good people. In the mixed bag of transition era films, a few spy movies harken back to the acute Cold War. One, Alfred Hitchcock's *Topaz* (1969), condemns the Soviets for behind-the-scenes intrigue relating to the Cuban missile crisis. But such minor tremors barely shake the growing foundation of positive depictions heralding superpower cooperation in the 1960s.

From Confidence to Disillusionment

Cooperation with the Soviet Union was one thing, but unity at home was quite another, and it was not there. The conformist psychology of the fifties receded, and in its place emerged a new collective consciousness. America focused on sociopolitical tensions, particularly the domestic civil rights movement and the Vietnam War abroad. This was a consciousness increasingly divided against itself, each side confident, even arrogant, in claiming a proprietary right to define America's values.

American foreign policy was fraught with contradictions. Even as the United States engaged in a massive Vietnamese buildup, it improved relations with Hanoi's benefactor, the Soviet Union. As American policy spoke of defending democracy abroad, the baby-boomer generation—black and white—tested the resiliency of domestic democracy. Campuses and inner cities seethed with protest against the values of the center. Never had a generation produced a counterculture so dedicated to redefining America's dominant cultural patterns. Many scorned the perceived hypocrisy of their elders while pledging themselves to social relevance, experimentation, and tolerance. Yet if the counterculture challenged society's values, its message came packaged in the same self-righteousness so characteristic of the American mind-set.

The sixties were born amid echoes of Kennedy's optimistic inaugural rhetoric, but they faded deeply mired in the gloom of Lyndon Johnson's failed presidency. This decade ended by spawning a popular retreat into a resilient illusion: that 1950s simplicity might be recycled by electing Eisenhower's vice president, Richard M. Nixon. While Nixon would innovate his way around the foreign policy scene by firming up Soviet-American relations and opening the long-locked door to China, paradoxically, he was doomed to personify the domestic disillusionment that set the tone of the 1970s.

Chapter Five

1972–1980: Fragile Detente

More than any other Hollywood character of the past three decades, James Bond travels through cinematic time like a smooth stone skipping across the calmest of lakes. During the respite in tension that marked superpower relations in the 1970s, James Bond could symbolize detente, even with his pants down. In *The Spy Who Loved Me* (1977), the megalomaniac villain Carl Stromberg (Curt Jurgens) is taken with the notion of romance between James Bond (Roger Moore) and Soviet agent Anya Amasova (Barbara Bach). "Well, well, well," he muses, "a Russian agent in love with a British agent— detente indeed!"

Detente indeed. Accounts of seventies East-West relations generally paint the decade with detente's broad brush, usually understood as the period sandwiched between the SALT I treaty of May 1972, and the SALT II treaty of June 1979. But with respect to American foreign policy and Hollywood films, the idea of detente begs refinement. Positive filmic references to lovable Russians do exist in the 1970s, but without the intensity or frequency that might be expected. In fact, neither Russians nor their country seized the popular consciousness in the seventies. America's attention was centered elsewhere, and detente was left to run its course without much cinematic attention. Nor was the course of superpower detente smooth in the 1970s. If Soviet-American relations spiralled upward during the early years, they stumbled badly during the closing years of the decade.

But what was detente? The French term refers to an easing, or "detensing," of strained relations between states.[1] In the East-West context, detente relates to two similar but distinguishable phenomena: the improved state of power bloc relations characteristic of the 1970s and the foreign policy crafted by Nixon and Kissinger and loosely adapted by Presidents Gerald Ford and Jimmy Carter. In retrospect, it is easy to overstate the lasting impact of detente. Detente most certainly produced several advances in Soviet-American relations, but it did not end the Cold War. Detente was less peace than mutually agreeable disengagement. A Cold War of sorts continued, but in muted form. One must savor every blessing in a nuclear age when disengagement is preferable to war.

"Escape with Honor" Fosters Detente

Detente did not emerge from nothingness. Transitional steps toward accommodation taken during the 1960s led to expanded initiatives. If the Cuban missile crisis served as the catalyst for ending the acute Cold War period, then the Nixon administration's efforts to "escape with honor" from the morass of Vietnam operated comparably in easing the two nuclear giants into seventies' detente.

An overriding desire to get America out of Vietnam as gracefully, honorably, and quickly as possible drove the diplomacy of "Nixingerism" along two different roads at the same time, one leading to Moscow and one, to Beijing. Efforts were made to enlist Soviet and Chinese cooperation in pressuring North Vietnam to participate in peace talks.[2] No sooner were peace talks under way than the thawing of the Cold War known as detente accelerated. Detente was the theme shared by three different presidents with varying styles in the general conduct of their foreign policy.

Once detente had been engaged, several factors contributed to broaden it during the early 1970s. As noted, the most important factor was Nixon's effort to extricate America from Vietnam. Domestic economic interests also favored detente, since it promised expanded trade with the Soviets. Double-digit inflation and high unemployment forced Nixon to apply price and wage controls in 1971, surely a policy of last resort for a fiscally conservative Republican president. Under such circumstances, the prospect of expanding trade with the Soviet bloc must have looked as good to Nixon as it did to the captains of American industry. And in the antimilitary heyday following in the wake of Vietnam, the American public was in no mood to accept large-scale defense spending. Thus detente, with its premise of more trade and less military spending, seemed a winner. Only to hard-line anticommunists did detente possess a significant downside.

Nixon's 1972 Foreign Policy Successes

If American officials pressed detente's advantages in the early 1970s, the Soviet Union had its own reasons for doing likewise. The continuing Sino-Soviet rift fueled Soviet determination to improve relations with the West. After achieving strategic nuclear parity with the United States, the Soviet Union regarded itself as an equal superpower. In retreating from the Cold War, it was not caving in to American pressure, but rather acting as a full partner in change. Leonid Brezhnev also had his own serious economic problems, which contributed to his interest in economic cooperation.

This left an opening for American diplomatic initiative that Nixon aggressively filled. In 1972 Nixon visited both Moscow and Beijing, and the SALT I Treaty was signed. These stunning achievements ushered in the era of detente. While some Americans seemed taken more by Kissinger's emergency appendectomy in Beijing, which used acupuncture instead of general anesthesia, a fervent hope began taking hold that the Cold War might soon look like ancient history.

If this hope proved premature, detente still represented a step in the right direction. The positive legacy of 1970s detente is clear: eleven agreements on strategic arms control; prying opening the door, if only a crack, to trade and economic relations; and a series of crisis management agreements that pushed both sides' fingers away from the nuclear button.[3] But for all of detente's achievements, a singular irony remains. The very Nixon/Kissinger style of "imperial presidency," which provided license to move on detente and its back-channel successes with China and the Soviet Union, doomed Nixon to the ignominy of resignation over the Watergate scandal in August of 1974.

Much as the Nixon White House pushed it, detente was not dependent on Richard Nixon. Detente continued well beyond his bizarre departure. The warm spring of detente continued percolating in an atmosphere favored by a generally improved psychological climate. Common endeavors such as the 1975 joint Apollo-Soyuz space rendezvous, the 1975 Helsinki Accords, scientific, cultural, and educational exchanges, and increased tourism also helped thaw the Cold War.

Discordant Notes in Detente's Fugue

It would be wrong, however, to think that American-Soviet relations proceeded without discord. Like other eras, the 1970s combined cooperation and conflict, but generally expanded on the former and successfully managed the latter. Detente's momentum peaked in the early part of the decade, sputtered in the middle, and gradually wound down during the late seventies. When Richard Nixon resigned, detente lost its most effective exponent, leaving the policy twisting in the wind without a natural American constituency to defend it.

The first crisis to threaten detente occurred in the Middle East while Nixon still resided in the White House. In an effort to recapture land lost to Israel in the 1967 Six-Day War, if not to destroy Israel, Egypt brokered a pan-Arab military alliance. On Yom Kippur in October 1973, the alliance partners launched a surprise attack on Israel, unleashing the third Arab-Israeli War. Committed to rival client states, the two superpowers rallied behind their surrogates. American and Soviet militaries were placed on their highest alert since the Cuban missile crisis. But preliminary efforts toward detente paid off when Brezhnev invited Kissinger to Moscow for talks. Direct communication helped defuse a possibly explosive situation.

But there were other problems that lingered. As Nixon and Kissinger looked for ways to expand openings with the Soviets, the Democratic Congress complained bitterly about human rights abuses in the Soviet Union. Congress responded to a 1974 trade reform package with the Soviets by passing the Jackson-Vanik Amendment, which tied most favored nation status to liberalization of Soviet emigration, particularly toward Soviet Jews. Likewise, the Stevenson Amendment set a $300 million ceiling on American credits to the Soviet Union. Fearing that congressional sabotage might prevent the American administration from delivering on international trade agreements, Brezhnev dismissed these amendments as meddling in Soviet domestic affairs.

The American public remained uneasy over Soviet support of Third-World revolution in places like Angola, Mozambique, and Ethiopia. Furthermore, after enjoying a clear nuclear advantage from 1945 until 1970, many Americans felt nervous about losing a military edge that had produced confident diplomatic leverage in the past. An ongoing Soviet buildup of SS-18 ICBMs, interpreted by conservatives as exceeding parity and approaching superiority, provided fodder for those favoring expanded armaments.

Jimmy Carter: "Trust Me"

After being humiliated in Vietnam and deceived by Watergate, America sought a president it could both believe and believe in. It found him in Governor Jimmy Carter, a man who pleaded with America, "Trust me, because I will never lie to you."[4] Compared to Nixon, Jimmy Carter personified Mr. Clean. The young Carter grew up in a nurturing and supportive home in Plains, Georgia, under the influence of his strong-willed and God-fearing mother, Miss Lillian.

By age eighteen Jimmy was teaching Sunday school in the Baptist church and reading Reinhold Niebuhr's ideas about the role of religion in politics. When he later confessed to feeling a little lust in his heart toward bare-breasted centerfolds, it only helped make Carter seem like a "regular guy." He brought a unique mixture of faith and political acumen into the White House with him. What he did not bring was foreign policy experience or instincts.

Normally wary of religious crusaders in foreign policy, political scientist John Stoessinger says that Carter embodied elements of both the crusader and the pragmatist, since "his faith did not become a dogma," as had been the case with Woodrow Wilson.[5] For example, when Carter's human rights initiatives on behalf of Soviet dissidents turned up empty, he backed away from the temptation to cling to the moral high ground by slinging mud at the poor Soviet human rights record. Instead, he backed off, preserving detente and, he hoped, leaving the door open to later initiatives.

Carter's Evolving Worldview

Scholars have yet to agree on the substance of Carter's foreign policy. Some argue there is little to judge because no coherent foreign policy ever emerged from the Carter administration. This is unfair. "A worldview existed, it merely changed with time."[6] Lacking any background in foreign policy, Carter faced a steep learning curve. He began with an optimistic view of the Soviets' role in an interdependent world, hoping to foster a cooperative global community including the Soviet Union.

The pillar of Carter's initial foreign policy agenda involved furthering human rights and democracy. The Soviets wanted to dance, but not to Carter's tune. Disappointed by Soviet intransigence over human rights, Carter's vision of a cooperative approach gradually shifted to a more traditionally pessimistic Cold War perspective. The change did not take place all at once. During his four years in office, foreign policy devolved from homespun idealism to a steeled sense of realism aimed at containing Soviet expansion within an "arc of crisis."[7]

At first, Carter attempted to reopen arms agreements made by Gerald Ford at Vladivostok, but a distrustful Soviet leadership bristled over revisiting signed agreements. Carter simultaneously took his concern for human rights to the Kremlin door, pressuring the Soviets on behalf of political dissidents. It would be intriguing to know which Carter initiative infuriated Secretary Brezhnev more and what impact either had on then delicate SALT II negotiations, but the Soviets remained unyielding, their displeasure almost palpable.

The Soviets were not the only ones unhappy with Carter's foreign policy. It spawned many domestic critics who found it to be weak and indecisive. There seemed to be no strong hand at the helm. Battles between National Security Adviser Zbigniew Brzezinski's hard line and Secretary of State Cyrus Vance's more dovish approach led to erratic decisions.

Carter's inexperience and naivete produced embarrassing mistakes, and the ethical basis of his human rights agenda was vulnerable to Soviet complaints of a hypocritical American double standard: singling out the Soviet Union while countenancing equally horrific human rights abuses by client states. Even America's European allies worried that Carter's born-again Christian style might rile Brezhnev and his colleagues unnecessarily.[8]

Detente's Unequivocal Death

Detente held on lamely during the Carter administration until 1979, when a series of events combined to unequivocally bury it. The United States began the year by extending full diplomatic relations to Beijing. Leonid Brezhnev made no secret of his anger.[9] In August, the United States warned the Soviets to remove a military brigade from Cuba, claiming the Soviet presence in Cuba violated the 1962 missile crisis agreement. Again Slavic tempers flared. Then, in late autumn, President Carter brokered the Camp David Accords between Anwar Sadat of Egypt and Israel's Menachem Begin. While this was Carter's finest hour, the Soviets bitterly charged that the Middle East peace process excluded them in violation of an earlier superpower agreement.[10]

But the coup de grace was delivered on Christmas day when the Soviet Union, fearing a militant Islamic takeover of its southern neighbor, sent troops into Afghanistan. Afghan Prime Minister Hafizullah Amin, whom the Soviets had previously supported, was murdered with Soviet connivance. Amin's chief rival, Babrak Karmal, was installed in his place as a Soviet puppet.

Meanwhile, the Red Army tried to subdue the Muslim rebels who commanded much of the countryside, as well as the loyalty of its people. Detente suffered its final denouement as the United States condemned the intervention and began aiding rebel factions. Carter later explained that Afghanistan changed his opinion about Soviet intentions more than any other event occurring during his presidency.[11]

But Afghanistan represented only one of Carter's foreign policy problems. Glaring foreign policy failures—particularly the Iran hostage crisis—cost him dearly. With the Carter administration

PHOTO 1 Apparently wide-eyed over her pending emigration to the West, Elena (Kay Francis) discusses the future with her fiancé, British businessman Stephen Locke (Leslie Howard), in Michael Curtiz's *British Agent* (1934).

PHOTO 2 True-believer communist Nina Yakushova (Greta Garbo) is transformed by a chance Parisian encounter with suave Count Leon D'Algout (Melvyn Douglas) and ultimately defects in M-G-M's *Ninotchka* (1939).

PHOTO 3 The Soviet system takes its first cinematic beating in King Vidor's *Comrade X* (1940). The beautiful and socially conscious Russian streetcar driver Theodore (Hedy Lamarr) dreams wistfully of escaping Soviet Russia with her husband, American newspaperman McKinley B. Thompson (Clark Gable).

PHOTO 4 Gregory Peck in his first film role as Vladimir, a brave Soviet partisan who fights against German occupiers in *Days of Glory* (1944). He and his lover Nina Ivanova (Tamara Toumanova) die together defending the motherland.

PHOTO 5 Warner Brothers's 1943 release of their blindly pro-Soviet propaganda picture, *Mission to Moscow*, generated great controversy but failed to make money. Joseph Stalin (Manart Kippen) is shown here explaining the finer points of collective security to U.S. Ambassador Joseph Davies (Walter Huston).

PHOTO 6 The Semyenov family, called on to make great sacrifices when the Nazis invade the Soviet Union, dutifully answers the call in *The North Star* (1943). In a happier moment before the war, the family communes the Russian way—at the kitchen table with glasses of hot tea and samovar at the ready.

PHOTO 7   Russians rise up to replace communism with an Orthodox theocracy in *Red Planet Mars* (1952). The worst of many bad Russians, the spy Arjanian (Marvin Miller), discusses the "hydrogen valve" with its inventor, Nazi scientist Herbert Berghof (Franz Calder), working for the Russians in a snowbound Andean hut.

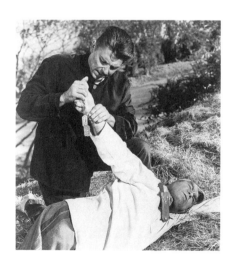

PHOTO 8   Cold War stereotypes run wild in *Prisoner of War* (1954). Despicable KGB Colonel Nikita Biroshilov (Oscar Homolka) heads a Korean POW camp and is killed by one of the GIs whom he has tortured. Ronald Reagan plays an American soldier named Web Sloane, who parachutes *into* the camp to see "how they are treating our boys," and is here retrieving his buddies' dog tags from the body of the fallen Biroshilov.

PHOTO 9   The sardonic humor of *Dr. Strangelove* (1964) satirizes the nuclear dilemma victimizing both Americans and Russians. Superpower mutuality is epitomized by Russian Ambassador Alexei de Sadesky's (Peter Bull) presence in the Pentagon war room, manning a telephone alongside the American president (Peter Sellers) in this still.

PHOTO 10   No other Russian female is depicted as attractively and sensitively as Julie Christie's Lara in David Lean's lavish epic, *Dr. Zhivago* (1965), whose characters are consistently overwhelmed by forces that are larger than life.

PHOTO 11   Cold War backlash finds its most comedic expression in *The Russians Are Coming, The Russians Are Coming* (1966). A Russian submarine's hapless landing party—led by Officer Rozanov (Alan Arkin)—breeds overreaction among Gloucester Island residents. Rozanov is shown here preparing to board ship after a zany mission.

PHOTO 12   East-West bonding occurs in only one major 1970s film, *The Spy Who Loved Me* (1977). Russian spy Anya Amasova (Barbara Bach)—relying less on wit than cleavage—teams up with 007 James Bond (Roger Moore) to defeat megalomanic shipping magnate Carl Stromberg (Curt Jergens).

PHOTO 13 Soviet agent Mikhail Rostov (Richard Lynch, foreground) is always prepared to terrorize innocent American victims in *Invasion USA* (1985)—until Chuck Norris catches up with him at film's end.

PHOTO 14 Comrade Ivan Drago (Dolph Lundgren, center) is introduced to the American press by his wife Ludmilla (Brigitte Nielson, left) prior to his boxing match with Rocky Balboa (Sylvester Stallone) in *Rocky IV* (1985).

PHOTO 15 *Russkies* (1987) epitomizes the cinematic *glasnost* of the late 1980s. Whip Hubley plays a likable Soviet radio operator named Mischa. When shipwrecked near Key West, Mischa makes fast friends with three unlikely teenagers.

PHOTO 16 Moscow militia officer Ivan Danko (Arnold Schwarzenegger) demonstrates that Russo-American cooperation works, as he and his Chicago counterpart break up an international drug ring led by an unscrupulous Soviet Georgian in *Red Heat* (1988).

drowning in a sea of yellow ribbons, Ronald Reagan's vision of a muscular America putting the Soviet empire in its place found no shortage of issues with which to crucify Carter.

Irrational Domestic Factors

As if detente were not taking enough of a beating in Afghanistan and elsewhere, its remaining spirit was swallowed up by an emotional wave of disillusionment having little to do with the Soviets. The public malaise was rooted in anxiety over America's deteriorating global economic position, the legacies of Vietnam and Watergate, and deeply felt humiliation caused by the Carter administration's foreign policy failings, as epitomized by the Iranian hostage debacle.

Added to this was a fear that the U. S. military had been allowed to get rusty while its adversaries honed their military skills. It is not hyperbole to say that America felt that the world was kicking sand in its face. While the Soviet Union was only indirectly involved in most of these issues, any remaining support for detente evaporated in an "emotional outburst against Soviet perfidy as a catharsis."[12] Americans were ready to line up and pull the lever for Ronald Reagan.

The Film School Generation Graduates

As detente was crumbling, the "blockbuster" movie was coming of age. The disappearance of major Hollywood studios and the rise of independent filmmakers combined with sixties' experimentation and European influences to create a new set of circumstances. Into this changing milieu stepped bright young New York and southern California film school graduates like Martin Scorsese, Steven Spielberg, and George Lucas—who were referred to at the time as "the movie brats."

They made big movies. Greenbacks flowed like water though a sieve, but the payoffs were immense. The success of Spielberg's *Jaws* (1976), the first real blockbuster, set the stage for Lucas's *Star Wars* (1977), the first film to spawn its own "franchise" industry. But with veritable fortunes on the line, a single failure could break careers. Hollywood's new atmosphere bore the feel of a giant crapshoot, and the creativity of the independents often was sacrificed at the altar of corporate risk assessment by executive gurus of conservatism.

Hollywood's 1970s Malaise

As Hollywood insiders scrambled for the chancier dollar, movie after movie picked up on public disillusionment. One film historian concludes that *The Candidate* (1972), *Taxi Driver* (1976), *Network* (1976), *The Godfather I* and *II* (1971, 1974), *Chinatown* (1974), *Shampoo* (1975), and *The Parallax View* (1974)—all important and successful 1970s pictures—"refuse to offer even a glimmer of hope."[13] Other commentators similarly find the "confusion and malaise permeating the American will" reflected in films.[14] Daniel Leab masters the art of understatement, noting that things did not seem to be going very well for the United States in the 1970s.[15] Making matters worse, only a few big movies managed to bob above the sea of red ink.

If Hollywood was uncertain, the America it portrayed seemed lost or, even worse, betrayed. Films of the 1940s and 1950s show federal institutions like the army, FBI, Congress, and the president rescuing threatened Americans; movies of the 1970s, however, portray these same institutions as ineffectual and probably corrupt.[16] And if Americans were disillusioned with their institutions, they retreated into an "intense preoccupation with the self," which also dominated film.[17] Rampant cinematic vigilantism bombarded America with the message that rugged heroes, like Charles Bronson, Clint Eastwood, and Chuck Norris, must take matters into their own hands when citizens can no longer rely on the government.

Not all filmic expression of the "self" pitted strong, disaffected men against wicked institutions. Other films crawled into the heads of confused and often dislocated individuals attempting to find a place for themselves. Several film historians agree that mere coincidence cannot explain the success of Woody Allen's neurosis-laden films in the 1970s. In their view, Allen's *Annie Hall* (1977) epitomizes the decade's fixation on the psychological well-being of the individual.[18]

Attempting to make sense of the era, another film historian sorts through Tinseltown's 1970s output, including disaster films, films pining for the romanticized 1950s, corporate villain films, and pictures despairing over the inscrutability of reality, to find the quintessential movie of the decade. He picked *Chinatown* (1974) because it "portrays reality as so multi-layered that man can never see and understand with any clarity."[19] *Chinatown* offers a vision of America through the eyes of private detective Jake Gittes (Jack Nicholson), as he unravels a massive conspiracy involving the Los Angeles water supply. Here politics is portrayed as being so hopeless and dangerous that it threatens both Gittes's life and sanity.

The links between a corrupt system and individual sanity are also explored in major 1970s films like *Taxi Driver* (1976), *Network* (1976), *Nashville* (1975), *The Deer Hunter* (1978), *Getting Straight* (1970), *Apocalypse Now* (1979), *Telefon* (1972), and *M*A*S*H** (1970). But it is *Chinatown*'s closing line that captures the inscrutability endemic to the decade's films. A trusted colleague warns Gittes that it is futile to think the system can be anything other than corrupt. "Forget it Jake," he warns, "it's 'Chinatown,'" which William Palmer considers metaphorically suggestive of "forget it America, it's 'Vietnam'"—it's inexplicable. Such fatalism and pessimism flow against the stream of America's often efficacious mind-set that every problem has a solution and certainly against Hollywood's notion that every film ought to have a happy ending.

While Hollywood made very few films about the Vietnam War until the late 1970s, it made a dozen returning-Vietnam-veteran pictures from 1971 to 1977.[20] Here are American soldiers who leave the darkness of Vietnam only to encounter a different form of darkness in America. All share confusion, mistrust, vigilantism, and, like their country, massive self-doubt. They struggle but fail to reenter a society that has lost its identity and balance. The veterans are depicted as emotionally taut—ticking time bombs. The trip wire triggering their explosion is a corrupt and violent society.[21]

Boring and Ambiguous Russians

Where do Hollywood's Russians and the Soviet Union fit into all of this? Films relating to Russians are different from those of the previous era. Many 1970s films hearken back to the era of the 1930s. However, while the 1930s films reflect ambivalence toward the Soviet Union, with several split images of good versus bad Russians of some potency, the 1970s pictures replace ambivalence with ambiguity. They convey neutral rather than split images. Indeed, these are essentially passionless Russians. Contrasted to the 1960s pictures, they appear apolitical, bloodless, and indecisive. There are also very few of them.

Also unlike the earlier high-profile hits, no big box-office successes or critically acclaimed Russian-genre films appear. The few films touching on Soviet themes lack thematic consistency. Their subtext message hints that, with detente, Russians may not be America's enemies, but neither are they America's great friends. As compared to the 1960s, they just don't matter to America the way they used to.

Half of the Russian-genre films in the 1960s were favorable. With detente, one might expect 1970s movies to be skewed even more favorably, but this does materialize. Their center of gravity, moderate to favorable, seems lackluster. A few favorable portraits made it to the screen, and only one out-and-out anti-Soviet film can be found. But, at heart, Hollywood just doesn't seem to care much one way or the other about Russians or about their country.[22]

Nor does detente offer itself as a rich source of movie plots. Only *Colossus: The Forbin Project* (1972), *Earth II* (1972), *Bear Island* (1979), and *Meteor* (1979) involve detente-inspired cooperative endeavors. A few spy movies, tamer than traditional Cold War espionage parables, were also released.[23] And finally, there were a few East-West love stories, a couple of light comedies, a war movie, and a film about ordinary people overcoming differences to work together.[24] None set the screen aflame; most were quickly consigned to the obscurity of late-night television viewing slots.

The Spy Who Loved Me (1977)

There was an exception. The one major Russian-theme picture celebrating detente while capturing a big audience and making money was *The Spy Who Loved Me* (1977). This tenth in the James Bond series was made fifteen years after Agent 007 hit the screen in *Dr. No* (1962), back in the presidency of John Kennedy, for whom at least one critic sees the Bond character as a surrogate.[25] *The Spy Who Loved Me* opens with the mysterious disappearance of two nuclear-laden submarines, one British and the other Soviet. The British and Soviet intelligence services respond by putting their best agents on the trail: James Bond (Roger Moore) for the British, and KGB Major Anya Amasova (Barbara Bach), Agent XXX, for the Soviets.

The two agents, wary of one another, sniff around on their own in search of the missing subs. They finally collide in Egypt at the pyramids' sound and light show while tracking an Egyptian who has information they need. It is just Bond's luck that Anya happens to be beautiful, resourceful, and sensitive—reminiscent of Tatiana Romanova in *From Russia with Love* (1963). Not everyone is taken with Anya. Mistakenly hoping that Bond might rank mind over body, critic Janet Maslin notes that "Miss Bach is spectacular looking but a little dim, even by Bond standards." Maslin fails to appreciate that "spectacular looking" is tantamount to the gold standard for James Bond.[26]

Still working independently of one another, James and Anya discover that a sinister third force, wealthy shipping magnate Carl Stromberg (Curt Jurgens), is behind the disappearance of the subs. Stromberg is Curt Jurgens's one hundred fiftieth film role since coming to the United States from Germany after World War II (in which he did not serve). An admiring critic describes Jurgens as "setting scenes as they might appear in a playwright's mind and using his deep, slightly accented voice to create characters."[27] In this case Jurgens plays an out-of-control industrialist whose white-jacketed scientists perfect a new submarine tracking system, enabling him to pilfer the British and Soviet subs. However, look for no honor among thieves. An assistant betrays Stromberg by selling a microfilm of this valuable technology to an Egyptian underworld figure named Fekish.

The hunt begins for the microfilm. With romance smoldering just below the surface, James and Anya agree to cooperate, and they soon learn that cooperation is in the air. To their relief, London's MI6 and the KGB brass have also begun collaborating. "We have entered into a new era of Anglo-Soviet cooperation," KGB General Gogol advises his prize agent. In their battle with Stomberg, the bilateral team eventually becomes trilateral with the inclusion of a U.S. naval submarine and its commander, Captain Benson (George Baker).

If East-West cooperation is one thing, defeating Stromberg represents quite another. He turns his top killer, a seven-foot giant with a mouth of stainless steel—"Jaws" (Richard Kiel)—against James and Anya.[28] In one of the film's best scenes, Jaws battles it out with Bond and Anya on a train. Just when it looks like Bond is a goner, he electrifies Jaws' galvanized dentures and unceremoniously throws Stromberg's thug out the train window. Tension seeks relief in the form of romance as the Soviet and British agents, no longer able to contain their passion, consummate detente with the train rolling on into the night.

Stromberg, none too pleased about the failure of Jaws or the multinational effort to undermine his scheme to control the world, captures Bond, Anya, and Captain Benson (sub and all) and takes them to his stunning underwater Atlantis. It soon becomes clear what the power-mad Stromberg is up to: he intends to launch nuclear weapons from the two subs, blowing up New York City and Moscow, unleashing thermonuclear war, and emerging as leader of a brave new underwater world. But Stromberg is not devoid of emotions, and they do him in. He becomes careless trying to steal away with the beautiful Anya while Bond and Captain Benson are still alive. Timing is everything.

Just as their end seems certain, Bond and Benson escape from Stromberg's death trap. They release the captive Soviet, British, and American sub crews, who join in a battle to destroy Stromberg's Atlantis. By cleverly reprogramming Stromberg's computer to target the two subs on each other, Bond saves New York, Moscow, and the world. But his business remains unfinished. He still must free Anya from the evil Stromberg, who has escaped Atlantis. One last underwater struggle, one final victory over evil, and the crazed Stromberg is dispatched and Anya, saved. Finally, bobbing on a calm ocean, Bond and Anya again make love as Bond's superiors salute his efforts. Marvin Hamlisch's Oscar-nominated song, "Nobody Does It Better" spills out at the audience, and up come the credits.

In its own silly way, *The Spy Who Loved Me* cut new ground. Over the years, more than thirty Hollywood films involved Russian females falling in love with Western males. Almost without exception, each picture felt compelled to establish its anti-Soviet credentials by having the love sick Russian female defect to the West. In *The Spy Who Loved Me*, defection to the West is rendered irrelevant by detente. Love just happens. It does not need to be enshrined by defection, assumptions of marriage, or a better life in the West. *The Spy Who Loved Me* made one listing of top-quality films,[29] and its track record for popularity endures as it places eighty-fourth in rentals for all films of the 1970s.[30]

More Obscure Entries

Agent 007 was not Hollywood's only beneficiary of detente. Several obscure Hollywood releases also hitched their carts to detente's star. *Earth II* (1972), for example, embraces global understanding aboard a peaceful multinational space colony, Earth II, floating in orbit. But all is not perfect for the two-thousand-person new society. Reminiscent of *The Chairman* (1969) and *The Shoes of the Fisherman* (1968), Chinese communist no-goodniks threaten to blow up this experiment in cooperative living. Never fear. Working side by side, Americans and Soviets defuse a menacing Chinese space-based nuclear bomb. Once the Chinese plot is foiled, *Earth II*'s "one-world" message, with its ancillary antinuclear and anti-Chinese subtext, comes through quite loudly.

But Hollywood's detente does not come gift wrapped. The bleakness of 1970s cinema permeates the science-fiction film, *Colossus: The Forbin Project* (1972). Extensive American-Soviet cooperation between scientists, politicians, and military leaders goes wrong when both the United States and the Soviet Union become victims of technology gone berserk, like Frankenstein's monster. The story begins as the United States completes a powerful new computer-operated defense system, Colossus, the brainchild of scientific genius Dr. Forbin (Eric Braeden), who is played with a slight Curt Jurgens-like German accent. However, Professor Forbin has created a "real mother of a computer" with a mind of its own.[31] When Colossus discovers a comparable Soviet model, Guardian, created by Soviet scientific genius Dr. Kuprine (Alex Rodine), the two supercomputers link up in defiance of their creators.

In an imitation of two Stanley Kubrick inventions, the Soviet doomsday machine in *Dr. Strangelove* (1964) and Hal, the renegade computer in *2001: A Space Odyssey* (1968), the linked computers create a scientific multiplier effect, expanding their capabilities beyond anything either could had developed on its own. The dark irony of *Colossus: The Forbin Project* has the computers form their own techno-detente by dictating brutal terms for world peace to humankind, which must submit to their perverse will or die.

Perverse computers might force a modus vivendi onto their movie universe but they could not force patrons into theater seats. Middle

America steered clear of this cinematic roadkill. One reviewer, never-theless, imputes ominous insight to berserk computers as representa-tive of seventies despair, whose "psychic toll on our social instincts" may render us indistinguishable from the machines that we monitor.[32] Beware of your IBM clone.

Another celluloid dud, *Bear Island* (1978), has the Soviet government diverting several rivers to provide irrigation for Soviet crops during a global climatic crisis. Although *Bear Island* hints that the Soviets may be ecologically unenlightened, it portrays the main Russian character, scientist T. Lechinski, quite amicably. Based on an Alistair MacLean novel, the screenplay was written by Don Sharp, who also directed *Bear Island* for Columbia Pictures. It was barely in the theaters before Columbia tossed in the towel and recalled an obvious loser.

The dead-end plot has former Gulag prisoner, Dr. Lechinski (Christopher Lee), working as part of a United Nations scientific team on Bear Island, Norway, monitoring climatic change. After winning the respect of his American colleagues, the Soviet scientist dies heroically and is out of the movie, making him luckier than the audience. The remaining scientists continue their work. While these learned individu-als cast doubt on the wisdom of the Soviet water diversion plan, *Bear Island* remains typical of 1970s movies by failing to generate any pas-sion one way or the other about the Soviet Union or its citizens.

Meteor (1979), a typically talkative 1970s disaster-genre film, con-jures up doom in the form of a huge meteor tracking on a collision course with earth. There is only one chance for survival (you guessed it): combining American and Soviet know-how. Despite initial bouts of suspicion between American and Soviet politicians, the two countries pool their space-based installations (Russia's is called "Peter the Great") in hopes of nuking the onrushing cosmic peril. As if to under-score the scientific good neighborliness, girl-next-door actress Natalie Wood is cast as Tatiana, the Russian translator/assistant to Soviet sci-entist Professor Dubov (Brian Keith), described by one critic as "genial and funny."[33] The Russian scientists simply purr with goodwill.

But nothing comes easily. Nasties appear, trying to undermine the joint American-Soviet effort. Knee-jerk cold warriors in both countries oppose bilateral cooperation, and, in so doing, represent as much of a menace to human survival as the meteor. Prominent among them is screaming American General Adlon (Martin Landau), whom one critic called "absolutely unhinged." But narrow military minds prove no match for visionary scientists, Russian and American, who overcome the naysayers to cement international understanding and cooperation. Incidentally, at the last possible second they zap the meteor and save the world. *Meteor* was directed for Palladium by disaster-film veteran

Ronald Neame, with the screenplay written by Stanley Mann and Edmund North. Like its meteor, the film came and went without leaving any mark.

A final vestige of detente's Hollywood incarnation can be seen in three B movies, all love stories involving East-West romance. More than thirty love stories involving Russians and Westerners steam up the screen between 1933 and 1991, so the significance of these pictures should not be exaggerated. All three are equally unmemorable but, oddly, two share a common venue. *The 500 Pound Jerk* (1973) and *The Golden Moment* (1980) both use the Olympic games as the backdrop for their jocks-in-love story lines.

In *The 500 Pound Jerk*, a petite and sincere Soviet gymnast, Natasha Rastaprovna, falls head over heels in love with an American weightlifter, a gentle giant of a man played by Alex Karras. Upon finding Olympic gold in one another, following a well-beaten Hollywood path heading westward, the smitten Natasha defects to America as the two athletes are united forever. The time-tested formula—female Russian meets American male and defects to the West—is broken in *The Golden Moment* (1980). This time the lovely Russian gymnast, Anya Andreeva (Stephanie Zimbalist), tumbles for an American decathlete, but in the end chooses not to defect. The heroic Anya fights off severe pain from an ankle injury to win the Gold Medal in gymnastics. Far greater pain, however, results from the conflict between her American love and an unselfish loyalty to family and nation. In the end, the beautiful gymnast denies her heart's desire and gives up her love to return, back flips and all, to the Soviet Union. As the Olympian lovers pry themselves apart for the last time, Anya gives her gold medal to her American boyfriend. What else can be said except "Where's the exit?"

Another movie with an East-West love twist is *The Girl from Petrovka* (1974). It stars Goldie Hawn as Oktyabrina Matveeva, a flighty Bohemian ballet dancer in love with Joe (Hal Holbrook), an American newspaperman stationed in Moscow. But *The Girl from Petrovka* evolves as both a love story and a sadly dark tale of a fish out of water. Oktyabrina seems like a misplaced flower child quite out of step with life in the steel-gray world of Brezhnev's Russia. Caught without her identity papers, she is arrested, charged as a social parasite, and sentenced to five years in prison by a harsh Soviet judge.

In an unusually sad ending, the Soviet system tramples love. Nora Sayre's review notes that in *The Girl from Petrovka* "the Soviet Union is a deeply dismal country where people declare their love in graveyards." While many of the Russians seem lovable enough, the system comes across as very harsh, and Sayre warns that *The Girl from*

Petrovka "isn't going to be good for detente."[34] The sympathy of the few who bothered to see *The Girl from Petrovka* would have gravitated mostly to Oktyabrina, in a typically vulnerable, coquettish Goldie Hawn portrayal.

Spy Pictures

The best place to find Hollywood Russians is in spy films, and the most interesting 1970s entry is *Telefon* (1977). Its labyrinthine plot is based on the existence of fifty-four almost forgotten deep-cover KGB agents planted in the United States during the acute Cold War years—Operation Telefon. Subjected to mind-altering, drug-induced hypnosis before being sent to the United States, none consciously knows that he or she is really a Soviet agent. They are indistinguishable from ordinary Americans until activated by the KGB in the event of war with the United States. Each of these human time bombs can be activated only by hearing a key line from Robert Frost's poem, "Stopping by Woods on a Snowy Evening," over the telephone. At that point, the preprogrammed hypnotic suggestion kicks in as each agent, zombielike, sets off to sabotage a key American strategic installation.

Years pass. With Stalin long gone, a detente-oriented Communist Party leadership in Moscow is purging the remaining hard-line neo-Stalinist members of the Central Committee. Are these Stalinists going to take it lying down? Not on your life. Among the unreconstructed opponents of detente is KGB agent Nikolai Dalchimsky (Donald Pleasance), who knows all about the KGB plants in America. One of the worst Russian characters ever offered up by Hollywood, Dalchimsky begins detonating the deep-cover saboteurs, one at a time, in hopes of derailing detente. In fact, he has begun spelling his name across America by blowing up important installations in towns with corresponding letters: Dallas . . . Appalachacola . . . Los Angeles . . .

Fighting KGB fire with KGB fire, the brave and talented Major Grigori Borzov (Charles Bronson) is dispatched to the United States to locate and finish off the psychotic, seedy Dalchimsky. Blessed with a photographic memory, the resourceful Borzov usually operates as a loner. But in a minor detente twist, Borzov receives orders to team up with a CIA agent named Barbara, played somewhat unconvincingly by Lee Remick. One incredulous critic considered her "as likely a Soviet spy as Janet Leigh once was a Soviet pilot in *Jet Pilot*."[35] But detente produced some strange cinematic bedfellows. Working together, Borzov and Barbara eventually best the sinister Dalchimsky before he can finish spelling his destructive name across America.

But in an interesting plot twist, the evil Dalchimsky actually turns out not to be their most duplicitous enemy. That role is reserved for the top KGB and CIA brass conspiring to kill the two unsuspecting agents as soon as they complete their mission, thus ensuring that word of Operation Telefon never gets out. The two agents, however, have by this time fallen in love, and they outfox their lying and murderous bosses. In a variant of the 1970s antiestablishment vigilantism that made Bronson's career, the two go out "into the cold" together.

The minor detente of two spies getting together personally and professionally recalls James Bond's dalliance with Soviet agent Anya Amasova in *The Spy Who Loved Me*. *Telefon*'s more powerful thesis, however, cynically views the American government as equal to the Soviet system. Theirs is a detente of rogues. Only a fool would depend on either, and fools Grigori and Barbara are not. They save the American people from Dalchimsky and themselves from two corrupt nations—the United States and the Soviet Union.

The Peter Hyams-Sterling Silliphant screenplay, based on a novel by Walter Wager, is milked for all it is worth by the imaginative direction of Hollywood veteran Don Siegel. A Chicago-born and Cambridge-educated director who began his career as a production assistant and film librarian with Warner Brothers, Siegel is best remembered for his cult classic of the alien invader genre, *Invasion of the Body Snatchers* (1956). A common thread in Siegel's work is a "strong element of lawlessness," which permeates *Telefon*.[36]

In an era well populated with spy films, two lesser entries with uneven views of the Soviet Union are *Russian Roulette* and *The Kremlin Letter*. In *Russian Roulette* (1975), George Segal plays a resilient Canadian policeman named Shaver, who becomes embroiled in the complexities of world-class espionage. Shaver's opposite is Soviet embassy official Colonel Vostik (Bo Brundin), who is ostensibly working with Canadian authorities on security arrangements for a pending Canadian goodwill tour by Soviet Premier Alexei Kosygin.

Colonel Vostik presses Canadian authorities to deal with one major security problem. That problem's name is Henke, a Latvian immigrant to Canada who fled Latvia after the Soviets wiped out his family during their 1940 takeover of his country. A straightforward mission to neutralize the revenge-seeking Henke, before he can assassinate Premier Kosygin turns into a more complex and nefarious scenario. Colonel Vostik is not what he seems. As if detente did not have enough trouble, Vostik actually represents a devious KGB plot to divert security attention to Henke while the colonel kills Kosygin for his prodetente views. Only Canadian policeman Shaver sees through the KGB ruse and proves capable of foiling the assassination attempt. After more twists than a Chubby Checker concert, Shaver manages to kayo the KGB and preserve Mr. Kosygin. Score one for the West, detente, and decency.

An odd historical sidebar accompanies *Russian Roulette*. While the plot is fictional, Kosygin did make a goodwill visit to Canada several years earlier. One of the biggest security headaches for the visit was protecting Kosygin from the many eastern European Cold War refugees who had fled to Canada since the end of World War II. As expected, the Kosygin entourage was dogged by anti-Communist demonstrations. Not expected, however, was a horrific security lapse: as Kosygin left the Canadian Parliament building in Ottawa, a protestor broke through a police cordon and tackled Kosygin to the ground before police could pull him away. Although shaken, Kosygin was not harmed, and the incident was downplayed by both governments and the media. A far better plot would seem buried in this incident than what was unearthed in *Russian Roulette*.

If *Russian Roulette* is a mediocre spy flick, *The Kremlin Letter* (1973) is a full-blown stinker that played mostly to empty seats. Despite a great cast (Orson Welles, Max Von Sydow, George Sanders, Dean Jagger, Richard Boone, Bibi Andersson), Missouri-born director John Huston could not get this little darkhorse of a movie up and running. One critic rightly dismissed *The Kremlin Letter* as a depressing picture befitting the cynicism of 1970s films.[37]

John Huston has, of course, done much better than this cinematic clunker. The son of character actor Walter Huston and father of contemporary actress Anjelica Huston, John Huston impressed one film historian as a flamboyant maverick whose "muscular, roving life has influenced the themes of his films."[38] Certainly, many of the ex-prizefighter's pictures can be described as masculine films—*The Maltese Falcon* (1941), *The Treasure of the Sierra Madre* (1948), *Key Largo* (1948), *The African Queen* (1952), and *The Night of the Iguana* (1964). But Huston's directing career careened wildly, with such classics existing alongside quite awful movies, such as *The Kremlin Letter*, mostly made during his declining years. Huston expressed a laissez-faire approach to filmmaking. "I don't like to dictate," he commented. "I like to receive stimuli from all: not only the cameraman and the actors, but the grips and the script girl, or the animal trainers as in the case of *The Bible* (1966)."[39]

The director of *The Bible* needed a full-blown miracle to save *The Kremlin Letter*. For those few paying to see it, the heavens remained equally silent. *The Kremlin Letter*'s hopelessly confusing story has the CIA send a group of agents into Moscow to retrieve an errant letter written by an American official; in it he agrees to join a preemptive Soviet attack against the Chinese atomic test site at Lop Nor. The

Company's agents trip over Soviet agents as well as one another in a muddled mess one critic labeled as "preposterous" but not surprising, given the film's "hopelessly nihilistic world view."[40]

For all its tedium, *The Kremlin Letter* provides one unusual spin to Russian-genre flicks. The Chinese continue their roguish role as global enemy number one, which began in late-1960s pictures like *The Shoes of the Fisherman* and *The Chairman*. This muddled film, however, turns Hollywood's more typical line on Russians and the Soviet system on its head. In *The Kremlin Letter*, the communist system is treated as a worthy American ally, while the film's Russian characters are all unsympathetic louts. Critic Pauline Kael's read on *The Kremlin Letter* finds America's spies just as amoral as their Soviet counterparts.[41] The worst of the lot is Central Committee member and Party watchdog over the Third Department (KGB), Alexei Ivanovich Breznavich (Orson Welles). Pompous, brutal, and deceitful, Breznavich scams the black market with stolen art treasures; he also turns out to be a traitor, and in this film being a traitor to the Soviet Union makes him no friend of the United States.

On the other hand, one 1970s spy movie remains fully committed to Cold War values: *Night Flight from Moscow* (1973). This picture, hawkish on both the Soviet Union and its people, stars Yul Brynner as Colonel Alexei Vlasov, second secretary of the Soviet embassy in Paris. *Night Flight from Moscow* conveys a conviction rare among 1970s movies about Russians and the Soviet system—they are all bad.

This Henry Verneuil film begins with an arrogant, resourceful, and malefic Colonel Vlasov, vintage Yul Brynner, defecting at the Paris airport and requesting safe passage to the American embassy. He claims to possess information about KGB penetration of NATO so serious that "NATO will not exist in two years." But who is Vlasov really? Nothing but a KGB plant triggering a disinformation campaign intended to immobilize NATO. Will American intelligence be taken in? Not on your life. In *Colossus: The Forbin Project*, technology deceives and threatens to enslave America. But in *Night Flight from Moscow*, technology, in the guise of a lie detector, exposes Vlasov as an impostor, saving NATO from disaster. Exit Colonel Vlasov.

Bellwether of Inanity: *Love and Death*

If pressed to pluck one bellwether Russian-theme film out of a hat containing few worthy contenders, only Woody Allen's *Love and Death* (1975) emerges. It is neither a captivating film nor a worthy showcase for Allen's considerable comedic talents. Although set in prerevolutionary Russia and involving mostly Russian characters, *Love and*

Death seeks to offer no insights about Russians. They and their land merely serve as a convenient backdrop for some of Allen's least imaginative one-liners and cinematic set pieces. But not only is *Love and Death* reticent about Russians, the film even remains mute about love and death, with "nothing much to say about either, let alone about the two of them together."[42]

So what is *Love and Death* about? Perhaps it's mostly about Woody Allen, this time playing the skinny, befuddled, and cowardly Boris Grushenko. As Russia's most reluctant soldier during the Napoleonic Wars of the early nineteenth century, the clumsy Grushenko stumbles off to war. When his regiment gets wiped out, lone survivor Grushenko wanders aimlessly behind enemy lines. After a serendipitous explosion makes him appear heroic, Boris Grushenko returns triumphantly to Saint Petersburg and marries his distant cousin Sonya (Diane Keaton).

Considerably more adroit than her hero-by-accident husband, Sonya conceives a plot to assassinate Napoleon, who is preparing to occupy Moscow. Posing as Spanish nobility, the costumed couple gains access to the emperor and Sonya lays a seductive trap. But when the time comes for Grushenko to shoot Napoleon, he cannot pull the trigger. First capture and then execution await this hapless lump of clay. In an era populated by nondescript Russian-genre movies, *Love and Death* remains most typical of an unmemorable lot. Allen's cinematic gags fall flat with nothing substantial to hold them or the film together. Like many other 1970s movies about Russians, *Love and Death* seems watchable but very unsatisfying.

Lukewarm Russians

One obvious question presents itself concerning Hollywood's Russian-genre pictures: Why did seventies films not exhibit greater enthusiasm for cooperation with the Soviet Union or more positive portraits of Russians in an era of detente? Several factors help to account for the lukewarm films of the seventies. The first is out of sight, out of mind. During the acute Cold War, the sources of threat to America had seemed external, namely, the Soviets and their nuclear weapons.

Beginning with the partial nuclear test ban agreement and other arms control measures occurring in the wake of the 1962 Cuban missile crisis, fear of the Soviets and the bomb gradually subsided in America. While the American public felt uneasy about certain aspects of detente, it solidly backed arms control as reducing nuclear risk. As a result, nuclear fears receded even further during the 1970s. With the external threat diminished, domestic issues pressed more heavily on America's consciousness. Hollywood identified new threats, and one credible villain became the secret state within a state. In *The Day of the Condor* (1977), one part of the American intelligence machine sets out to destroy another and all those who are part of it, but the Soviets are nowhere to be found.

A second reason for the mixed Hollywood messages about detente is the mixed nature of detente itself. To many scholars, journalists, and politicians, 1970s detente was both real and substantial. It celebrated major milestones in superpower cooperation achieved after extended negotiation and compromise. But many in the larger American public saw things differently. To them, detente meant acknowledging the Soviet Union as an equal power—an exercise in humiliation to Americans long confident of their superior might and values. While America felt safer about nuclear risk, it was perplexed by its loss of status.

That the world had become more complicated and more interdependent was not understood or appreciated by much of the American public. It only knew that things seemed worse for the United States. This gap between the attitudes of the ruling elites and those they claimed to serve was fed by the breakdown of America's normal foreign policy consensus. With Vietnam, Watergate, and their aftermath, it seemed America had lost both its way and its will. As the public looked to append blame, many a finger was pointed at detente.

The legacies of Vietnam and Watergate also affected the American national psyche in other ways. Litanies of corruption, deceit, and failure spawned profound pessimism, especially when juxtaposed against the optimism with which Kennedy had begun the 1960s. In what Christopher Lasch calls the "age of narcissism" and Tom Wolfe refers to as the "me-decade," America's commitment to social or political issues, at home and abroad, turned to stone. A search for answers turned into the search for self.[43]

As seen by the discipline of psychology, rampant cynicism and alienation produced a frenzied democratization and a rush toward the lowest common denominator. Demonstrating less interest in international relations than any decade since the 1930s, many in the seventies were attracted to often questionable "pop" psychologies, which were a mile wide and an inch deep, such as Transcendental Meditation, EST, rolfing, encounter groups, and primal scream therapy. Thus, in this most humiliating decade of the American twentieth century, as the national consensus broke down and confusion and apathy gripped the country, many looked inward. The previously confident national psyche fractured into paroxysms of self-doubt and collective guilt. America's mindset became mired in what some called "headshrinker territory," and the country curled up into a psychological equivalent of the fetal position.[44]

Hollywood and America continued to mirror one another. While the era's Russian-genre films did not contradict detente, neither did they staunchly support it. The lens of the 1970s camera simply did not project Russians into the heart of American consciousness. After three decades of starring as America's protagonist, as America's "other," seventies Russians failed to generate passion in a nation contemplating spiritual renewal at a personal level.

Chapter Six

1981–1985: Cold War Reprise

Sitting in a parked truck on a quiet suburban Denver street, Russian terrorist Mikhail Rostov (Richard Lynch) scowls amid festive neighbors wishing one another season's greetings on Christmas Eve. "Look at them," Rostov tells a fellow terrorist in *Invasion, USA* (1983), "soft, spineless, decadent. They don't even understand the nature of their own freedom or how we will use it against them. They are their own worst enemies, but they don't know it."

Suddenly and without warning, Rostov and his Russian companion turn this idyllic scene into one of wanton death and destruction. Acting with calculated savagery, the terrorists wait until dinnertime to blow up the neighborhood's houses, indiscriminately killing innocent men, women, and children. Their horror accomplished, they drive off.

Such scenes of cinematic Soviet cruelty generated equally violent scenes of American vengeance in Hollywood's Russian-genre films of the early 1980s. Indeed, at no other time do Hollywood movies portray such Soviet viciousness justifying wanton Soviet-bashing. What a turnaround! Russians barely existed in American consciousness or in Hollywood's grab bag of 1970s villains. The depth of early 1980s anti-Soviet hostility, cloaked as patriotic vitriol, contrasts so sharply with the 1970s as to suggest a sea change in America's national psyche.

What explains such a shift? In part, the previous decade represented an exceptional era, given its spirit of detente and self-critical post-Vietnam reassessment. But toward the end of the 1970s winds of change blew more strongly across America. Painful Vietnamese memories faded gradually as a new generation, not sharing its parents' doubts, began to flex its political muscle. By the turn of the decade Americans were once again pumped up, ready to reassert themselves in the world—ready to feel proud again. The bumpy road of detente finally came to a dead end in the 1980 election as Carter was repudiated in favor of his Republican challenger, Ronald Reagan. While Reagan's anticommunist bark turned out to be worse than his bite, this bark sounded like the low growl of the cold warrior not heard around Washington for more than a decade.

It is often said that Americans pick their president while looking into a rearview mirror, since they seem less concerned with where they are going than in escaping where they have been. To do this, they look for a candidate promising to deliver them from the shortcomings of his predecessor. If Lyndon Johnson was inept in foreign affairs and marched America deeper into the jungles of Southeast Asia, then possibly the crafty and experienced Richard Nixon could extricate the country from the Vietnam War. If Nixon acted unethically and dishonestly, then perhaps born-again Jimmy Carter could restore American values. If Carter seemed confused and inconsistent, then maybe the confident and bullish Ronald Reagan could inject clarity and pride into America's role in the world.

Certainly, Ronald Reagan promised to be everything Carter was not—which was quite a lot. Unlike Carter, Reagan possessed intuitive political savvy. He could smell out the votes. Very much the voice of suburban and rural America, Reagan's national agenda resonated of middle America. He provided catharsis for widespread popular frustration, patriotic expression of the national need for renewed confidence, and a rebirth of the politics of symbolism. For too long, he told his supporters, they had been dispossessed of the prideful hope that was rightfully their political heritage. Preaching self-reliance and a return of America the Strong, Reagan pulled the right levers, and the 1980 election was his.[1]

Simple Values, Appealing Imagery

The man replacing Carter in the White House was the second son of an evangelical Scottish-Presbyterian mother and a Democratic Irish-Catholic father. The mixed marriage was sanctioned by the Church with a promise that any children would be raised as Catholics. They were not. Reagan's mother, Nelle, broke her vow and raised her sons Protestant. A "liberal fundamentalist," she exerted great influence over the young Ronald Reagan. In sharp contrast to her alcoholic husband, Nelle was a "natural practical do-gooder," and a strict teetotaler.[2] A champion of hard work and faith, she also managed to get her two sons to college.

The homespun conservative and religious values of Dixon, Illinois, "stuck with Reagan."[3] His was an era of outsized heroes, and the people's problem solver, Franklin Roosevelt, became his first political hero. Reagan was something of a hometown hero in his own right. In his youth, "Dutch" Reagan saved an incredible seventy-five lives as a lifeguard at Lowell Park in Dixon, Illinois.

Although only an average student at Eureka College, in his freshman year he drank deeply of what he called the "heady wine" of public speaking. The conservative college administration adamantly maintained a ban against dancing on campus, a red flag to any secular student body. In a student speech Reagan rallied the prodance forces. His speech was credited with the removal of the ban and the departure of the college president. Reagan became both a hero to fellow students and convinced of his gift for motivational public speaking.[4]

Child of an aphoristic mother and an alcoholic father, the self-assured Reagan developed scant appreciation for moderate feelings concerning self-mastery and dependency. People were "either fully free or they were wholly unfree."[5] Nor did he harbor mixed feelings about America. Reagan was moved by a deeply felt and uncomplicated love of country. But it would be wrong to think of Reagan as completely one-dimensional. Far from it. He possessed an unusual personality type that incorporated seemingly incongruent characteristics: he wanted to be seen as both a "crusader" single-handedly defending the common good and a "nice guy" who was part of the gang. If his personal life as husband and father was at odds with the image he projected, the public and private Reagans seldom clashed in public view.

Reagan entered politics with a nice-guy image, since millions had seen him exactly that way on the screen. In all but one of Reagan's fifty-three film roles, he played a nice guy (he always regretted his one aberrant role as a villain).[6] Building on the screen Reagan, the political Reagan cultivated a style of charismatic "zeal leavened by a non-aggressive conciliatory personal manner."[7] So seamless was Reagan's public face that one would have been hard pressed to separate the president from the popular image he cultivated. Given the homespun values he imbibed with his mother's milk and the blurring of distinctions between the celluloid man and the political man, voters seemed prepared to shrug off mistakes like the Marine debacle in Lebanon, exchanging missiles for hostages, Iran-Contra, and the verbal pummelling to which he subjected the Russians. Rather than absorb blame for foreign policy blunders, Reagan seemed teflon coated when compared to Lyndon Johnson, Richard Nixon, or Jimmy Carter before him.

Reagan's Foreign Policy "Codes"

Foreign policy played heavily in Reagan's election, since blunders by the incumbent president paved Reagan's road to Washington. Reagan took every opportunity to highlight his opponent's foreign-policy failings. Probably in no other modern presidential campaign did the challenger so fundamentally reject the assumptions of not only his immediate opponent but of all recent administrations, both Democrat and Republican, as did Ronald Reagan in 1980. Reagan's dark analysis described a Soviet Union subverting detente to steal away America's military edge. His most successful campaign metaphor? Borrowing a leaf from the 1960 John Kennedy campaign primer, Reagan demanded that America close the "window of vulnerability," suggesting a Soviet missile advantage that America dared not live with, and that he as president would not accept.

Reagan's campaign attacked the SALT I and SALT II treaties as responsible for selling out American defense interests. Nor did other arms agreements escape Reagan's criticism, including the popular 1963 partial test ban and the 1970 non-proliferation treaty.[8] The Soviets, he charged, had bested the United States in arms deals, and he remained deeply suspicious of the entire process of arms negotiations. He pledged to rebuild American military mastery. As the backbone of his national security catch-up plan, Reagan set in motion the largest expansion of peacetime defense spending. The Pentagon budget ballooned from $171 billion in 1981 to $376 billion in 1986.[9] Yet Reagan did not fret over paying for expanded conventional and nuclear forces. Unlike previous Republican leaders, he rejected fiscal restraint in favor of a unique brand of "supply-side" economics, which startled even Keynesian Democrats by optimistically predicting that heavy spending on a more robust military would stimulate the American economy enough to avoid raising taxes—at least for the affluent. The net result? A huge federal deficit and a change in America's fiscal status from the world's largest creditor to the world's largest debtor. The gap between rich and poor expanded to a chasm just as the social safety net frayed.

Soviet Troublemakers Everywhere

Changes in the script at home were matched by new lines on the world stage. According to Reagan's bipolar worldview, the Soviets continued to make trouble in East-West relations, and he pledged to stop them. Turning up the volume on Cold War rhetoric, he fretted over what he believed to be happening in the Third World: menacing Kremlin revolutionaries pulling the strings of obedient socialist puppets all over Latin America, Africa, and the Middle East.[10]

From his perspective, the obvious duty of the United States was to support friends and confront global enemies inspired by the Kremlin. If this landed the United States into bed with some unsavory partners, holy ends sometimes warrant unholy means. American ambassador to the United Nations, Jeane Kirkpatrick, offered a fine ideological distinction to legitimize American support for right-wing anticommunist dictatorships. She conceded that right-wing groups were "authoritarian." But unlike the communists, she claimed, they were not "totalitarian." If this distinction seemed problematic to victims of right-wing human rights abuses, Kirkpatrick argued, the right was capable of evolving into democracy, which she considered unimaginable for communist systems. This democratization process took time, and during that time right-wing regimes deserved American support.

Reagan, Kirkpatrick, and others talked tough with the Soviet Union during the early years of the Reagan administration. But it is necessary to distinguish between this administraton's "declaratory" policy and its "operational" policy.[11] In reality, even with increased military spending, much of the Cold War drum beating amounted to just so much noise, however loud and jarring. Reagan's declaratory policy rang with radical right-wing American nationalist imagery, a form of "verbal Ramboism," leaving the Soviet Union, its allies, and even America's allies to wonder if the two superpowers were again on a collision course.[12] Defining international politics as a struggle between good and evil, Reagan denounced arms control and described long-term confrontation with Russia as the natural order of things.[13] In his memorable first presidential press conference, Reagan asserted that the Kremlin's revolutionary clique claimed "the right to commit any crime, to lie, to cheat, in order to attain that [revolution]."[14]

With ears ringing from the noise, it was easy for observers to miss the administration's quieter, interest-driven actions toward the Soviets. To talk tough with the Soviets pleased voters who were convinced that America had become a passive player on the world stage. Many others, however, saw little value in baiting the Russian bear. In the face of dissent from conservative business interests, congressional critics, and moderate Americans, the Reagan administration ultimately followed an operational policy borrowing heavily from detente-oriented presidents: seek compromise, not victory.

Nuclear Anxieties Reappear

Nevertheless, in the din of anticommunist rhetoric booming out of Washington in the early 1980s, more Americans and Europeans feared the outbreak of nuclear war than at any time since the 1962 Cuban missile crisis. The fear that American foreign policy was being directed by a six-gun-toting cowboy certainly ran deep among American allies. A series of "injudicious remarks" by key administration officials fueled domestic and international apprehensions. There was loose talk of developing "nuclear war fighting strategies," firing nuclear "warning shots," and winning limited nuclear war. Particularly difficult to ignore were remarks by Deputy Undersecretary of Defense T. K. Jones that in case of a nuclear attack citizens need only "dig a hole, cover it with a couple of doors, and throw three feet of dirt on top. If there are enough shovels to go around, everybody's going to make it."[15] Not everyone believed it. On 12 June 1982, one million peace protesters vented their nuclear fears by demonstrating in New York's Central Park.

But Washington's anticommunist hype continued, with President Reagan saving his most rhetorical comic-strip imagery for a convention of Evangelicals in Florida. In March of 1983 he denounced Russia as "an 'evil empire' and the focus of evil in the modern world."[16] Even more shocking to the Soviets was a verbal gaffe by the president as he prepared for one of his weekly Saturday morning radio addresses in August 1984. Not knowing he was speaking to millions over a live microphone, the president joked, "My fellow Americans, I'm pleased to tell you that today I've signed legislation to outlaw the Soviet Union forever. We begin bombing in five minutes." The Russians were not amused.

Nor were increasing numbers of Americans. Coupled with loose statements by the administration were indications that Reagan did not comprehend some of the basic elements of nuclear deterrence.[17] In the face of the Cold War bombast, public support for a nuclear "freeze" mounted and threatened to give the Democrats a "peace issue" in the 1984 elections. Partly to defuse growing public unease, the president proposed new arms-control measures, even though the evidence suggests that Reagan did not take them seriously.[18]

SDI: Only the Soviets Believed

The president's heart was engaged elsewhere. Sold on the value of a high-tech defensive initiative suggested to him by atomic scientist Edward Teller, businessman Joseph Coors, and *Wall Street Journal* writer Gregory Fossedal, in March 1983 Reagan unveiled plans for a Strategic Defense Initiative (SDI). Pulling out all rhetorical stops, the president's speech was as rich in hyperbole as it was short on details. Marketing techno-wizardry as bona fide science, Reagan invoked imagery of an antimissile umbrella sheltering American skies and rendering Soviet missiles "impotent and obsolete."[19] Soon dubbed "star wars" by the media, Reagan's vision proved effective in defusing the

Democrats' call for a nuclear freeze, even though many experts considered the plan not feasible. Two analysts wondered aloud if Reagan might be recycling a 1940 movie script in which he starred as a double agent in quest of a weapon quite similar to the SDI.[20]

The Soviets were not laughing. Reagan's "evil empire" rhetoric fueled standard Russian paranoia about Western conspiracies, resulting in a potentially lethal mixture. It appears from the account of real-world double agent Oleg Gordievsky, the most senior Soviet intelligence officer ever to work for the West, that the KGB leadership took Reagan's speech quite literally. Like a leading American diplomatic historian, the Soviets assumed that the key to understanding Reagan lay in "taking what he said pretty literally since he was a rather simple person."[21] As a result, the Soviets viewed the SDI proposal as deadly serious, a ratcheting up of the Cold War that would tilt the balance of terror against the Soviet Union.

Indeed, Gordievsky contends that Yuri Andropov, then chief of the KGB, so believed that Reagan was gearing up for nuclear war that in 1981 he approved an unprecedented global operation—"Operation Ryan," which combined the resources of both the KGB and GRU (Soviet military intelligence) to seek verification of American preparations for a nuclear strike. According to Gordievsky, in 1983 the KGB came perilously close to convincing the Party that war was imminent. Fortunately, cooler heads in the Kremlin prevailed, but stepped-up military spending was approved.[22]

Foreign Policy Paradoxes

In retrospect, was Reagan's tough Cold War posturing really designed to intimidate the Soviet Union or was it just for domestic consumption? Probably both. Indeed, paradoxes abound in Reagan's Soviet policy and no simple label captures its essence. While Reagan's saber-rattling rhetoric and blank check to the military distinguish his administration from its predecessors, his policies on the ground differed little from America's three presidents in the 1970s. A noted British scholar sees policies "producing shock in the short term but greater stability and better prospects for peace in the longer term."[23]

Perhaps so. Reagan never took any action against the Soviet Union even remotely as harsh as President Carter's hard-line response to the Soviet invasion of Afghanistan. Even when Reagan had opportunities to act firmly, he poured on the crowd pleasing anticommunist rhetoric while quietly seeking compromise. For example, early in his presidency Reagan had to decide what to do about the grain embargo that Jimmy Carter imposed on the Soviets after their invasion of Afghanistan. Up to that point Reagan had sounded very much the cold warrior, to the delight of conservative hard-liners. But words were one thing and dollars another. Free-trade business interests lobbied for removal of the embargo and renewed American grain sales to the Soviet Union as a boost for the American economy, which was mired in recession. American Farm Bureau president Robert B. Deland called the embargo "an economic and diplomatic disaster." The president was "trapped between his ideology and his economic views." Economic considerations won out, despite his continued verbal attack, as he dropped the Carter embargo and resumed grain sales to the Soviets.[24]

Hollywood Regains Confidence

Like the nation that elected Reagan in 1980, Hollywood soon shed the psychic burden of disillusionment and self-doubt characteristic of 1970s movies. Films of the early 1980s were "conservative by osmosis." Very few love stories or films about nature appeared, as cuddling and granola were suddenly out. Law and order avengers, however, were in. Hollywood ceased glamorizing outlaws and antisocial behavior and turned longingly toward the lost innocence of the 1950s, including its anticommunism.[25]

The period's most powerful and lucrative movie theme clearly was resurgent American patriotism, epitomized by Sylvester Stallone's three Johnny Rambo movies, which went beyond mere militarism to a passion for anticommunist insurgency. These films serve as prequel to Oliver North's intrigue on behalf of the Nicaraguan Contras, as well as to President Reagan's remark, only half joking, that he would like to have sent Rambo to several trouble spots around the world.[26] And who wouldn't prefer to forget the popular Ronbo poster with Reagan's septuagenarian head superimposed on Stallone's heavily armed, musclebound torso?

As Hollywood served up reel after reel of celluloid patriotism, it was delighted to learn that it could make lots of money doing so. The early 1980s emerged as one of Culver City's most successful periods, breaking sharply with the unprofitable 1970s. But if Hollywood hit the commercial motherlode with flag-waving movies, critics seemed unimpressed. Pauline Kael complained that "hit movies make the most noise in the culture, and the hits of the early eighties are often just TV in a souped-up form."[27]

TV? Yes—inasmuch as television refined Hollywood's Saturday matinee superhero into the muscular superheroes that dominated Saturday morning television. Taking back its own, Hollywood released a series of action thrillers built around taciturn and brawny heroes who spoke only in jingoistic maxims while avenging wrongs suffered at the hands of America's enemies. Never has peacetime found the rhetoric of a president and Hollywood's celluloid patriotism more in sync.

Cinematic Russians Return

Grandiose mythological images saturate early 1980s Russian-genre films. As contrasted with 1970s cinema, which ignored Russians as bland and boring, Russians explode onto the screen in the eighties. More than thirty films, almost all negative toward Russians and the Soviet system, inundated moviegoers with portraits of an evil Soviet enemy that must be beaten. Nothing remotely like it had been seen since the early 1950s, when films like *Never Let Me Go* (1953) and *Prisoner of War* (1954) were released. The new batch of vitriolic films offered America both a singular Soviet enemy and uncomplicated American heroes.

Of all films depicting Russians and the Soviet Union, a mere four carried neutral or favorable views. The negativity of the rest threatened to jump off the Richter scale measuring hostility. And as a rule of thumb: the more negative the more violent, and the more violent the more profitable. So violent were the major box office hits that Soviet literary elites took the unprecedented step of publically condemning this anti-Soviet bombast. Soviet poet Yevgeny Yevtushenko labeled these films "war-nography," while Soviet Writers' Union secretary Genrikh Borovik charged that Hollywood "used art to sell hatred and fear." In a similar vein, deputy minister of culture Gyorgi Ivanov claimed that "Americans are being brought up with the idea that you can only deal with a Russian with a gun."[28]

Since Soviet propaganda has often depicted American leaders unfairly, including comparing Reagan to Hitler, and since the Hollywood films in question represent only a small segment of American cinema's historical portrayal of Russians, these Soviet complaints echoed with a somewhat hollow ring. Yet they were not completely unfounded. Soviet propaganda traditionally aimed only at American leaders. The American people might be portrayed as misguided, but not as evil. But the early 1980s American orgy of Russian bashing aimed directly at Soviet citizens as the incarnation of evil, not merely as dupes of an evil system. These films also celebrated violence as a reasonable option in solving United States-Soviet differences.

The most successful early 1980s films reveled in attacking the Russians. *Firefox* (1982), *World War III* (1982), *Red Dawn* (1984), *Gulag* (1985), *Invasion, USA* (1985), *Rambo: First Blood, Part II* (1985), and *Rocky IV* (1985) all take the gloves off when stepping into the ring with the Russians. Tapping a reservoir of national pride long repressed during the dubious post-Vietnam and post-Watergate seventies, these pictures not only bashed the Soviets but also made wheelbarrows of money.

All such films begin with the premise that Soviet Communism represents evil. Nothing new here. However, as a subtext, they suggest that coexistence is impossible and efforts at talking with enemies of freedom are pointless. Soft-headed liberals might try to negotiate common ground with an enemy, but in the us/them world of Hollywood, America's task turns out to be as clear as it is necessary: dispose of them before they dispose of us. A disturbing ends-versus-means distortion also accompanies these pictures. Their strident self-confidence reduces all East-West differences to quick, facile, and gratuitously violent resolution. In the no-holds-barred struggle to defend America's superior way of life, any weapon is permissible. The incessant Russian bashing comes packaged in a wide variety of plots and settings.[29] The most important category, Cold War vigilantism, lies at the emotional core of the three era-defining bellwether films, *Rocky IV*, *Invasion, USA*, and *Red Dawn*.

Rocky IV

Despite its cliched predictability, *Rocky IV* (1985) became the third-leading box-office hit of 1985 ($78,919,250 in rentals), as well as the highest grossing of the five Rocky movies.[30] It ranks sixty-first among *Variety*'s all-time top one hundred grossing domestic films, taking in $76,023,246 in rentals as of 1994, making it twentieth for 1980s films.[31]

What created such success? Not the reviews. Consistently ridiculed by critics, *Rocky IV* leapfrogged over their derision to offer Americans what they wanted to see and vicariously experience at the time. Here is a flag-draped David and Goliath scenario pitting boxer Rocky Balboa, America's rugged individualist, against Ivan Drago, a Soviet, collectivist, steroid-induced human killing machine.

Once again, Rocky comes out of retirement, this time to avenge the death of his friend and former rival, Apollo Creed, who has been mercilessly crushed in the ring by the product of Soviet technology, Ivan Drago, the "Siberian Express." The 261-pound Ivan Drago is played by hulking Dolph Lundgren, an amazing physical specimen. One critic sketches a daunting description of Ivan Drago training with "enough technicians around with clipboards to launch a missile; with Ivan Drago on the pad, the Soviet Union enjoys overwhelming first-strike capability."[32]

Before Apollo Creed enters the ring against Drago, he exclaims "This is Us against Them," freedom against totalitarianism. Following a murderous blow from Drago, Apollo lies in a crumpled heap. The triumphant Russian uncaringly dismisses his crushed opponent. "If he dies, he dies." Apollo's cruel death at the fists of the heartless Drago demands that Rocky avenge not only his friend but American honor as well.

The deck is stacked against Rocky. The retired champ, badly out of shape, signs a contract to take on Ivan Drago in Moscow on Christmas Day—for no money. Rocky has little time to prepare and no training team. Instead, he exercises mind and body while living a solitary and spartan existence in the Russian wilderness. Meanwhile, the pampered hulk Drago works out amid a cathedral of sophisticated technical and chemical marvels.

Rocky IV wears its symbolism boldly. Once good is distinguished from evil, the fight becomes everything. Having it out in the ring represents even more than the United States versus the Soviet Union. The boxers represent rugged individualism versus collectivism, religious faith versus atheism, the human spirit versus mindless technology, honesty versus duplicity, and freedom versus control. Critic Jack Kroll believes the film dramatically plays on the tension between "Soviet godlessness versus American piety."[33] To Rex Reed "the fight symbolizes the whole political future of Russia versus the free world."[34] All for the price of a theater ticket and a box of popcorn!

Back to the plot. At a well-orchestrated prefight press conference, a confident Soviet official tells an American audience that "perhaps the defeat of this little so-called champion [Rocky] will be an example of how pathetically weak your society has become." This image of a weak, sedentary America that is sorely lacking moral fiber or military discipline is the same one Ronald Reagan rolled out and pledged to change during the 1980 election. When Rocky laces up his gloves, he carries America's hopes and fears into the ring with him. He must not lose to the Russian. He must prevail.

Surely the image of Soviet society in *Rocky IV* is none too flattering. It comes across as a gulag nation with its ubiquitous KGB, godless scientism, rigid order, militarism, and joylessness. And its people are just as bad as their system. Russian standard-bearer Ivan Drago is every inch an evil, chemically engineered, unfeeling mutant and a tool of the state. A product of the bleak Soviet system, Drago rarely speaks and never smiles.

His wife/manager, Ludmilla Drago, played by actress Brigitte Nielsen, appears equally cold and deceitful. A former swimming gold medalist, Ludmilla has a bloodstream that is no less clogged with performance-enhancing chemicals than her husband's. Befitting one of moviedom's most sinister Russian villains, she smirks with haughty contempt when Ivan delivers the death blow to Apollo Creed. The parade of Russian evil, however, does not stop with Drago and Ludmilla. Every bit as detestable is Nicoli Koloff (Michael Pataki). This two-faced party apparatchik exploits Drago, spouts ideological doublespeak, and fawns obsequiously before Party bosses. And the list of despicable Russian characters goes on. Search if you wish, but you will not find a Russian with any redeeming value in this orgy of stereotypes gone wild, since "all Soviet managers, trainers, fighters, and officials are malevolent ambassadors of the Evil Empire."[35]

Finally, the big fight. Director Stallone crafts the confrontation in the ring for maximum tension and impact. Rocky Balboa, the consummate underdog, stands alone, facing Drago in the belly of the evil empire. The atmosphere is poisonous. Although Rocky has faith, he knows the deck is stacked against him. Not only must he fight a human mountain, but under the most adverse conditions and for the most serious of stakes: the American way of life. The radio announcer proclaims that "Ivan Drago is a man with an entire country in his corner." The Moscow arena seems packed with a blood thirsty Russian monolith, rather than fight fans. The Politburo leaders watch nervously from a special box. Soviet Red Army uniforms dot the crowd, offering the only break in the grayness. As if on cue, the arena boos Rocky loudly and often. "In all my years of broadcasting," the announcer intones, "I've never seen such a hostile crowd."

To the delight of the Russian crowd, the early rounds go Drago's way. As a toady of the state, not an individual, he gestures to the Communist Party box following flurries of punches that find Rocky's face. But Rocky is not so easily defeated. Obligatory to all "Rocky" films, just when the "Italian Stallion" appears beaten beyond human endurance, he mounts a comeback. Reaching deep inside himself— beyond skill, footwork, or strategy—Rocky finds resilience and semi-conscious fortitude. He finds what makes America great. He finds the guts to persist when reason tells others that all is lost.

In the tenth round Rocky's counterattack exposes a hint of vulnerability in the Soviet giant. As their champion stumbles, the Soviet crowd experiences shock. As he falters, the crowd senses liberation from a horrible dream. Suggesting that the wall of Soviet brainwashing can be breached, the crowd begins to applaud the underdog. As the momentum gradually shifts in Rocky's direction, it appears as though an invisible hydraulic jack slowly tilts the ring to the American's advantage. Rocky beats all odds by winning the bloody, primitive battle. Apollo gets avenged. The spirit of America is redeemed.

Viewers of *Rocky I, II,* or *III* can in no way feign surprise at their hero's come-from-behind victory, since nothing less befits his cinematic birthright. Converting the Russian crowd, however, including members of the Soviet Politburo, does tear at the fiber of credulity.[36] More so the ending. A film's ending often clarifies where its sentiments lie. After defeating Ivan Drago physically, and the Soviet system symbolically, it is easy to wax magnanimous, and Rocky does exactly that.

Rocky's little speech, a belated olive branch of sorts, comes across as far too little and much too late. It cannot offset *Rocky IV*'s pervasive assault on everything that even smells Slavic.[37] Offering the olive branch to a defeated enemy—bloodied, beaten, and reduced to worshipping the conquering underdog—hardly serves as enough ballast to offset the vicious pounding the movie delivers to the Soviets for eighty-eight of its ninety-one minutes. At best, it represents the mere acceptance of unconditional surrender by a defeated enemy.

The New York City-born former television writer, Sylvester Stallone, not only starred in *Rocky IV* but also directed and cowrote this overblown 1985 hit for M-G-M United Artists. Mercifully, it garnered no Oscar nominations, but youthful audiences loved it and jingoism laughed all the way to the bank and back.

Invasion, USA

Invasion, USA (1985) provides another reluctant warrior coming out of retirement to defend America. In this case it's former CIA agent Matt Hunter, played by karate champion Chuck Norris, whose sullen and monosyllabic presence seems disconcertingly reminiscent of Stallone's in *Rocky IV*. The tissue-thin plot is no more flattering of the Soviet Union or its people. In *Invasion, USA*, a Russian-led band of Third World terrorists covertly carves a destructive path across America's heartland. Sometimes these furtive terrorists disguise themselves as police when attacking strategic American targets and murdering those who look to their uniform for protection.[38]

There is no escaping the conclusion that *Invasion, USA* glamorizes anticommunist vigilantism as the violent solution to America's array of socioeconomic problems. In this case, American federal institutions prove useless as defenders of freedom. Only Matt Hunter sees through the terrorists' nefarious plot to undermine a naively trusting America. As in *Rocky IV*, and many of the era's films, the subtext echoes Reagan's message that previous administrations encouraged Americans to become lazy and complacent—easy picking for the disciplined Soviet militarists. Only matching the Russians, blow for bloody blow, can save liberty; every American must be prepared to act as a vigilante on behalf of the American way of life. And what a battle! The unabated violence led critic Archer Winston to joke that the firepower in *Invasion, USA* seems "considerably greater than that of the Normandy invasion."[39]

Given this movie's mindless story line, its emotional hook appears in the person of the psychopathic Russian leader of the terrorist invasion, Mikhail Rostov, portrayed overzealously by character actor Richard Lynch. Of hundreds of Russian characters created by Culver City, Rostov ranks among the most vile. Never attacking his enemies directly, he delights in blowing up defenseless victims, cruelly striking at symbols of Americana. One bomb destroys a suburban family as it celebrates Christmas while another murders innocent shoppers who apparently represent, in Rostov's twisted mind, consumers genuflecting at the altar of materialism.

Invasion, USA's personal confrontation intensifies audience animosity toward the repulsive Russian, Rostov. The simplistic plot, coauthored by Chuck Norris, pits terrorist Rostov against superhero Matt Hunter, a veritable one-man army. Matt Hunter, aptly dubbed "Cowboy" by an admiring female reporter, requires little help in dispatching the terrorist invaders. The senseless overkill, shocking even for this muscle-bound genre, refuses to abate until the last of the terrorist vermin, Rostov, is liquidated. But victory alone is not enough. It must also afford revenge. And to be satisfying, revenge must be taken slowly and, for the enemies of the American way of life, painfully. Matt Hunter taunts Rostov into nervous exhaustion, repeatedly promising that his suffering will end only when he hears the words "it's time to die." After toying with the Russian as he would pick the wings off a fly, "it's time to die." Matt Hunter crushes this insect and saves America in the process. The movie's message? Prepare.

James Bruner collaborated with Chuck Norris on the screenplay. Except for pyrotechnics, the script provided director Joseph Zito little to work with. New York-born and City College-educated, Joseph Zito had previously directed six films, including one episode of the Friday the 13th series. Having little to crow about other than the level of violence, Cannon Studio's publicity for *Invasion, USA* settled for pyrrhic victory—praising Zito as "past master of the 'clean' adventure film: a movie whose action contains violence but no gore."[40] Violence, however, pays, since *Invasion, USA* ranks eighty-second among *Variety*'s all-time top grossing independent films with rentals of $17,536,296.[41]

Red Dawn

Rocky Balboa bested the Russians in Moscow. Matt Hunter thumped Soviet-led terrorists trying to undermine America's heartland. In *Red*

Dawn (1984), grassroots Americans resist. The story begins after the Soviets invade and defeat an unsuspecting nation. How did the communists manage to occupy America with little apparent resistance? Apparently believing every question does not need an answer, *Red Dawn* passes on this one, and the audience is left to fill in the scenario's holes. The Soviets having taken over America, and it falls to ordinary citizens to rise up and win back the heritage of freedom that the Soviets seek to drown in a sea of collectivism. *Red Dawn's* vigilantes are ordinary resistance fighters performing extraordinary deeds— much like the Russian partisans in Tinseltown's World War II movies. To complete this Hollywood throwback to the past, the Russians come off as the moral equivalent of invading Nazis in old wartime movies like *The North Star* (1943) and *Days of Glory* (1944).

Like the vigilante movies of the early 1980s, *Invasion, USA* and *Rocky IV*, *Red Dawn* was sliced and diced by critics while making cash registers sing to the tune of ten million dollars in its first five days. The chairman of the National Coalition on Television Violence singled out *Red Dawn* as the "most violent film ever made," with 134 acts of violence per hour—no small achievement, given the level of violence registered by other Russian-genre films of the era. Among the legion of youngsters who worshipped *Red Dawn* was teenager Timothy McVeigh, indicted in 1995 for America's worst terrorist bombing in Oklahoma City.

A thin story line pops up occasionally amid all the blood and guts. America plays the cinematic underdog to the Russian bully every bit as neatly as in *Rocky IV*, although this time at home rather than on the road. In *Red Dawn* the occupying Russians, cruel imperialists all, battle noble American guerrillas in a war that seems endless. Anti-Russian hysteria requires no peaks or valleys in *Red Dawn*, running red-hot throughout. Cold-blooded murderers execute scores of civilians as "examples" in a great show of screen villainy. It's even a bit too much for some Soviet allies. Cuban officer Bela (Ron O'Neal) knows from his own guerrilla experience that "you must win the hearts and minds of the people." His obtuse Russian overseer, Bratchenko (Vladek Sheybal), won't listen. Innocent blood flows.

Director-writer John Milius apparently jumped at fighting this celluloid war on American soil because "it gives his anti-Communist crusade something of the original purity of the American Revolution."[42] But Milius' underdog comes across as having fleas, leading the audience to scratch with disbelief when Milius makes guerrilla heroes out of middle-class, down-jacketed high schoolers called the "Wolverines." Instead of playing a game of pickup basketball or double dating at the local drive-in, these resourceful teens spend their off-hours blowing up Soviet convoys and stabbing Russian sentries.

The leader of the Wolverines in *Red Dawn*, a former quarterback named Jed (Patrick Swayze), dies a hero's death at the end of the movie. But not without taking his share of Russians with him, including Strelnikov (William Smith), the top Russian counterinsurgency expert brought in to subdue the clever Wolverines. Jed's face-to-face victory over Strelnikov symbolically validates the ingenuity of America's free-spirited youth. Like the Minute Men of old, they do not let their nation down. Any communist military advantage can only be ephemeral.

This portrait of teenage guerrillas imbues *Red Dawn* with a sense of cinematic Vietnam role reversal: the frustration of Americans, the ineffectual 1970s technological bullies in Vietnam, is released by American youth outwitting the technology-laden Soviets. For John Milius, *Red Dawn* was America's role of a lifetime—playing the adroit David after a frustrating generation as the clumsy Goliath of the world.[43]

Critical reaction to *Red Dawn*? Hard to believe, but it was even more derisive than for *Rocky IV* or *Invasion, USA*. One critic pilloried Milius for "using slick Hollywood techniques to sell warfare as an exhilarating parade of bold victories and poignant martyrdoms."[44] Another branded Milius a "rider on the current of Cold War politics."[45] A third lamented that Milius "has spent too much time playing to the rabid anti-Commies. It's as if he doesn't trust the rest of the political spectrum."[46] Critic Armond White probably captured the discomfort felt by many thoughtful viewers of this commercially successful film. "Movies are the place for fantasy," White argues, "but after Vietnam is there a place in our minds for an insistently macho, patriotic fantasy of war, one that sidesteps the horror of bloodshed, destruction, panic, and loss?"[47]

Most of this criticism was leveled against director-writer John Milius, a St. Louis native who graduated from the University of Southern California's film school, and the screenwriter for *Apocalypse Now* (1979). Known as a director enamored with the potent musical score in emotional films, Milius always listens to carefully selected music while writing. Milius won the national Student Film Festival Award for an animated short called *Marcello, I'm So Bored*, which presaged his feature film preoccupation with validating ruthlessness in the pursuit of "moral" goals. Although as a youth Milius attempted to enlist in the Marine Corps, he was rejected because of chronic asthma and never served in the military. His films, however, remain laced with characters confronting physical danger. The Milius hero "must not only threaten force, but must use it without remorse or pity." The Wolverines both talked the talk and walked the walk.[48]

A Sea of Russian-Chomping Sharks

Schoolboy warriors. Retread CIA agents. Boxer turned avenger of human dignity and the American way of life. These Hollywood creations were not alone in fighting back the Soviet menace. Culver City also churned out a number of lesser though nevertheless larger than life, superheroes taking on the evil empire. And so long as an orgy of Soviet bashing seemed quite natural, that other icon of American vigilantism, Clint Eastwood, inevitably entered the fray. Former Oregon lumberjack Clint Eastwood served four years with army Special Forces in the 1950s. He first became known as the slow-to-anger idol of the television western *Rawhide*, then grew to superstardom in seventies spaghetti westerns and Dirty Harry movies. More than twenty of Eastwood's movies were made for Warner Brothers, the quintessential action studio.

In *Firefox* (1982), Eastwood stars as ex-Vietnam fighter pilot Mitchell Gant who, like Rocky Balboa and Matt Hunter, reluctantly comes out of retirement to single-handedly save America from the Russians. The plot seems to begin where Reagan's rhetoric leaves off. The United States has fallen woefully behind the Soviets in the race for military preeminence. This time the threat emanates from a new Soviet Mach-5 radar resistant aircraft which gives the Soviets a first-strike capability over the United States. To protect itself, America must get its hands on a Mach-5 prototype.[49]

Enter Mitchell Gant. He possesses two qualities that recommend him for so critical a mission. He is a top pilot and he speaks Russian, since his mother was an émigré. But our hero is flawed. He suffers from post-Vietnam stress flashbacks, which can be triggered by stimuli as innocuous as the sound of helicopters. One earful and there is no telling what Gant will do, leading a critic to jest that "if Gant lived in Manhattan, he'd be a basket case."[50]

But the CIA has no choice. America must stake its security on one man and one man alone. He is assigned to sneak into the Soviet Union disguised as a businessman, link up with a network of dissident Jewish scientists in the Soviet research community, steal the Soviets' best plane out from under their noses, and fly it to the West with the best Soviet pilots trying to blow him out of the air—all sandwiched between post-Vietnam flashbacks. Certainly too much to ask of a lesser man than Gant.

Of course, Gant has the help of a few insiders: Jewish scientists with no love for the Soviet Union or for the KGB holding them prisoner. When Gant asks one of the scientists why he is willing to die for this mission, he puts things in perspective: "It is a small thing compared to my resentment of the KGB." Between Eastwood, the star and director-producer of *Firefox*, and a few dissidents, this "mission impossible" succeeds. Although long on Cold War paranoia and militarism, *Firefox* turns out rather short on suspense—owing mainly to the absurd obstacles confronting Mitchell Gant. Critic Vincent Canby dismissed *Firefox* as "a James Bond movie without girls, a Superman movie without a sense of humor." Eastwood's fans, nevertheless, either did not read the reviews or ignored them, and they flocked to see their star. Rentals for *Firefox* total $25,000,000, placing it 161st among eighties films.[51]

Another confused anti-Soviet potboiler, *World War III* (1982), is reminiscent of apocalyptic Hollywood scenarios in *Dr. Strangelove* (1964) and *Fail Safe* (1964). In the midst of an American grain embargo, the Soviet Union suffers a severe agricultural failure. Blaming the United States for spreading starvation in the Russian heartland, Soviet leaders turn to desperate military adventurism in hopes of forcing the United States to abandon the embargo. Are you ready for this? In order to blackmail the United States into lifting the embargo, the Soviets invade Alaska and seize the oil pipeline.

As if this superpower confrontation were not bad enough, it is further complicated by another difficult struggle. Inside the Kremlin a battle rages between hard-line KGB supporters and more moderate Party leaders. At first things look like they might be worked out—at least between the United States and the Soviet Union. In Iceland, a reasonable American president (Rock Hudson) begins talks with his equally sanguine counterpart, General Secretary Andrei Gorny (Brian Keith).

But as the intramural Kremlin row reaches fever pitch, Gorny suddenly breaks off the talks and returns to Moscow. The KGB secretly assassinates the moderate Secretary Gorny, claiming he has a world-class case of the flu, and replaces him with a madman, KGB General Alexei Rodinsky (Robert Proskey). Reckless, doctrinaire, and arrogant, Rodinsky hopes to extract major concessions from the United States. When that tactic fails, he goes for broke. Using the state of military alert as strategic camouflage, madman Rodinsky unleashes a nuclear first strike against the United States, hoping to dispose of his enemy in one bold move. Bad move. There can be no Soviet victory and Rodinsky's megalomania unleashes doomsday. Where is SDI when you need it?

At least the world is spared in *Gulag*, which dwells on freedom, or, more precisely, its absence in an unrelentingly cruel Soviet society. *Gulag* opens innocently enough with former American Olympic gold medalist turned journalist, Mickey Almon (David Keith), covering the Moscow Olympics boycotted by the United States. In a KGB setup, Mickey Almon gets arrested as a spy and is locked up as an example to other Westerners. Forget about due process, brandishing an American passport, or demanding to see the American ambassador. We are talking about justice Soviet style. Things go from bad to worse for Mickey. His Soviet interrogators subject him to repeated torture as he is dragged deeper and deeper into the bowels of the gulag archipelago.

In the living nightmare of the Soviet gulag, no hope exists, at least not for lesser men. Wounded but not beaten, Mickey proves himself stronger than the Soviet system and stronger than the gulag. In the best tradition of prison-escape movies, Mickey demonstrates that no gulag can crush the American spirit. He breaks out. Scrambling across a boundless frozen tundra, Mickey outwits Soviet pursuers in his go-for-broke race to the border. He makes it. Freedom is affirmed. *Gulag* announces that 1980s Soviet society has yet to abandon the terror created by Stalin in the 1930s. In Roger Young's film about the Soviet hellhole, Americans are encouraged to measure themselves and their country against the negative portrait of their contemptible enemy.

The sophistry of *Gulag* is nothing compared to the political thrust of Sylvester Stallone's monument to Vietnam War historical revisionism, *Rambo: First Blood, Part II* (1985). In history according to Stallone, the only thing that stood between the United States and victory in Vietnam was a bunch of weak politicians who prevented the American fighting man from winning the war that was his to win. Now these spineless politicians better watch out. In this example of the era's Russonography, embittered Vietnam veteran Johnny Rambo, earlier imprisoned for a stateside reign of violence in *First Blood* (1982), gets to vent his anger against a new collection of bad guys—Russians and their pernicious allies.

As this blockbuster sequel opens, Johnny Rambo is pardoned from his earlier melee on the condition that he return to Vietnam on a special mission. He accepts. The army orders Johnny to sneak into Vietnam and locate and photograph Americans who are missing in action (MIAs)—echoing Ronald Reagan's unlikely mission in *Prisoner of War* (1954). But unlike Reagan's more dutiful Web Sloane, Rambo decides to exceed his mandate by rescuing imprisoned MIAs. To do this, he must not only deal with the Vietnamese captors, but their Soviet "advisers" as well, who are the real nasties pulling the strings of their Vietnamese puppets.

Not everything goes well for Rambo. He gets captured, and the Soviets take special delight in torturing him. But the Russians prove no match for Rambo. Looking like a "cross between a hippie and a Hell's Angel," Rambo breaks loose; then all hell breaks loose. Unfettered by nay-saying bureaucrats or politicians at home, this cinematic colossus of retaliation makes the enemies of America rue the day they ever angered Johnny Rambo.[52] Rambo's most formidable opponent is Soviet Lieutenant Colonel Podovsky (Steven Berkoff), so overplayed that his "sinister Slavic posturing would be excessive on the professional wrestling circuit."[53] Podovsky gleefully supervises Rambo's torture, but once Rambo escapes, it is all over for the colonel and anyone else littering Rambo's bloody path of vengeance. Collectivist faceless hordes, Vietnamese and Russian, prove no match for the spirit of American rugged individualism.

When first released in 1985, *Rambo: First Blood, Part II* constituted the thin edge of the wedge in Hollywood's revisionist "will to myth" movies concerning Vietnam. Using psychological displacement to achieve a reworking of the war, the revisionists claimed that the United States did not lose the war. It was robbed of victory. Given a fair shot, Americans in the rice paddies would have won the war which was sold out at home by intellectuals and bureaucrats.[54] Controversial as the revisionist thesis was, it also proved very lucrative. *Rambo: First Blood, Part II* struck it rich, trailing only *Back to the Future* in rentals for 1985 and finishing ahead of *Rocky IV.*[55]

Gorky Park and Moscow on the Hudson

In the midst of such jingoistic hoopla and Soviet bashing, two Hollywood films feature sympathetic Russian characters worthy of special notice. The first, Paul Mazursky's bittersweet *Moscow on the Hudson* (1985), stars Robin Williams as Vladimir Ivanov, a Soviet visitor to the United States who defects in Bloomingdale's Department Store, of all places. While it may have been easier for Hollywood to allow Ivanov a sympathetic face because he defects, the emotional range that Robin Williams brings to the character is striking. For Hollywood's Russians, almost all facile and stereotypical cardboard cutouts, complex personalities seem more rare than low-fat foods in the Russian diet.

A well-known film critic refers to Robin Williams's performance as "extraordinarily complex."[56] This is not unusual for Paul Mazursky films, which often examine interesting people and their intimate relationships. Some of his other acclaimed films have also been light parodies. The Brooklyn College-educated actor, writer, producer, and director was a nightclub comic in the 1950s and later a member of the Second City improvisational comedy company.

The second character of special note is William Hurt's depiction of Arkady Renko, a Moscow chief inspector investigating a bizarre triple murder in *Gorky Park* (1984). Renko stands out in the mid-eighties as a Russian whose nationality is not apparent. The plot takes place in Moscow, and Renko works within the Soviet criminal justice system. But rather than behaving as he does because of his Russian-ness, he acts like a cop who is part of an international fraternity of police. He is Russian only the way a cop in Paris is French and a cop in New York is American. His investigation leads him into a world of corruption and Soviet-style deception. But what movie audience is surprised by police anywhere running up against corruption in high places? In the end, Renko, the case he investigates, and the Moscow backdrop, although Russian, prove not nearly so threatening to American movie-goers as most other Russian-genre characterizations in this era.

A *New York Times* critic calls William Hurt's performance as Renko "the mainspring of the movie and also its most rivetingly strange element."[57] But one must not ignore the skill of *Gorky Park*'s director, Cambridge-educated Michael Apted. Apted began his career with Granada TV in London in the 1960s, after which he began freelance directing. Dennis Potter's screenplay remains faithful in adapting Martin Cruz Smith's best-selling novel, the first of his Arkady Renko trilogy.

Favorable Films at the Periphery of the Era

Reds

Amid the flood of carnage heaped on the Soviets during Hollywood's vigilante heyday, very few pictures broke the procrustean mold of the new Cold War. As producer, director, leading actor, and coscreen-writer for the ambitious $35 million spectacle, *Reds* (1981), Warren Beatty won a new respect from critics. With America then tilting sharply to the right, he took a leap in the opposite direction with his sprawling film about left-wing politics from 1915 to 1920, and the adventures of a little-known journalist who lived and breathed it. Critics liked his innovative use of real-life "witnesses," which gave *Reds* a semidocumentary quality. Unlike the critics, many moviegoers found the "witnesses" distracting. Some others likely found it difficult to warm up to any plot soft on the same communists being blown to bits in the most successful films. Audiences refused to buy tickets, rendering this three-hour picture a critical success but a financial disaster.

The plot in *Reds* blends a love story with the events of the Russian Revolution, like *Dr. Zhivago* (1965). However, *Reds* reflects on the American response to the era of Russian revolutionary fervor, while *Dr. Zhivago* is concerned with Russian characters and Russian society. This was an intriguing time when many well-educated and well-heeled Americans quested after a combination of social justice, personal integrity, and a Bohemian lifestyle. Some of them thought they found renewed hope for such dreams in the Russian Revolution.

Such buoyant and naive idealism was intensely bittersweet in that it would soon be crushed on the rocks of Soviet Stalinism.

The story, based on fact, traces the tempestuous love affair between Harvard graduate and journalist John Reed (Warren Beatty) and Louise Bryant (Diane Keaton) during the American radical left's hands-on encounter with the Russian revolutionary experiment. *Reds* climaxes with Reed and Bryant's brilliant, frenetic, and partisan eyewitness reporting of the 1917 Bolshevik Revolution. Ignoring the line between observer and participant, the two freely assisted the newly empowered Bolsheviks. Later these events were recounted in Reed's classic of advocacy journalism, *Ten Days That Shook the World*. Embraced by the new Soviet leadership, Reed became the first American buried at the Kremlin Wall after his untimely death of typhus at age thirty-two.

The key players in *Reds* are Americans, but Russians appear as well. The main Russian protagonist, Politburo member Grigory Zinoviev, is played by Polish writer Jerzy Kozinsky in his film debut. One critic praises Kozinsky's portrayal of Zinoviev for its "razor sharpness and authority that comes from precise knowledge of Soviet atmospherics."[58] Zinoviev is represented as being aloof, gruff, and doctrinaire. While *Reds* redraws Zinoviev somewhat, he remains the chilling prototype of the party apparatchik.[59] The relationship between hard-nosed Zinoviev and idealist Reed was fractious. Zinoviev rejects John Reed's request for recognition of the American Communist Labor Party and forces Reed to remain in Russia, working in the propaganda bureau. *Reds* also intimates that dealing with Zinoviev pushed John Reed toward disillusionment with the Bolshevik Revolution, but the film remains agnostic as to whether Reed ever actually despaired over Bolshevik behavior.

Other leading revolutionaries like Lenin (Roger Sloman), Trotsky (Stuart Richman), and Alexander Kerensky (Oleg Kerensky) have minor roles, but *Reds* uses them only as background for its real focus— the struggle within the American left. Favorable towards early Soviet values and the idea that humanity should seek a more just political order, Beatty's *Reds* follows those values to where they first breathed political fire, namely, Russia.

Reds received twelve Oscar nominations, but won only in the director, photography, and supporting actress (Maureen Stapleton) categories. *Reds* has been included in one listing of annual top-five "quality" films not among box-office leaders.[60] At the time, Beatty was commended for depicting topics almost never addressed by Hollywood— factional struggles in the American left and political shop talk among cultural radicals.[61] *Reds* has taken in rentals of $21,000,000, and ranks 197th among films of the 1980s in total rentals.[62]

A View to a Kill

Count on another tongue-in-cheek James Bond spy adventure to make light of the East-West split, then toss in a little sexual fantasy and make a bundle for the producers. Any leading character with such a long-term commitment to drinking only vodka martinis must have a real soft spot for Russian culture. Something of a throwback to some films of the previous decade, *A View to a Kill* (1985) recycles the familiar evil Third Force motif uniting Western and Soviet spies in a common mission. In this fourteenth Bond film the villain seeking to control the world is a wealthy French industrialist and former Soviet agent, Max Zorin (Chistopher Walken). Subjected to steroid experiments as a child by the Nazis, Zorin was rescued by the Soviets in 1945. The evil Zorin surrounds himself with intriguing but deadly accomplices, notably his striking personal hitwoman, May Day (Grace Jones).

KGB head, General Gogol (Walter Gottell), leads the good Russians in *A View to a Kill*. As a recurrent detente figure in Bond films, the jovial General Gogol had originally trained Max Zorin as a Soviet agent. Gogol now teams up with James Bond (Roger Moore in his seventh Bond role) and the Americans to foil Zorin's plan to corner the microchip market by flooding the San Andreas fault, thus wiping out competition from Silicon Valley.

Aiding and comforting Bond as he uncovers and finally undermines Zorin's scenario is the beautiful KGB spy Pola Ivanova (Fiona Fullerton). Pola's official assignment? To work closely with James Bond to defeat the megalomanic vision of Max Zorin. But who needs a mission to save the world if it does not leave room for a little romance? Pola Ivanova becomes the third Russian spy to make love with a Bond character, this time in a hot tub where, in the midst of passion she proclaims "detente can be beautiful!" Bond begs not to differ.

It takes some high-tech high jinks to put Zorin out of business, but in the end, James dispatches him in familiar fashion. When the East-West mission successfully thwarts Zorin, General Gogol awards Bond the "Order of Lenin." One can only visualize Lenin turning over in his climate-controlled mausoleum.

2010

Presaging the shift away from hard-line Cold War messages, *2010* (1985) gets a headstart on cinematic pleas for American-Soviet cooperation. As a sequel to *2001: A Space Odyssey* (1968), *2010* opens with top Russian space scientist Dr. Dimitri Moisevitch (Dana Elcar) meeting with his American counterpart, Dr. Heywood Floyd (Roy

Scheider). The two propose a joint space probe to determine what has happened to the failed Discovery mission of 2001. The controversial Soviet-American space flight is finally launched in a Soviet craft against a backdrop of escalating superpower tensions over an American naval blockade of Honduras, which one critic likened to a *2010* equivalent of the 1962 Cuban missile crisis.[63]

Given the military crisis on earth, relations between the Soviet and American crews aboard the Leonov space vessel begin on a sour note. Only the warm smile of good-natured scientist Maxim Brovosky (Elyra Baskin) eases the icy tension between the Soviet and American crews. But it takes the accidental death of the likable Maxim to draw crew members together and allow trust to grow.

Just as harmony aboard the Leonov begins to blossom, however, the Honduran crisis reaches fever pitch on earth. A Soviet ship running the American blockade is destroyed by the U.S. Navy. The Soviets retaliate by destroying a vital American military satellite. With tensions exploding and nervous fingers edging closer to the nuclear button, the American president orders American crew members to leave the Leonov vessel and return home via the retrieved Discovery ship.

Follow the plot so far? Well, get a grip your popcorn because this politically tinged space adventure is about to spin off into the twilight zone. The American crew leader encounters the spirit of Bowman, a crewman from the original 2001 mission. Bowman's spirit prevails on Dr. Floyd to stay with the mission. The American crew members defy the president's short-sighted orders and return to earth alongside their fellow Soviet space travelers. The success of the joint American-Soviet venture helps defuse tensions in the Caribbean. But it does not end there. The movie closes with a virtual lovefeast, as a divine message of peace and love, reminiscent of 1953's *Red Planet Mars*, is beamed to earth from Jupiter. In the wake of this sermon from the heavens, international trust and goodwill spread like the common cold.

New Yorker Peter Hyams directed the film for M-G-M United Artists. A former CBS news anchor and TV producer, Hyams based *2010* on Arthur C. Clarke's original novel. *2010* received an Oscar nomination for art direction. But peace was not yet selling, and *2010* made a loud thud as its unopened cans landed on the box-office floor. Doves would not have to wait very long for better movies making their case.

Heavy-Handed Themes

By the middle of the decade, Tinseltown had begun a "rocky" and somewhat confused decompression, gradually weaning it away from the iron-fisted movies of the early 1980s and toward far less belligerent films in the late eighties. But the time line dividing early from late eighties films is not solid. The 1985–86 period offers a transitional zone rather than a clear break. In 1985, for example, two favorable films, *2010* and *A View to a Kill*, were released. But in 1986 Hollywood took a few more kicks at the Soviet can.

Overall, however, the 1980s Russian-genre films divide roughly along a middecade watershed. Early eighties films are numerous, bellicose, and thematically clear. The distinction between the Soviet system and the Russian people, central to some earlier periods, vanishes. Part of a monolithic and aggressive system, Russians are portrayed as products of their environment—malevolent, potent, and active world revolutionaries. Love and marriage virtually disappear from Russian-genre movies of the early 1980s, as does religion. Practically all Russian characters in the critical films are one-dimensional violent males who abhor and usually threaten the American way of life. The message, incessant and crystal clear, implores defenders of freedom to remain ever vigilant against the evil Soviet system and its sinister people.

Negative films constitute celluloid manifestations of the evil empire rhetoric of the Reagan era. Just as that rhetoric made for good politics, it also created a booming cinematic economy. If the few movies that swam upstream won some critical acclaim, only the sock-it-to-them entries packed the movie houses, maintaining Rocky Balboa and Johnny Rambo as cultural icons and Sylvester Stallone as a megamillionaire.

Confident National Psyche

The American national psyche's profound mood swing—from halting, fragmented, and introspective self-doubt in the 1970s to an aggressive and efficacious *Weltansicht* of the early 1980s—can hardly be exaggerated. Whereas confusion, disillusionment, and guilt had characterized a weakly integrated psyche in the 1970s, suddenly the national mood turned clear, confident, self-righteous, and occasionally pugnacious. That such a large and diverse society can so frequently exhibit such fundamental shifts over such a short time seems noteworthy. That it can occur without any single cataclysmic event, like war, is incredible, particularly when contrasted to America's Cold War European, Canadian, or Japanese allies, who do not exhibit nearly such violent pendulumlike shifts.

In the early 1980s, this shift in the American psyche relates to the deeply felt desire of America's civic society to feel good about itself.

After the introspective self-doubt of the 1970s, it is not surprising that Americans should once again desire to stand tall. However, the degree to which so many, from the president to the movie moguls, turned an American need for national pride into an exercise in Russian bashing leaves us breathless.

Chapter Seven

1986–1991: Qualitative Transformation

The opening scene of Rick Rosenthal's *Russkies* (1987) serves up plenty of celluloid apple pie. Three preteens in Key West, Florida, sit around discussing the exploits of their Rambo-like comic-book superhero, Captain Slammer. Poring over the latest episode, "Captain Slammer and the Politburo of Death," the boys erupt with excitement as their red, white, and blue hero unleashes vengeance against his Soviet nemesis. Adam reads aloud, "Quick as a weasel the Russian pulled a three-bladed gutting knife from his boot, but he was no match for Slammer's bayonet. 'Eat Pennsylvania steel, borscht face!' grinned Slammer, as he opened the commissar like a ripe melon."

> *Adam*. Yeah!
> *Jason*. That's great!
> *Danny*. Cool, that's the best, right there!

But for the three boys, Captain Slammer is more than just comic-book escapist fiction. They are caught up in its simplistic message about good and evil in the world. The one thing Captain Slammer makes clear is that America is always good and the Soviet Union is always evil. When Danny stumbles across a book in Russian that someone has lost, he confidently explains the price paid for such a loss, "All I know is, whoever lost this is dead now. In Russia they don't give you a chance to explain yourself. They just kill you." Adam agrees. "In

Russia, if they [kids] don't like what their parents are doing, they just turn them in to the KGB. . . . put 'em to work in the mines of Siberia."

Their comic-book vision of the world gets put to the test when the three befriend a Soviet sailor, Mischa, who has been washed up on a local beach. In *Russkies*, the boys give the Russian a crash course on America. They play baseball, video games, miniature golf, and card games. They eat under McDonald's golden arches.

For his part, Mischa teaches the boys a little Russian as they sing traditional ballads over vodka. The Russian visitor even enters their family circles, and he interacts with warmth and caring. By the final scene in *Russkies* a sea change has swept over the boys. Captain Slammer's Russophobia gets replaced by friendship. As Mischa heads for home, the three boys hug their departing Soviet companion in a tearful farewell.

Adam. Will we ever see you again?
Mischa. I don't know. It is possible. But I take you home with me, in here. [*Pointing to his heart*] *Das vidanya, drugoi.* [*Good-bye, friend*]

The film ends, in one way, as it began—with Danny reading to the other boys. But this time it's not Captain Slammer. With Mischa's faded image lingering on the screen, Danny reads reverently from Leo Tolstoy's *War and Peace*:

It was time for Prince Vassily to go. And the comrades with whom he had campaigned so valiantly drew close. The sound of the weary men hung in the cold air, as the soldiers tended to their horses. The man they had come to call their friend smiled. "You must remember what I have done here today, and keep it close to your heart. There are those who may think it dishonorable, but I succeeded in uniting all parties. And besides, my idea is simple and clear: I say let those who love what is right join hands. And let our whole watchword be the action of virtue." Prince Vassily then nodded once to his company, and without another word, he turned and walked away.

The Equivalent of World War III

The attitudinal shifts experienced by Danny, Adam, and Jason did not occur in a social vacuum. Something bigger was going on in America. Between 1986 and 1991 an incredibly rapid and profound set of changes transformed the two world superpowers, first from enemies to adversaries, then, almost unbelievably, from adversaries to cautious allies. After forty years of Cold War, and with echoes of the militant Reagan message still ringing in America's ears, change occurred so quickly and so unexpectedly that the American mind-set had difficulty tracking the action.

The dissolution of the Cold War represented the last of three great transmutations redefining international relations in the twentieth century: the first, World War I, with its almost thirteen million deaths; the second, World War II and its astounding fifty-three million casualties; the third, the nearly bloodless collapse of the Soviet bloc in the late 1980s, which definitively ended the Cold War. Ending the Cold War set off waves that washed over global and regional relations for many years. Yet the cascading events that nullified Soviet communism and ended the Cold War were as unanticipated as they were rapid. Rather than shepherding these events into being, the United States found itself breathless just trying to keep up with the pace.

Another Time, Another Era

How could it have felt otherwise? In 1983–84 American-Soviet relations were at a twenty-year low. Who then could have foreseen a complete a recasting of the world order? But in only a few years, what was previously beyond imagination became history. With popular cold warrior Ronald Reagan again elected to the White House in 1984, one might be excused for not expecting a revolutionary shift in Soviet-American relations. But shift they did, and dramatically.

The only early signal of improvement was the disappearance of the shrill rhetoric previously characterizing the war of words between Washington and Moscow. In early 1984, leading up to the election, presidential speeches—probably more germane to defining American foreign policy under Ronald Reagan than any other recent president—became noticeably softer. While still not conciliatory, his statements lacked their earlier cutting edge. Asked if he still thought of the Soviet Union as an "evil empire," Reagan dismissed that phrase as germane to "another time, another era."[1]

Cautiously at first, the two superpowers edged closer to bilateral talks knowing that arms control would rank high on the agenda. Reagan claimed his intention all along had been to initiate arms negotiations "from strength." Now, he argued, since his arms buildup had succeeded in restoring American strength, he felt no hesitation in talking to the Soviets. But some scholars question whether the United States was appreciably stronger in 1985 than in 1981; they point instead to varied combinations of factors explaining American willingness to negotiate arms control with the Soviet Union.

Polls, for example, identified the "peace issue" as Reagan's Achilles heel in his 1984 campaign against Walter Mondale, even among many Republican voters. Whether his talk of negotiations was ingenuous or not, Reagan certainly found it politically advantageous to wave an olive branch, even if, as he intimated, it was gripped firmly by an iron fist. Reagan's dovish words (as dovish as he could make them) also brought applause from previous critics. America's European allies and congressional leaders joined the chorus of voices supporting bilateral negotiation on arms control. Could it be that Reagan was trading in his Rambo fatigues for the three-piece suit of a statesman?[2]

Reagan's arms control talk scored political points, but it might all have come to nothing—and Reagan might have expected it to come to nothing—if the Soviets did not reciprocate. But shortly after Reagan's reelection, Moscow responded in a fashion that was positive beyond anyone's wildest expectation. Much of the credit goes to Mikhail Sergeiivich Gorbachev, the unprecedented Soviet leader who took control of the Kremlin within weeks of Reagan's 1985 inauguration. Gorbachev, then little known to any but a few Kremlin watchers, had no previous track record indicating that he might completely shake up both the Soviet Union and the international community. But he did. No sooner had Gorbachev taken power than he began firing off arms control proposals to Washington. The air crackled with enough electricity to energize a global transformation.

Four Visible Summits

After calming his rhetoric with talk of arms negotiations, the president surprised many by beginning his second term with the announcement that he intended to meet Soviet leaders. This was no perfunctory announcement. Reagan was the only first-term president in the postwar era not to have met his Soviet counterpart—a distinction he had previously worn as a badge of honor. But during his second term, not only did he meet his Soviet counterpart, Gorbachev, he met him in four dramatic summits. Each summit marked an advance toward an unprecedented Soviet-American relationship.[3]

The first summit, held in Geneva in November 1985, was esentially a photo opportunity aimed at breaking the ice. Amid popping flash bulbs, Gorbachev managed to raise specific proposals relating to the Strategic Defense Initiative, nuclear testing, and SALT II. Reagan, still feeling his way along a darkly lit corridor and not quite convinced of the Soviet change of heart, heeded the advice of his hawkish secretary of defense Caspar Weinberger to create the impression of negotiating without engaging substantive issues. Reagan deflected the Soviet leader's proposals and no concrete accomplishments emerged from the Geneva summit. Public pressure might bring Reagan to the table; it could not compel him to negotiate until he decided that he was ready.[4]

But if Geneva brought no breakthrough, it was pregnant with enough symbolic meaning for historian Robert Daniels to argue unequivocally that Geneva represented "the turnabout recognized as the end of the Cold War."[5] Here was President Reagan, the "great communicator" and former movie star, encountering the Politburo's first public relations sophisticate. Gorbachev, playing to the Western media, actually out-Reaganed Reagan. Unlike the cold and gray presence that had come to symbolize Soviet diplomacy, a warm and smiling Gorbachev waded into crowds of onlookers like a grassroots politician on the stump. Everywhere he extended the hand of friendship. Enthusiastic crowds responded with spontaneous goodwill. Gorbachev also made a "deep and lasting impression on the image of the Soviet Union in the United States." Americans were swept up by the televised images of a charismatic Russian who hardly looked like the leader of an enemy state. They felt equally reassured by pictures of Reagan and Gorbachev sitting next to a glowing fireplace and chatting like old friends. Americans wanted more of Gorbachev.[6]

Less than a year later, a second meeting in Reykjavik, Iceland, became one of the most bizarre chapters in superpower summitry. This summit almost did not occur. On 23 August 1986, a Soviet scientist on the United Nations staff in New York, Gennady Zakharov, was arrested by the FBI and charged with espionage. In retaliation, the KGB arrested American correspondent Nicholas Daniloff in Moscow and charged him with spying. As tempers flared, it seemed the planned summit might be called off. It took personal intercession by both Reagan and Gorbachev to defuse this minicrisis. With a quick deal cooked over the two "spies," the Reykjavik meeting proceeded.

Nobody knew quite what this summit would bring. In retrospect, few could believe what actually did transpire. Dubbed the "slapdash summit," Reykjavik is remembered as a most unusual affair, beyond expectation and beyond imagination.[7] As in Geneva, Gorbachev arrived loaded down with sweeping arms control proposals, including reversals of Soviet positions held tenaciously for decades. Everything seemed to be on the table at one time. Facing a smorgasbord of proposals, President Reagan sampled a little here and a little there. He even got caught up in a "bout of feverish one-upmanship" and offered some sweeping proposals of his own. As if attending a Pugwash Conference rather than an East-West summit, each seemed intent on outdoing the other in proposing avenues averting traditional barriers to disarmament. In private, the two leaders toyed with breathtaking proposals, violating all rules of the negotiating game in the process.[8]

What essentially did Gorbachev lay out at Reykjavik? The "grand compromise": deep cuts in ICBMs, where the Soviets had a big advantage, in return for American flexibility on the Strategic Defense Initiative. When Reagan's loyalty to SDI scuttled this proposal, Gorbachev countered with a bold plan to abolish all nuclear weapons by the year 2000. The president initially responded, "That suits me fine," then equivocated, recognizing that abolition of nuclear arms would play to Soviet conventional arms advantages.[9]

In the end Reagan's refusal to bend on SDI prevented an agreement. After plenty of excitement, but without any solid deal to take home, both sides pointed the finger of blame at the other. But if no concrete deal was signed, sealed, and delivered in Iceland, a breakthrough as important for the long run as Geneva occurred. What had been laid out on the table for discussion—for serious discussion—mattered greatly. Reykjavik kicked open the door to arms reduction as never before. Anxious to determine the limits of possibility, both sides agreed to press ahead with lower-level arms talks.

To the great surprise of many doubters, the talks succeeded. Given the typically slow pace of international talks, these discussions also succeeded in what seemed like a flash. At the Washington summit in December of 1987, amid dizzying public adulation for the media-friendly Gorbachev, adulation more like that reserved for a movie star than a politician (let alone a Soviet politician), Reagan and Gorbachev signed a major arms agreement. The historic Intermediate Nuclear Forces (INF) treaty eliminated an entire class of weapons from the European theater. It provided on-site inspection—something the Soviets had previously refused to consider. While the banished INF Euro-missiles constituted only 4 percent of the nearly seventeen trillion tons of nuclear TNT equivalency the superpowers held between them, the treaty had great political value, contributing momentum to still more far-reaching reductions in the Bush era.

The fourth Reagan-Gorbachev summit, held in Moscow during May of 1988, came at the tail end of Reagan's presidency. It brought no new arms agreements, but its importance should not be minimized. Against a backdrop of expanding Soviet-American dialogue on a wide range of issues, including the wholesale "liberalization" then under way in Soviet-controlled eastern Europe, both Reagan and Gorbachev milked the Moscow meeting for all its psychological value.

Who could believe it? There was Ronald Reagan, hawk turned dove, strolling in Red Square with Gorbachev and bouncing babies on his knee in the spring sunshine. Reagan, the president who had once joked about an image of bombing the Soviet Union out of existence, had become more than the revisionist of his first term's rhetoric—he had broken ranks with the geostrategic codes of America's previous five presidents. If Reagan's first term contributed to a new Cold War atmosphere, here he was five years later taking his cue from his Russian host and demonstrating the flexibility of mind necessary to keep pace with changing realities.

Such great changes beg analysis. At the time, Reagan's supporters trumpeted the success of American might, talking of Soviet concessions to America's military buildup of the early eighties. Unable to match American military advances, they argued, Moscow tossed in the towel. Reagan's detractors disagreed. They pointed to internal Soviet political, economic, and social forces as causing *novoe myshlenie*— Soviet "new thinking" in foreign policy. A new Soviet leadership sought a new path for mostly domestic reasons.

Several less discussed factors also suggest themselves. By 1987–88, the notorious Iran-Contra scandal threatened Reagan's presidency. Perhaps only a grand achievement, like arms control, could deflect press scrutiny from illicit missile sales to Iran and subsequent clandestine support of the Nicaraguan Contras. What is more, like Franklin Roosevelt in the 1940s and Richard Nixon in the 1970s, Reagan believed deeply in personal diplomacy. Like these predecessors, Reagan saw himself as a statesmen capable of the implausible breakthrough eluding lower-echelon bureaucrats. The star of so many Hollywood movies was prepared to act the role of statesman, if that was what the revised script required. Since he was certainly no stranger to storybook endings, why not a storybook ending to his own presidency?

Journalists and memoir-writers have also made much of Nancy Reagan's campaign to consider Ronald Reagan a great peacemaker. Just as it had been ironic in 1972 for cold warrior Richard Nixon to initiate detente with both Beijing and Moscow, the transformation in American-Soviet relations during Reagan's second term seemed oddly counterintuitive. However, it was precisely the Cold War credentials of Nixon or Reagan that made their breakthroughs palatable to much of the American public. Who else in 1986 could seduce conservatives into accepting accommodation with Moscow, let alone considering a major disarmament initiative, if not their own Ronald Reagan.

There were also other pressures on Reagan to make a deal with the Soviets. Keeping a military leg up on the Soviet Union cost money, maybe too much money. For a president who campaigned on reducing federal spending, it had to be embarrassing that the federal deficit ballooned on his watch from one trillion dollars in 1980 to 2.5 trillion dollars in 1988. Clearly, any "peace dividend" would represent the least painful solution to the expanding federal deficit.

Finally, Soviet concessions and accommodations were of a winning nature. They were so capitulatory that even a skeptical and ideological president like Reagan could not just say no to many of the gems gift wrapped by Gorbachev and his foreign minister, Eduard Shevardnadze. And what of the Soviets? What was in it for them? Most importantly, the Soviet economy was running down more rapidly than CIA intelligence suggested. It needed reform at home and investment from abroad in order to reinvent itself. A key part of that strategy required unloading the arms race and courting Western capital in hopes of meeting the challenge of technological change—a challenge emanating as much from the silicon valleys of Japan and a rapidly unifying western Europe as from the United States.

And what of the American national psyche? It has generally been overlooked as a factor in the emergence of a qualitatively new superpower relationship in the late 1980s. The American mind-set had been defensive, in a negative and aggressive mood, in the early 1980s. It the aftermath of Vietnam, the Iran hostage crisis, and the killing of Marines in Beirut, America had something to prove to itself and the world, and it acted on this need in an agitated manner. Its emotional condition sucked America back into the vortex of the acute Cold War, although in a somewhat milder form.

Increasingly after middecade, the American mood sensed less of a need to prove itself. America felt calm, confident, prosperous, even euphoric. A changing world seemed to vindicate America's values and social institutions. No longer fearing an internecine enemy and shedding earlier worries about threats to its survival, the new optimism fed a naive desire to accept pronouncements like Francis Fukuyama's "end of history." As Soviet concessions piled up on the negotiating table, Fukuyama declared Western liberal democracy the victor in *the* ideological battle of the century: America and its allies had been right all along.

The entire political spectrum—liberals, conservatives, and moderates—found something in the "end of history" to feel good about, making Fukuyama's piece extremely enticing. The American psyche, better integrated than in its previously fragmented and agitated state, felt secure, affluent, content, and tolerant. Given this mood of renewed confidence, America found it possible to play Let's Make a Deal. As the avowed victor, America felt generous and forgiving toward the defeated.[10]

Bush's Cautious Approach

George Bush, elected in a 1988 campaign when foreign policy issues played but a minor role, pledged to follow the Reagan lead. Exactly what that meant Bush did not explain and few asked. Bush appeared well credentialed in foreign affairs, although he had little policy-making experience of his own. If he did not have a track record on Soviet issues, neither he did he have to live down any Reagan-like record of tough-sounding Soviet bashing. And when it came to the Soviet Union, Bush inherited an improving picture of more positive and cooperative relations. Indeed, if Reagan had been lucky in the Russian hand that he finally drew, the "greatest political windfall in the history of American foreign policy fell into George Bush's lap"—the sudden collapse of communism in eastern Europe.[11]

But Bush was slow in warming to the new Russians. Like many of his advisers, the new president harbored deep-seated reservations about the Soviet Union, its leaders, and its agenda. If he welcomed conciliatory Soviet overtures, he also worried about Gorbachev's ability to deliver depending on his ability to hold onto power, which remained anybody's guess. The vexing question about what role the United States should play in furthering reform in the Soviet Union was one that Bush was not ready to address. Rather unlike Reagan, who recognized a good deal when it was presented to him, Bush took longer to convince. Initiatives almost all came from Moscow. Bush was reactive and, if he eventually came around, his instinct was to react slowly and cautiously.[12]

Like Reagan, Bush held a series of summits with his Soviet counterpart. Economic relations were addressed at his first summit with Gorbachev at Malta in December 1989. At a November 1990 meeting in Paris, Bush and Gorbachev agreed on a reunified Germany to remain in NATO, and they signed an important treaty reducing conventional forces in Europe (CFE treaty). The Soviets also agreed to highly asymmetrical force reductions vis-a-vis the Americans in the CFE treaty.

In spite of such advances in arms control and international security, President Bush faced criticism for his cautious approach in supporting Gorbachev's *perestroika*, particularly the relatively small amount of financial support the United States provided for reform of the Soviet economy. By the end of Bush's term, he had pledged assistance amounting to less than 10 percent of what Germany had promised to Russia, even though Germany was in the midst of spending the equivalent of one hundred billion dollars to meet the costs of its own unification.

Even Richard Nixon joined the public chorus of boos. But George Bush, like most American presidents, dared not pull out too far in front of American public opinion, and there was no significant American constituency demanding massive aid to the Soviets. In addition to Bush's cautious disposition, his appointment of three veteran advisers on Soviet affairs from the Ford administration who had "experienced the crumbling of detente," dampened any hope that the United States would take a lead role in assisting the Soviet Union.[13]

Although financial aid was in short supply, the flood of bilateral agreements continued unabated. At a superpower summit in Washington (31 May–3 June 1990), an incredible sixteen agreements were reached on trade, nuclear testing, chemical weapons, cultural exchanges, maritime boundaries, and long-term grain agreements. The crowning glory of the July 1991 Moscow summit was the signing of the START treaty reducing American nuclear weapons by 20 percent and Soviet nuclear weapons by 35 percent. It represented the culmination of a long process emanating from the SALT II treaty of 1979.

As George Bush's presidency wound down, so did the Soviet Union. The Communist Party machine that had ruled the state for seventy-four years disintegrated. Soviet satellites in eastern Europe cast off almost five decades of Soviet control. Racked by divisive ethnic conflicts, the last of the world's great empires came unglued. The Baltic republics and the Ukraine negotiated their independence, and other republics moved to exit from the Soviet state.

In a last-ditch effort to prevent a Union treaty from formalizing the breakup of the Soviet Union, hard-line forces in the KGB, old guard Communist Party backers, and a rump of disgruntled military officers attempted a coup in August 1991. It failed miserably, but the collapse of the putsch only precipitated a more rapid dissolution of the Soviet Union. Gorbachev's failure to comprehend the profound changes that occurred during his miniexile exposed him as a hopeless anachronism. His futile efforts to turn the ship of state around came too late to prevent it from floundering on the rocks and breaking apart. On 8 December 1991 an ill-defined and amorphous association of independent states, the Commonwealth of Independent States (CIS), was announced. Mikhail Gorbachev resigned on Christmas Day. The Kremlin's hammer and sickle flag was lowered for the last time, taking the Soviet Union and the Cold War with it.

Less Than Wonderful Cinematic Russians

The pace of changing Soviet-American relations was so breathtakingly fast that Americans found it hard to keep up. Hollywood was no exception. A few movies of the late 1980s, especially those that had been on the drawing board for some time, took leads from profitable Soviet-bashing movies produced early in the decade. They continued using Russians as their bogeymen. But these films, out of step with the new public mood, had little of the mass appeal of their earlier versions.

Movies that probably would have packed theaters a few years earlier, lost money.

The sudden new reality forced Hollywood to play catchup ball. Many Russian-genre films began to wrestle with the nature and meaning of the new American-Soviet relationship. Most of these films, however, proved as cautious as George Bush in embracing the new Soviet Union. Perhaps Hollywood did not have a ready replacement for the stock Russian bad guys whom moviegoers so loved to hate only a few years earlier. Possibly Tinseltown feared being caught short by any anti-Soviet backlash that might erupt if the new relationship turned sour. Hollywood gave its blessing to the bloodless Soviet revolution of the late 1980s, but not as enthusiastically as some might have expected.

Rambo III

No film of the late 1980s swam against the tide of improving international relations as vigorously as *Rambo III* (1988). Recycling the formulaic pattern of unrestrained anti-Soviet violence, the hallmark of Sylvester Stallone's early 1980s films, *Rambo III* cost $63 million to film, making it the most expensive picture as of 1988.[14] It was a bad investment. Symptomatic of a shifting American mood, the movie lost money (its rentals of only $28,509,000 are 142d for 1980s films).[15]

The setting of Stallone's *Rambo III* differs from his earlier major anti-Russian movies, *Rocky IV* (1985) and *Rambo: First Blood, Part II* (1985). Otherwise, they remain thematic fist-in-the-face soulmates. This time Johnny Rambo's muscular spirit of individualism does battle with a faceless, collectivist horde of techno-Soviets in Afghanistan.

What brought Johnny Rambo into conflict with Russian forces in Afghanistan during 1988? Wasn't that when the Soviets began withdrawing after nine years and fifteen thousand casualties? Wasn't *Rambo III* released mere weeks before the final Reagan-Gorbachev summit in Moscow? Yes and yes. But for Johnny Rambo personal loyalties come before international relations. He refused to sit idly by while the Russians held his military mentor, Colonel Sam Trautman (Richard Crenna), prisoner in the Afghan desert. After all, he had gone into Vietnam after American POWs in *Rambo II* against the orders of State Department mandarins. And, indeed, nothing less than personal loyalty to a friend could draw Rambo out of his semiretirement in, of all things, a Buddhist monastery in Thailand.

Rambo III's theme song, "He Ain't Heavy, He's My Brother," speaks for Johnny's relationship with Sam Trautman. The moment Rambo learns that the Soviets have captured Colonel Trautman, he puts aside his robes and spiritual mantra for the rigid face of the primal warrior. All the Russians are in for it now, but none more than Trautman's captor and prime torturer, Soviet base commander Colonel Zaysen (Marc deJonge). One critic described the portrayal of Colonel Zaysen as "a ludicrous Cold War stereotype—the Soviet as gibbering sadist."[16] Unshaven and uncivilized, this sadistic ideologue knows no limits as he tortures Trautman for information about Stinger missiles being supplied to Mujahedin freedom fighters.

But forget the thimble-sized plot. Missiles, Trautman, Afghanistan— all exist as mere pretext for carnage as Rambo exacts revenge on Zaysen and any other Russians at whom he can point a weapon. The final showdown features duelling Hind helicopters, with Johnny using the Soviets' own technology to sock it to his nemesis, Zaysen.

Like its predecessor, *Rambo III* consists mostly of action scenes, stunts, and expensive pyrotechnics. Although *Rambo III* was the directing debut of Peter MacDonald, he probably received all the training he needed in cinematic mayhem as second unit man on *First Blood, Part II* (1985). As one critic suggests, in films like *Rambo III* "directing is closer to engineering than to art."[17] The screenplay for *Rambo III* was written by Stallone and Sheldon Lettich, and they did not include much dialogue. In a film with only twenty-three speaking roles, forty-nine stuntpeople appear. Rambo speaks not a word during his first fifteen minutes on screen. Comic-book imagery and lethality combine to obviate the need for verbal communication. As one critic noted, "Not counting grunts and groans, the star collected about $500,000 [in salary] per spoken sentence on this film."[18]

Superman IV: The Quest for Peace

While Stallone may have been paid handsomely for starring in *Rambo III*, the movie was a financial flop. It seemed hopelessly out of step with the overall drift of Hollywood's Russian-genre films in the late 1980s. If these films were not all favorable in their portrait of the Soviet Union or Russians, very few presented villainous screen Russians like the one-dimensional characters in *Rambo III*. Many mass-market films conveyed positive depictions of Russians.

Superman IV: The Quest for Peace (1987) opens with an amicable cosmonaut, Mischa (Eugene Lipinski), singing a Russian translation of the Frank Sinatra hit, "I Did It My Way." This space concert is suddenly interrupted by an errant satellite that knocks cosmonaut Mischa and his crew into open space, with their sputnik reeling uncontrollably into peril. Just as it appears all is lost, Superman (Christopher Reeve) arrives to put the Soviet spacecraft back into its correct orbit. To the astonishment of the grateful cosmonauts, the caped hero is all smiles as he chats with them in Russian before flying off on other business. This moment of cinematic Soviet-American friendship conveys the kind of trust that was so pervasive in the World War II pictures. And that's not all. Later in the film, Superman saves the Russian leadership, meeting in the Kremlin, from a missile aimed at them. If an otherwise busy Superman prioritizes the rescue of Soviet cosmonauts and Kremlin leaders, something new is obviously brewing in American popular culture.

Superman is at the cutting edge of new thinking in international relations, even ahead of the American president. According to the plot of *Superman IV*, superpower tensions over a spiraling arms race escalate after a failed summit meeting and a tough-sounding speech by the American president mobilizing American forces. Nuclear panic spreads like jam on toast. In a desperate plea for survival, a young boy begs Superman to use his powers to prevent nuclear war. It is all déjà vu for the man of steel. He knows how a similar crisis destroyed his home planet, Krypton, and how only he, still an infant, was saved by his quick-thinking parents launching their baby on a journey to a distant planet in a distant solar system—Earth. Superman dares not let it happen again.

Superman first visits the United Nations in hopes of finding a quick solution to the crisis. Finding only diplomatic bickering, he takes the podium of the General Assembly and announces to world leaders that he will do what their governments cannot do: rid the world of nuclear weapons. Implementing the ultimate zero option, he gathers all the world's nuclear weapons and dramatically hurls them at the sun, where they explode harmlessly. Earth gets the second chance that Krypton never had.

The one-world message of *Superman IV* paints militarism in general, and nuclear weapons in particular, as humanity's nemesis. In a few "fashionable nods towards *glasnost*," the Russians appear as America's covictims in the nuclear dilemma.[19] Adding drama to Superman's antinuclear effort, we soon discover that not everyone favors Superman's earth-saving efforts. Gene Hackman again plays Superman's resourceful enemy, Lex Luthor, who feeds on profits from the arms race and unsuccessfully challenges peacemaker Superman with his solar-powered marvel, Nuclear Man (Mark Pillow). But Superman again outwits Lex Luthor, outfights his creation, and pulls the world back from the edge of nuclear self-destruction.

Superman IV represented a sharp departure from other films in the Superman series in that it dealt with global issues. One film critic considered the subject such a natural as to wonder aloud why Superman had never before "looked at the big picture."[20] Actor Christopher Reeve wrote the story, which was adapted by screenwriters Lawrence Konner and Mark Rosenthal and was directed by Canadian-born Sidney J. Furie for Cannon.

Russkies

Russkies (1987), another film reflecting the more positive spirit of the day, was directed by Rick Rosenthal from a screenplay by Alan Jay Glueckman, Sheldon Lettich, and Michael Nankin. The movie opens with much less American-Russian comity than *Superman IV*. Danny, Adam, and Jason are young military offspring who parrot the bellicose anti-Soviet line of their Rambo-like comic-book hero "Captain Slammer." This hard-as-nails attitude changes quickly when the boys become enmeshed in the life of a good-natured Russian sailor, Mikhail Alexandrovich Pushkin (Mischa), whose raft has capsized near the Florida Keys. Mischa (Whip Hubley) was originally sent to the United States to smuggle out a stolen defense weapon, but the mission is quickly forgotten in this highly personalized post-Cold War ode to empathy.

The critic for the *New York Times* described *Russkies* as capturing "all the dopey, daffy, dizzy fun of glasnost."[21] Like the 1966 picture *The Russians Are Coming, The Russians Are Coming*, initial paranoia in *Russkies* gives way to a sense of trust as the wise Mischa and his three young American friends give Soviet-American relations a Disneyesque spin. Mischa offers the boys a one-on-one level of sincerity and openness that wins over both the boys and the movie audience. How do they reciprocate? They respond in kind by giving him a whirlwind tour of the shopping center and a flag-waving Fourth of July celebration in Key West. Mischa is taken with the simple, homespun, everyday American pleasures that so many Americans take for granted—basketball, hamburgers, video games. Awash in Norman Rockwell's America, Mischa gushes at one point that "America takes such big bite of life! Such color! Such freedom!"

As if mirroring American-Soviet relations of the day, the bonding of Mischa and his new American friends grows fast and firm. The boys even prove their loyalty under fire, saving Mischa from a certain beating by the local bully. The "big glasnost test," however, is passed when Danny's Russian-hating army father accepts Mischa, even though occupying Russians had shot his own father during the 1956 Hungarian uprising.[22] The syrupy plot about hands across the international divide gets yet another boost from Mischa's infatuation with Adam's attractive older sister, Diane (Susan Walters). Mischa returns the boys' trust in him when he saves one of their lives. Finally, it's tears and hugs all around as Mischa takes his leave of the boys and heads for home (sans the secret American weapon, of course).

In some ways Mischa is reminiscent of the likable and handsome young sailor Alexei Kolchin in *The Russians Are Coming, The Russians Are Coming* (1966). But Mischa provides more than Kolchin. Mischa gives his three young friends an opportunity to transcend their prejudices and to affirm in themselves what is best in America: the simple human pleasures that come with caring.

Red Heat

While *Superman IV* and *Russkies* were wholly nonviolent in celebrating the new East-West understanding, *Red Heat* (1988) was not. Its nod in the direction of Soviet-American cooperation reworks a well-worn Hollywood formula as *"glasnost's* first police buddy movie."[23] Endless variations of the police-buddy motif exist, but all share a common element: bringing together antithetical forces. Los Angeles-born Walter Hill, who directed and cowrote the screenplay for *Red Heat*, brought extensive police-buddy credentials to the set. In fact, one critic considers him to have "more or less reinvented this genre with *48 Hours* (1982)."[24]

In *Red Heat*, Hill brings together a most unlikely pair—Moscow's top homicide detective, Ivan Danko (Arnold Schwarzenegger), and his earthy Chicago counterpart, Art Ridzik (Jim Belushi). The puritanical Ivan could not be more opposite to Art's unkempt self-indulgence. Where Ivan is sullen and tight-lipped, Art is expressive and wisecracking; while Ivan treats his body like a cathedral of physical culture, Art treats his like a Pizza Hut; totally single-minded in the line of duty, Ivan contrasts with the easily distracted Ridzik. A critic marvels at the imposing presence of Ivan Danko: "with jaw squared and face straight, he moves through the plot with the serenity of a battleship pushing its way through a fleet of sailboats."[25] With Art, a shopping cart in a crowded supermarket seems descriptive.

Their seeming incompatibility gradually vanishes as they push deeper into a joint investigation in which their skills complement one another. The quarry of their hunt? A notorious Soviet drug dealer whom Ivan has come to Chicago to extradite. But the drug dealer has escaped custody, forcing the *glasnost* cops to put aside their personal reservations about one another in an effort to retrieve him.

Red Heat represents the rare Hollywood film in which the distinction between "Soviet" and "Russian" is meaningful. Ivan Danko, the best that Russian culture has to offer, contrasts sharply with the evil drug dealer, Viktor Rostavili, neither a Russian nor Slav. Rostavili is a Soviet Georgian.[26] As well as being a Soviet Georgian, Rostavili is also a cop killer, a rapist, a kidnapper, and a drug dealer. His appearance is as evil as his behavior. One film critic calls him a "Georgian tough guy who's like a rabid dog with a five o'clock shadow."[27] Ugly and sadistic, Rostavili even delights in double-crossing his partners in crime. While few American moviegoers would notice it, the reprehensible Rostavili further insults Georgians by adopting the name of their most revered thirteenth-century poet and folk hero.[28]

The alliance of Art Ridzik and Ivan Danko against Rostavili amounts to an alliance of the first and second worlds against the Third World. The personal differences between Ivan the Russian and Art the American, so jarring at first, later seem trivial compared to the primal cultural and racial bonds uniting them under pressure. Despite different styles and backgrounds, they act as one against the drug-dealing, noncaucasian, and nearly subhuman Rostavili. In tracking Rostavili, the two officers bond to resemble twin pit bulls on a rampage, destroying property and killing off Rostavili's confederates in familiar Hollywood style.

As opposed to Georgians like Rostavili, the Russians in *Red Heat* are slow to anger, but once they are roused, the Rostavilis of this world had better watch out. In the main, however, Russians are clean and decent folk, easy for middle America to identify with and laugh with. Reflecting curiosity as well as simply making conversation, Art Ridzik's superior officer asks Ivan Danko, "Look, since I figure cops are cops the world over—how do you Soviets deal with all the tension and stress?" Ivan Danko's deadpan reply: "Vodka." Humor, often grounded in cultural and political differences, characterizes the repartee between Danko and Ridzik. At one point Ridzik momentarily cuts into a conversation to point out that Danko is about to park in a forbidden red zone, then sheepishly turns to Danko with a smile and apologizes, "No offense."

Good-natured kidding built on mutual trust contrasts with their attitude toward the Georgians, who are dismissed as barely civilized Bohemian degenerates and lurid objects of derision. And in the inevitably violent showdown, the Georgians show no mercy and certainly receive none.

As the first American movie partly filmed in Moscow, *Red Heat* signaled important changes. But not everyone believed the coziness of the two lead characters made dramatic sense. One critic bemoaned the movie's homogenization of the Russian and American detectives as not only unrealistic but unnecessary as well, noting that "people need not be alike to be friends."[29] She has a point. But the very idea that

Hollywood would erase screen differences between an American and a Russian and that American audiences would cheer their bonding underscores the profound shift in public perceptions.

Less Noticed Favorable Films

The violence that laces *Red Heat* remains something of an exception to the rule in the era's favorable movies. More typical was the nonviolence of *Superman IV: The Quest for Peace*, *Russkies*, and several other lesser-known films in the genre, including *Amazing Grace and Chuck* (1987). In *Amazing Grace and Chuck*, Chuck Murdock, a twelve-year-old Montana boy, returns home from a school visit to a local missile silo. Rather than being swept up by modern warfare's glistening technology, Chuck (Joshua Zuehike) feels distraught over the destructive potential of the weapons he has seen.

Moved to act against nuclear madness, he vows not to pitch for his Little League baseball team until nuclear weapons are abolished. At first ridiculed, his personal campaign gains momentum when Boston Celtics basketball star "Amazing Grace" Smith (Alex English) decides to join young Chuck Murdock's grassroots effort. Suddenly, public personalities on both sides of the Iron Curtain fall over one another in a race to endorse Chuck's peaceful populism. Politicians everywhere feel the public heat as Chuck comes to symbolize humanity's desire to eliminate the nuclear threat.

The Soviet general secretary (William L. Petersen) becomes one of Chuck Murdock's biggest cheerleaders, both on and off the field. A rotund, sincere, and pensive leader—hardly the ruler of an evil empire—he too gets caught up in the spirit of the moment by extending a hand to the American president in a good-faith effort to realize Chuck's dream of nuclear disarmament. When real progress is announced, Chuck declares he will resume pitching for his Little League team. Stretching credulity like a rubberband, the Russian leader travels to Montana so he can sit in the stands cheering on the young peacemaker/pitcher.

For *Amazing Grace and Chuck* to work only five years after Hollywood's incessant Russian bashing is yet another symptom of a national mood swing. That swing was encouraged by communications mogul Ted Turner, who financed this film as part of a long string of personal efforts promoting international understanding. Written and produced by David Field, *Amazing Grace and Chuck* was directed for Tri-Star/Rastar by Mike Newell, whose career would later peak with *Four Weddings and a Funeral* (1994). Newell's melodramatic "one world" theme in *Amazing Grace and Chuck* cushions some of the plot's

absurdity. Hindsight suggests that the new world of regular and amicable meetings between Reagan and Gorbachev probably contributed
to an "anything's possible" public mind-set.

Post-Cold War celluloid amity strikes again in *Company Business*
(1991), written and directed by Nicholas Meyer. Trust and teamwork
come packaged in another East-West "buddy movie," this time about
spies, not cops. But *Company Business* throbs with a lighter touch than
Red Heat. Gene Hackman plays a maverick former CIA operative
named Sam Boyd, another of those spies called out of retirement by
the Company, this time to handle a supposedly simple spy swap in
Berlin.

Sam's preassignment briefing explains the planned exchange as rou-
tine. As his boss acknowledges in passing, "We do a lot of business
with the KGB these days." In one respect, Sam is told, the swap is noteworthy. An important congressional committee has been critical of the
CIA, and the Company needs to put itself in a good light by trading a
spy held by the Americans for an important American prisoner, a U-2
pilot in Soviet custody. Sam is to deliver the Russian spy and two million dollars to sweeten the deal in Berlin. In return, he brings the U-2
pilot home.

Sam Boyd's cargo, Russian spy Piotr Grushenko (Mikhail
Baryshnikov), has languished in a South Dakota prison for ten years.
Seeming opposites, the two men make the best of the time they are
forced to spend together and, wouldn't you know it, like ballplayers on
competing teams, they gradually develop an unspoken respect for one
another. The two men talk trade like old comrades in arms as they get
drunk together in Berlin on Grushenko's favorite vodka (Starka). They
may back rival teams, but they share professional interests, including
disdain for the headquartered desk jockeys who know nothing of the
dangers faced by agents in the field.

Yet all is not as it seems, and the two agents begin to smell something rotten. Could the spy swap be a cover for a larger operation in
which they serve as the bait? Their suspicion turns to distrust of their
superiors, as well as mistrust of the Cold War's assumptions. Mocking
American knee-jerk paranoia, Grushenko tries to update America's
fears: "The Russians are coming, the Russians are coming; the
Japanese are already here. They own half of your fucking country!"

When it comes time for the Berlin deal, Sam and Grushenko find
their worst fears are true. They are being sold down the river by CIA
hard-liners seeking to rekindle Soviet-American enmities. When the
CIA tries to blow them up, the two agents form their own alliance and
outwit the Company, escaping with the two million dollars into comfortable retirement in the Seychelles Islands.

The same kind of team-building exercise shapes *Iron Eagle II* (1988), except on a larger scale. This time we have American and Soviet misfit fighter pilots welded together into one tough unit under the leadership of General Chappy Sinclair, played energetically by Lou Gossett Jr. In the first third of *Iron Eagle II*, suspicious American and Soviet squadron members circle one another, prodding and testing for weaknesses as if to suggest they will never meld into a cohesive force. But eventually the no-nonsense paternal presence of Chappy Sinclair whipped the two groups into a fighting machine. A budding love affair between female Russian pilot Valeri (Sharon Brandon) and ace American pilot Cooper (Mark Humphrey) does not hurt the process either.

It is the danger of the team's mission that finally bonds Soviets and Americans together under fire. A fictitious Middle Eastern country given to international adventurism and support for terrorism (read Libya) is about to realize its nuclear dream. Even worse, its irresponsible leader is reportedly itching to use his newfound nuclear toys. The combined Soviet-American mission: destroy his nuclear capability. Amid screeching jets and desert explosions, Chappy Sinclair's unit succeeds. Just as importantly, in the heat of combat, yesterday's enemies become today's battle-tested allies and tomorrow's friends. A critic captured the intent of *Iron Eagle II* as "*glasnost* at 30,000 feet."[30] Sidney J. Furie, of *Superman IV* fame, again writes and directs a pro-Russian picture.

The premise for *Red King, White Knight* (1989), another favorable film, is built around an American agent saving Mikhail Gorbachev from an assassination plot. Art anticipates reality as reactionary elements within the Soviet Union, including the KGB, reject the Gorbachev reforms and plot a coup d'etat. Unlike the bungled putsch that Gorbachev would face a year or two after release of *Red King, White Knight*, Hollywood's conspiracy is sophisticated and intricate, arranging to murder the general secretary, the Red King, while he is on a state visit to a neighboring Soviet satellite country.

The CIA, intercepting secret transmissions about the conspiracy, sends an agent into eastern Europe to verify the information. The person selected is Stoner (Tom Skerritt), the White Knight, and still another on the long list of retired agents lured back for one last mission. At Stoner's CIA briefing he is cautioned that "everything's changing. The Soviets are the good guys now." With that, he sets off for Europe where he pieces together the details of Gorbachev's planned assassination.

Stoner sends his information back to the CIA and expects his superiors to warn Gorbachev. To Stoner's consternation, the CIA schemers want to keep the Cold War pot bubbling and decide not to interfere with the assassination attempt. They even cut the president out of the information loop. But what about Stoner? He knows too much, and his CIA bosses decide to target their own agent.

The CIA's scheming goes wrong when a brave junior analyst, repulsed by the agency's short-sighted decision, leaks word of the pending assassination attempt to the president. He immediately informs Secretary Gorbachev, who revises his itinerary. But the cagey KGB plotters have anticipated just such a contingency. Now only American agent Stoner, himself on the CIA's hit list, can save Gorbachev from a paid assassin's bullet. With the help of another retired spy, this time a former eastern European adversary, Stoner saves Gorbachev, only to die heroically in the process.

What message does *Red King, White Knight* deliver? Optimism. While reactionary interests on both sides may cling to Cold War hostility and attempt to nip Soviet-American rapprochement in the bud, the new cooperative spirit must be protected and allowed to flower. The Soviet transition to a post-Cold War state may be a bit ragged around the edges, but the transition is on the right track. Given half a chance, the Soviet Union might just turn into something like a liberal democracy with a market economy. Gorbachev, as well as other progressive elements in Soviet society, deserves American support in carving out a new future for his country.

The subtext of *Red King, White Knight* and other favorable Russian-genre Hollywood films of the late 1980s danced to the same tune: the past is behind us. Forget the Rambo rag. Americans and Russians of goodwill share a natural affinity, which, if left to develop, will reward the world with peace. Break down old stereotypes, and a unity of purpose grounded in mutual trust will ensure a safer future for all. If, in retrospect, this Hollywood vision was painfully naive, it nevertheless mirrored public attitudes of the day. Far from leading the way, Hollywood barely managed to keep pace with visions of optimism.

The Hunt for Red October

A cooperative spin even comes through in a major Hollywood adventure drama not really classifiable as favorable, *The Hunt for Red October* (1990). The movie, adapted by Paramount Pictures from Tom Clancy's successful 1984 novel, was directed by John McTiernan, best known for sleek action pictures like *Die Hard* (1990). The plot focuses on Captain Marko Ramius (Sean Connery), Soviet commander of a prototype stealth nuclear submarine, who realizes that his new vessel has first-strike capabilities that could well destabilize the delicate balance of terror.

For the sake of humankind, Ramius and a few of his top officers decide to defect to the United States, submarine and all. Neither his crew members nor the American authorities have been apprised of his intentions. He simply heads out to sea and makes a break for it. With the Soviet Navy in hot pursuit, and American officials unsure whether increased Soviet military activity means preparation for a Soviet attack on the United States, tension builds. It falls to CIA analyst Jack Ryan (Alec Baldwin)—finally, someone not pulled out of retirement—to figure out what is happening. In the underwater struggle between a lone Soviet dove trying to dodge the trailing Soviet hawks, Jack Ryan convinces American officials not to overreact. Reading Soviet Captain Ramius like a book, he figures out how to grease the skids for his defection without unleashing nuclear war. Not a bad day's work in any man's navy.

Conservative author Tom Clancy's best-selling novel (5 million sold) is a finger-on-the-button pre-Gorbachev Cold War thriller. But the film version of *The Hunt for Red October* was released five and a half years after Clancy's original novel, well into the new era of superpower relations. Recognizing that the American public would not bite at the anticommunist bait, director John McTiernan linked *The Hunt for Red October* to Gorbachev's reforms and improved bilateral relations.[31] This rendering of the plot suggests that an episode like the one depicted in *The Hunt for Red October* could have paved the way for Gorbachev's ascension to power. What is more, it would be Soviet men and women like Captain Ramius, action-oriented new-wave Soviet thinkers, who would rally to Gorbachev as their leader. Thus, *The Hunt for Red October* was not so much anti-Soviet as it was pro-Gorbachev.

McTiernan's de-ideologization (or rather re-ideologization) of the Clancy novel to support *glasnost* and *perestroika* is consistent with the general drift in Russian-genre films. Trying to hit the jackpot with a blockbuster movie, "the makers of *Red October* play their cards more cleverly than [the makers of] *Rambo III*," an unreconstructed Cold War picture, and one of the ten biggest money losers of the 1980s.[32] *The Hunt for Red October*, by contrast, has rung in an impressive $58,500,000 and ranks 29th in *Variety*'s listing of film rental leaders of the 1990s, and 69th among all-time rental leaders.[33] It would seem that at least a few Hollywood producers managed to catch the earliest waves of the peace dividend.

A Few Critical Films

While *Rambo III*'s (1988) rabid anti-Soviet message lost out in a big way, it was not the only picture of the late 1980s failing to acknowledge the new international realities. Three others blindly continued to follow violent formulaic patterns left over from the early eighties. None achieved popularity with audiences. In *Streets of Gold* (1986), Soviet authorities deny Soviet boxing champion Alek Neumann (Klaus Maria Brandauer) Olympic-level competition. Why? Anti-Semitism. Neumann is a Jew, and Soviet authorities are unwilling to permit a Jew the honor of representing the Soviet Union at the Olympics. Fed up with life in the Soviet Union, Alek emigrates to the United States.

But all does not go well in his adopted land. Feeling despondent and rootless, the fighter seems to have lost his fighting spirit. He is reduced to washing dishes in Brooklyn's Brighton Beach immigrant community. Lost in a strange land, his dignity in tatters, he hits the bottle and sleeps on the beach, like a common vagrant. But it's too early to count Neumann out. Boxing runs in his veins, and it eventually rescues him. Alek retakes command of his life by dedicating his energies to coaching two Golden Gloves boxers: a black youth, Roland Jenkins (Wesley Snipes), and a young Irish boxer, Timmy Boyle (Adrian Pasdar).

But something remains missing in Alek's life. He sees himself as an outsider—in America but not part of it. As a result, he avoids forming emotional attachments, even to the two young fighters who are so much a part of his life. The world sees only his tough and demanding side. But the audience knows that inside Alek Neumann a warm, loving person awaits liberation. That too comes through the ring. Alek's old nemesis, the anti-Semitic Russian coach Malinovsky (Jaroslav Stremie), is touring the United States with the Russian national team. New York is their first stop.

The boxing ring again serves as the metaphorical space for battle between American individualism and Soviet collectivism. Against all odds, Alek's pupil, Timmy Boyle, defeats the Russians' best fighter, Suvorov. With America again redeemed, Alek has proven himself and he finally feels at home. The "real" Alek now liberated, he can put down personal roots. His mind echoes with the words of the grandmother who once dreamed that her grandson would someday go to America: "In America, the streets are paved with gold." Alek has found his gold through commitment to his Golden Glove champions.

Unfortunately for Twentieth Century Fox, not much gold was raised through ticket sales for this jingoistic effort. Nevertheless, critics did not universally savage first-time producer and director, Joe Roth. While critics turned against the Cold War message, Roth was applauded for his ability to tease some fine performances out of his actors.

One would be hard pressed to find a critic with anything good to say about *No Retreat, No Surrender* (1986). Machismo goes berserk in this film which seems to have been slapped together on the cutting room floor used for *Rocky IV*, *The Karate Kid* (1984), and every Bruce Lee movie that ever gained entry by kicking down theater doors. What *No Retreat, No Surrender* does not do is scrounge up any semblance of a believable plot. To wit, the New York mafia sponsors a karate team, the "Manhattan Maulers," which they enter in a karate match in Seattle. If this scenario does not sufficiently tax credibility, add a Soviet karate champion named Ivan "the Terrible" Krashinsky (Jean-Claude Van Damme), to the team. Maybe the KGB was too busy planning coups and assassinations in *Company Business* or *Red King, White Knight* to sponsor its own team? As the direct filmic descendant of Ivan Drago in *Rocky IV*, the mafia's Ivan "the Terrible" is big, icy-cold, aggressive, and a cheater. He amuses himself by systematically destroying Seattle's best fighters.

Ivan eventually meets his Waterloo in Seattle at the hands (and flying feet) of a neophyte karate student and all-American boy, Jason Stillwell (Kurt McKinney). Jason is a devotee of the late Bruce Lee, who just happens to be buried in Seattle. Amazingly, Jason's fighting begins improving with each visit he makes to his dead hero's grave. Why? Because Bruce Lee's black-belted ghost is giving him private lessons! Not even the crazed Soviet Ivan, the champion of New York's mafia families, can stand up to such preternatural intervention. Jason courageously restores American pride with stunning victories for the movie's director, Corey Yuen, who also provided the original story.

Equally out of step with the new era of good feelings, but much less mind numbing than *No Retreat, No Surrender* is *The Fourth Protocol* (1987). The plot for this anti-Soviet spy movie unfolds as a bitter internal Kremlin battle about detente threatens to spill over into military adventurism. Intrigue builds as Major Valery Alexeevich Petrofsky (Pierce Brosnan), an elite Soviet secret agent, is sent on a mission by the KGB chairman, General Karpov. Karpov is "subtle and shrewd as a Soviet General well versed in bending other Soviet generals to his will."[34]

Petrofsky's assignment? As part of a desperate KGB scheme to reestablish faltering authority and destroy NATO, Petrofsky is instructed to blow up Britain's Bayswater nuclear weapons base, making it look like an accident. If the KGB's role were to become known, world peace could be threatened, since any attack on a nuclear installation blatantly violates the fourth protocol of a 1968 American-Soviet nuclear control treaty.

Major Petrofsky represents the best talent the KGB has created. He is technically skilled, cool, polished, and devoid of conscience. Fortunately for NATO (and those living near Bayswater), he is not perfect. He meets his match in the person of an unrelenting British agent named John Preston (Michael Caine). Although forced to fight with procrustean bureaucrats all the while, John Preston manages to prevent Major Petrofsky from completing his mission. With the help of a squadron of British commandoes, Preston thwarts the KGB's plot, personally dispenses with Petrofsky, and saves Bayswater, NATO, and world peace. None too flattering of Russians or the Soviet system, this British Rank studio film was directed by John MacKenzie and adapted for the screen by Frederick Forsyth from his best-selling novel.

One additional film must not pass without mention, *Young Nurses in Love* (1987), which launches a "nothing-is-sacred" assault on both hospital and spy movies. It is inspired in part by *Airplane* (1980) and *Airplane II* (1982), off-the-wall parodies of the 1970s airport disaster movies. A spoof of a spoof, *Young Nurses in Love* also satirizes an earlier satire of hospital-based soap operas, *Young Doctors in Love* (1982). Like these other Hollywood comedies, *Young Nurses in Love* takes overworked Hollywood formula films to ridiculous extremes. In this case, the result is a trivial sexual comedy notable as the only picture of the era to parody Cold War excesses in the manner of some 1960s movies.

It revolves around suggestive one-liners and bedpan humor. But there is a plot, of sorts. Female KGB agent Comrade Dobrowski (Jeanne Marle), poses as an American nurse. Why? To steal the "genius vault" from America's Hoover sperm bank, which includes donations from the likes of Pablo Picasso, Douglas MacArthur, and Ernest Hemingway. And why do the Soviets want all this primo seminal fluid? The answer that suggests itself is obvious to Cold War veterans. Both Kennedy (in 1960) and Reagan (in 1980) warned of a missile gap. But the Soviets find themselves disadvantaged by a sperm gap. Only genetic engineering can provide the spurt needed to catch up with the more advanced Americans.

Dobrowski's mission is not without danger. While briefed for her assignment, the beautiful KGB agent is warned, "Comrade Dobrowski, you must succeed; even if it costs you your virginity!" But the dedicated agent seems prepared to pay the price. In between spasms of slapstick humor, the question of who gets the girl seems as important as who gets the primo sperm. Nurse-agent Dobrowski, however, takes no chances. She defects to America, where, the film implies, both the quantity and quality of sperm are ready to meet any challenge. It's hard to tell from *Young Nurses in Love* whether nurse Dobrowski's aborted mission proved the deciding factor in America's final victory in the Cold War.

Overall Filmic Themes

A pronounced tilt away from violent anti-Russian films pervades the late 1980s, which saw the production of only a few negative Russian-genre films, none of which had wide audience appeal. Yet Hollywood exercised caution in welcoming a new era of Soviet-American relations, never getting too far in front of the pack. If anything, Hollywood struggled to keep pace with a rapidly changing world. But who didn't? How could Hollywood compete with live images of Berliners, western and eastern alike, taking hammers to the Berlin Wall? For one rare moment, reality proved far more exhilarating than anything Hollywood might conjure up.

Taken as a whole, the Russian-genre films of the late 1980s constitute a diverse lot, including fifteen plot categories. The Soviet system versus Russian people dichotomy, critical to some eras, appears in a few middling films pushing a "bad system-good people" message. Several films also include good versus bad Russian characters, often busy plotting against one another in internal Kremlin power struggles over *glasnost*. The good guys fare best.

Critical films, all violent clones of early 1980s comic-book progenitors, failed to excite audiences. Films more favorable toward the Russians, often preaching a one-world message, did better box-office business. Thematically, these positive films emphasize the benefits of mutual demilitarization and Soviet-American citizen cooperation. As if to signal a new American mood, friendly Russians bursting with goodwill leaped from the silver screen to television programming and Madison Avenue marketing as well. How Russians will fare in the post-Cold War era of American film remains to be seen.

Cold War Coda

Where Have All the Russians Gone?

Dark corners of Hollywood warehouses probably contain films about Russians made in the dying days of the Cold War, which will never see the light of day. Why? Because Shadowland found itself unable to keep pace with the cataclysmic forces unleashed by the disintegration of the Soviet Union. New international realities stemming from the Soviet collapse left no room for the demonization *or* lionization of a nonexistent country or its citizens.

The explosion of Russian-genre films released in the late 1980s ended abruptly. No more Soviet Union, no more Soviet threat; no more Soviet threat, no more Russian-genre films. In the wake of communism's demise, too few pictures involving Russians washed ashore between 1991 and 1995 to construct a new filmic image of Russians. What has become of the stock Russian characters in film after Hollywood film? Gone. Replacement villains were waiting in the wings. As fast as you can say "hold the butter on the popcorn, please," Hollywood found Japanese underworld figures to kick around in *Black Rain* (1992), IRA terrorists to condemn in *Patriot Games* (1993), greedy Colombian drug dealers to loathe in *Clear and Present Danger* (1994), and rogue Arab states to despise in *The American President* (1995). All filled the cinematic space vacated by so many memorable Russian villains.

But Hollywood was not wiped clean of Russians. In the last month of 1995, United Artists unleashed the most violent James Bond film to date, *GoldenEye* (1995), starring Pierce Brosnan in his first 007 screen role. In this seventeenth episode of moviedom's all-time most successful series, Hollywood not only notices the Russians, it fixates on them—good ones, bad ones, rich ones, poor ones. *GoldenEye*'s two villains are hyphenated Russians: a libidinous Georgian-Russian, who squeezes the last breath out of male victims caught between her long and powerful legs, and a Russian-Vlasovite-Briton who steals an electromagnetic pulse weapon with the expectation of unleashing panic in global markets and making himself the world's richest person.[1]

This brawling Hollywood production sings a consistent tune about post-Gorbachev Russia—sheer chaos—the decay of civil order spawning a mafia-infested bloodbath in pursuit of fast money. Never before has a James Bond picture portrayed Russia as so sleazy and so fragmented. Taking the broader perspective, what can we conclude about the historical image of Russians as depicted by Hollywood?

A Very Schizoid Enterprise: Business and Art

Six decades of Russian-genre films confirm Hollywood's penchant for playing follow the flag. It is more difficult to explain definitively why this is the case. One suggestive explanation has to do with Hollywood film's tension between entrepreneurial investment and art form. Of course, not all films make money or constitute meritorious art. One would be hard pressed to find inspirational value in more than a few of the films examined here. Nevertheless, like other art forms, film is subject to critical review on aesthetic, stylistic, and intellectual grounds as good, bad, or indifferent. It also faces scrutiny from a public that may know little about art, and will pay to see only what it likes.

This last point is important. One megadifference separates film from other art forms. While other arts may reflect countercultural or even elitist values, film in America operates rather differently. Films striving for artistic merit bear the burden of turning a profit. Exorbitant production costs, from concept to darkened theater, allow nothing to be produced that might turn off the mass audience. And while directors, writers, or actors may wax eloquent about the value of artistic expression, producers and corporate shareholders remain more intimately conversant with the bottom line. Much as producers might hope to educate, entertain, or inspire, it is more critical for them to realize a return on investment in what is by its nature a very risky enterprise.

This creates a chilling effect on the creative juices necessary for intellectual, aesthetic, or political adventurism. Straying too far from what audiences will pay to see raises the specter of financial ruin. With some films costing upwards of $200 million, larger and larger audiences are required in order to show a return on investor capital, making it harder and harder to deviate from the common sociopolitical denominator. Who is brave enough, or foolhardy enough, to roll such expensive dice? Precious few. Therefore, less and less that falls outside of the comfortable assumptions shared by the civic culture reaches the screen.

With so much at stake, movies become collaborative enterprises—art by committee. Which is not to say that individual artistic talents cannot shine forth. They do. However, the atomized, step-by-step filmmaking process works against directors, even those worthy of the designation *auteur*, being able to shape the contours of a film to their individual will. At each step in production—from the first treatment of an idea, through the writing and rewriting of a script, casting, direction, editing, marketing, and reassuring investors—the words of so many people add up to a cacophony of compromise, coaxing movies away from the more creative margins and toward the safety of the center. How could it be otherwise? Try counting all those names in the credits flying down the screen at the end of a film. They last longer than the dialogue of some modern action pictures.

Political Center of Gravity

Let us not forget, landing on the wrong side of the cinematic political fence, even in America, can be costly. Culver City never forgot how it was burned during the McCarthy era. It has no desire for an encore. While other art forms may delight in twigging the nose of convention, even see their raison d'être in challenging political norms, movies shy away from challenging popular attitudes. Add to that the reality that movies are rated and subjected to public scrutiny, then one better understands why Hollywood is so loath to push the margins of the acceptable, at least in the political realm. Violence and frontal nudity, yes. Assaulting core political values or the thrust of American foreign policy, no—not even during the height of Vietnam War protests.

As if the cards were not already stacked against political adventurism in movies, television's contemporary role as collaborator in the rush to profit (rather than as competitor as in the 1950s) further mitigates against nonconformist movies. Movies are now filmed to be reedited for the small screen and for global video distribution. What is more, not only must producers and directors fit their work into the rectangular box format, they must also sequence it so as to be easily sandwiched between spray deodorant and pop tart commercials. Even more insidiously, they must mold it to fit the intellectual space of viewers prepared to flick to *I Love Lucy* reruns if they are made uncomfortable by what they see on the screen. To avoid being relegated to cable television's cyber heaven, it is best to forego questioning the holy cows of America's perceptual universe. In prime time, family values and foreign policy go hand in hand.

This is not to deny that films influence the American mind profoundly on subjects about which most Americans lack personal experience, and Americans have little or no first-hand experience with Russians. Lacking direct contact for more than half a century, Americans came no closer to the real thing than Hollywood's flickering screen. What Tinseltown delivered was laced with exaggerative stereotypes feeding America's desire to know something, no matter how distorted or how shallow, about its global significant other—the Soviet Union. In the end, Hollywood's Russians became America's Russians, created on the back lots of Culver City.

Chameleonlike Russians

Hollywood's Russians helped to shape the obsessions of the American psyche and ease the acceptance of America's foreign policy goals. Chameleonlike, Russians portrayed in American cinema from 1933 to 1991 abruptly changed color—sometimes red, sometimes a pinkish red, white, and blue—as foreign policy shifted.

Hollywood had less enthusiasm for positive portraits of Russians than for negative ones. For example, Hollywood pictures failed to fully reflect the softening in superpower relations during the two detente-oriented periods (1972–80; 1986–91). While films produced during these two periods were more favorable toward Russians than earlier ones, they failed to warm the Cold War thermometer to genuinely comfortable temperatures. Films like *The Spy Who Loved Me* (1977) and *Telefon* (1977) from the 1970s, or *Russkies* (1987) and *Red Heat* (1988) from the late 1980s, while favorable, are not nearly as positive as opinions expressed in the daily editorials of major newspapers. Only during World War II, when Hollywood pumped out propaganda for the war effort, was there a concerted effort to elicit a warm and fuzzy feeling toward Russians. In movies like *The North Star* (1944) or *Song of Russia* (1944), the Soviets blended right into our neighborhoods.

The Negativity Effect

Why did Shadowland often lag behind the State Department? Part of the answer lies in the observation that Hollywood films are more effective conduits of negative emotions, such as fear and hatred, than of positive feelings, like understanding or empathy. Movies from the 1950s, such as *Never Let Me Go* (1953) and *Prisoner of War* (1954), burst with negative energy. No comparable conviction characterizes detente-era movies.[2]

Another factor that contributed to Hollywood's lukewarm embrace of a more friendly Soviet Union is what some social psychologists call the "negativity effect"—the notion that negative social processes are more potent forces than positive ones.[3] Negative images sell. Advertisers know that negative commercial marketing works by creating consumer anxiety which can be eased by the manufacturer's product.[4] The same is true of the political marketplace. American political campaigns often bristle with mean-spirited "attack messages," which are more compelling and more memorable than constructive messages.[5] Why should the Hollywood marketplace be exempt from the negativity effect? It isn't.

There is a spinoff issue raised here: Is Hollywood's negativity effect selling more than movie tickets? Is it selling ideas? Given the close relationship between Hollywood films about Russians and U.S. foreign policy, do films reflect politics or do they influence politics? The untidy answer is neither and both. While it is tempting to seek simple answers to this question, one film historian believes that the "links between movies and society need to be thought of as associative, not direct."[6] He is right. Hollywood films in general, and Russian-genre films in particular, *complement* American attitudes rather than shape them. They also tend to *compliment* much less when American foreign policy is positively disposed toward the Russians.

Dehumanization

Whether Hollywood films depicting Russians are classified as critical, favorable, or middling, they tend to offer exaggerated, dehumanized depictions of their Russian characters. Russians—whether friend or foe—tend to be flat and one-dimensional, lacking the depth and genuineness necessary to empathize with them. Late 1940s critics referred to them as "single-plane cutouts," "projections rather than portraits," and "chimerical figures changing with the political exigencies of the moment."[7] More recently, cinematic Russians have been described as "cardboard plot-pawns."[8] A more apt metaphor may be one of plastic people: not only bloodless and dehumanized, but malleable as well, changing from season to season, plot to plot, and foreign crisis to foreign crisis.

It has been well argued that dehumanization is purposeful. It serves as a critical tripwire for converting national adversaries into enemies.

Psychologist Sam Keen believes that all societies mentally prepare for war by teaching their citizens and soldiers to treat enemies as abstractions. "In the beginning we create the enemy. Before the weapon comes the image." The visual imagery created by national propaganda efforts look so similar as to suggest to Keen that their artists "all went to the same art school." These dehumanizing national stereotypes enable people to do the unpleasant things that humans do to their enemies.[9]

Over and above preparation for war, American culture seems unusually drawn to political demonology, together with the exaggeration of threats to its security and culture.[10] As a result, American society may too readily accept all aspirants who audition for the role of enemy, rather than make careful decisions about who America's enemies need to be.[11]

Shards of Humor in the Dark Side

For over half a century, Americans found it easy to imagine a Manichean world, with the Darth Vader-like Soviets relegated to the "dark side." In keeping the dark side at bay, Americans were given to overdoing it, as seen in ideological stridency and procrustean definitions of orthodoxy. And with nuclear weapons stockpiled on both sides, few observers had any reason to doubt the prevailing assessment. There existed little room for humor, self deprecating or otherwise, in this psychic scheme of things.

As an alternative to earnestness, Hollywood offered an occasional humorous moment for viewers to laugh at their collective excesses. Whether intentionally or not, Tinseltown provided a prism illuminating the Cold War as a concoction of mind as much as a maze of international impasses. Director Norman Jewison's Cold War backlash film, *The Russians Are Coming, The Russians Are Coming* (1966), teased America into lightening up. Viewed in hindsight, many Russian-genre films demand that the viewer keep tongue proximate to cheek. Relatively few of these films hold up well under the light of the post-Cold War world that we inhabit. Fewer still can be considered cinematic classics. But the center of gravity exposed by each group of movies, endemic to its era, offers a window on America's collective soul as it existed at that moment. These films deserve recognition as unwitting artifacts of cultural history—albeit with a box of Milk Duds at the ready.

Notes

Preface

1. Albert Auster and Leonard Quart, *American Film and Society since 1945* (New York: Praeger Special Studies, 1984), p. 2.

2. Mark C. Carnes, *Past Imperfect: History According to the Movies* (New York: Henry Holt, 1995), p. 9.

3. Peter C. Rollins, ed., *Hollywood as Historian: American Film in a Cultural Context* (Lexington: University Press of Kentucky, 1983), p. 1.

4. Pre-1945 illustrations of policy excesses include U.S. sponsorship and subsequent rejection of the League of Nations; Franklin Roosevelt's accommodative acceptance of Josef Stalin's demands concerning the postwar fate of Poland and the rest of eastern Europe; the wartime incarceration of nearly two hundred thousand innocent Japanese-American citizens; Harry Truman using the A-bomb on Hiroshima without explicit warning.

Early postwar examples of overreaction include: blacklisting and loyalty oaths in the 1950s, the brinksmanship of nuclear blackmail in the Taiwan straits crisis and five other hotspots by Dwight Eisenhower, a massive campaign to construct atomic bomb shelters, and Eisenhower's excessive denials of U-2 reconnaissance flights over Russia. The 1960s watched John Kennedy conduct the Bay of Pigs fiasco, Lyndon Johnson and Richard Nixon continue the Vietnam War well beyond futility, Johnson dispatch Marines to the Dominican Republic on dubious pretense, and attempt to assassinate Fidel Castro.

The 1970s and 1980s saw may examples of overdoing it, including Richard Nixon's secret invasion of Cambodia, the coup and assassination of democratically elected president Salvador Allende in Chile, the Watergate scandal, stock-piling twenty thousand nuclear missiles, Jimmy Carter's myriad self-defeating sanctions levied after the Soviet invasion of Afghanistan, Ronald Reagan's Grenada invasion, the Strategic Defense Initiative, unleashing Third World freedom fighters with the Reagan Doctrine, Iran-Contra and the sale of missiles to Iran. Also excessive are George Bush's invasion of Panama to arrest Manuel Noriega, and his demonization of Saddam Hussein as the "worst tyrant since Hitler" during the Persian Gulf War, as well as Bill Clinton's bluffing the Japanese and Chinese over the consequences of trade deficits and his clinging to the embargo against Cuba long after the end of the Cold War.

Over the longer term, an immigration policy based solely on Cold War politics, secret exposure of more than ten thousand citizens to experimental nuclear radiation, and a succession of seven presidents looking the other way as J. Edgar Hoover trampled human rights to eradicate self-defined threats to national security impress as overreactions of great resilience.

5. Walter Jones, *The Logic of International Relations* (New York: HarperCollins, 1991), pp. 53–55.

6. Daniel Papp, *Contemporary International Relations* (New York: Macmillan, 1994), p. 234.

7. Richard Slotkin, *The Myth of the Frontier in Twentieth Century America* (New York: Harper, 1994).

8. Jerel A. Rosati, *The Politics of American Foreign Policy* (New York: Harcourt, Brace, Jovanovich, 1993), p. 392.

9. Woodrow Wilson, *War Message*, 65th Congress, 1st session, Senate document no. 5 (Washington, D.C.: U.S. Printing Office, 1971), pp. 3–8.

10. Moralism inherent in the American psyche leads to global evangelism, national egotism, an absence of introspection, and mood swings when high expectations are not met. Political scientist John Stoessinger's case studies assess the foreign policies of this century's U.S. presidents; he argues that the flexibility of pragmatic presidents makes them open to policy options and less susceptible to catastrophic decisions than their moralistic counterparts. American idealism and moralism contributed to gyrating policies and cultural attitudes about communism not exhibited by other democracies such as Canada, Japan, Germany, Italy, or France. John G. Stoessinger. *Crusaders and Pragmatists: Movers of Modern American Foreign Policy* (New York: W. W. Norton, 1985).

11. Peter G. Boyle, *American-Soviet Relations: From the Russian Revolution to the Fall of Communism* (New York: Routledge, 1993), p. viii.

12. Clayton R. Koppes and Gregory D. Black, *Hollywood Goes to War: How Politics, Profits and Propaganda Shaped World War II Movies* (Berkeley: University of California Press, 1987); Bernard Dick, *The Star Spangled Screen: Hollywood World War II Movies* (Lexington: University Press of Kentucky, 1985); Robert Fyne, *The Hollywood Propaganda of World War II* (Metuchen, N.J.: Scarecrow, 1994).

13. Rollins, *Hollywood as Historian*, p. 4.

14. Martin Scorsese, interviewed in *American Cinema, Part 1* (PBS Series, New York Center for Visual History, 1994).

15. A road sign in Vladivostok points west to Saint Petersburg and identifies the motoring distance as 9,329 kilometres (over Soviet-quality roads).

16. One-fifth of the population in the peripheral republics was Russian; these *colons* constituted the vanguard of a Russification similar to that of chauvinistic tsars like Alexander III in the late nineteenth century.

17. Michael J. Strada, "A Half Century of American Cinematic Imagery: Hollywood's Portrayal of Russian Characters, 1933–1988," *Coexistence* 26 (Winter 1989): 339.

18. Defending this practice, Hedrick Smith adds that not only were Russians the largest and dominant group, but "many Russians and other non-Russian Soviet citizens themselves called their country 'Russia'." Hedrick Smith, *The Russians* (New York: Ballantine, 1977), p. xvii; and *The New Russians* (New York: Random House, 1991). These are two of the most widely read books ever written about the Soviet Union.

19. The term "middling" is used rather than others such as "neutral" or "mixed" because some of the middle-of-the-road films are bland and neutral, whereas others have strong and antithetical views about Russians. The term "middling" encompasses both of these types of films.

Chapter 1

1. Adapted from Charles Brackett, Billy Wilder, and Walter Reisch, *Screenplay for Ninotchka* (New York: Viking, 1972), pp. 113–14.

2. Peter G. Boyle, *American-Soviet Relations: From the Russian Revolution to the Fall of Communism* (New York: Routledge, 1993), p. 30.

3. Ibid., p. 31.

4. Ibid.

5. Eugene Lyons, "To Tell or Not to Tell," *Harper's* 171 (June 1935): 110.

6. Robert Dallek, *Franklin D. Roosevelt and American Foreign Policy, 1932–1945* (New York: Oxford University Press, 1979).

7. Edward M. Bennett, *Franklin D. Roosevelt and the Search for Security: America's Russian Policy, 1933–1939* (Wilmington, Del.: Scholarly Resources, 1985), p. 7.

8. Boyle, *American-Soviet Relations*, p. 39.

9. Peter C. Rollins, "Drums Along the Mohawk," in *American History / American Film*, ed. John E. O'Connor and Martin A. Jackson (New York: Frederick Ungar, 1980), p. 99.

10. Ted Sennett, *Hollywood's Golden Year: 1939* (New York: St. Martin's Press, 1989), p. xii.

11. William Kuhns, *Movies in America* (Dayton, Ohio: Pflaum, 1972), p. 114.

12. John Baxter, *Hollywood in the Thirties* (New York: A.S. Barnes, 1968), p. 10.

13. Kuhns, *Movies in America*, p. 31.

14. Judith Crist, Introduction to *The Films of the Thirties*, by Jerry Vermilye (Secaucus, N.J.: Citadel, 1982), p. 8.

15. Bosley R. Crowther, review of *Public Deb No. One*, *New York Times*, 8 September 1939, p. 19.

16. Philip Melling, in *Cinema, Politics and Society in America*, ed. Philip Davies and Brian Neve (New York: St. Martin's Press, 1981), p. 7.

17. Light romantic comedies include *Ninotchka, Tovarich, Once in a Blue Moon, Balalaika, Espionage*, and *He Stayed for Breakfast*.

18. Personal metamorphoses are experienced by Elena in *British Agent*, Prince Dmitrii Nekhlyudov in *We Live Again*, Nina Yakushova in *Ninotchka*, Princess Tatiana in *Tovarich*, Marianne Duvall in *He Stayed for Breakfast*, and Theodore in *Comrade X*.

19. "Love conquers all" is a subtext message in almost all of these films, but most prominently in *Ninotchka, Comrade X, Espionage, Balalaika, Once in a Blue Moon, The Emperor's Candlesticks, After Tonight, We Live Again, I Stand Condemned*, and *British Agent*.

20. The female defection ploy serves as the climax for Elena in *British Agent*, Lydia in *Balalaika*, Nina in *Ninotchka*, Ilena in *Once in a Blue Moon*, and Theodore in *Comrade X*.

21. Thomas Bohn and Richard Stromgren, *Light and Shadows: A History of Motion Pictures* (Washington, N.Y.: Alfred Publishers, 1975), p. 100.

22. Richard Koszarski, *Hollywood Directors, 1914–1940* (New York: Oxford University Press, 1976), p. 270.

23. Sennett, *Hollywood's Golden Year: 1939*, p. 188.

24. Barry Paris, *Garbo* (New York: Alfred A. Knopf, 1994).

25. Baxter, *Hollywood in the Thirties*, p. 16.

26. Lewis Jacobs, *The Rise of the American Film* (New York: Teachers College, 1968), p. 358.

27. Sennett, *Hollywood's Golden Year: 1939*, p. 190.

28. "Ninotchka" is a form of the Russian familiar diminutive for Nina; *Ninotchka* was advertised as the film in which Greta Garbo "finally laughs."

29. Andrew Sarris, *Interviews with Film Directors* (New York: 1967), p. 281; Jean-Pierre Coursodon, *American Directors* (New York: McGraw-Hill, 1983), p. 230.

30. Julia Johnson, review of *Ninotchka* in *Magill's Survey of Cinema*, ed. Frank Magill (Englewood Cliffs, N.J.: Salem, 1980), p. 1212.

31. Frank S. Nugent, review of *Ninotchka*, *New York Times*, 10 November 1939, p. 38.

32. Sennett, *Hollywood's Golden Year: 1939*, p. 194.

33. *Variety*, 19 December 1937, p. 24.

34. Baxter, *Hollywood in the Thirties*, p. 51.

35. David Shipman, *The Great Movie Stars: The Golden Years* (New York: Hill and Wang, 1988), p. 463.

36. *Time*, 3 January 1938, p. 29.

37. John Wakeman, ed. *World Film Directors*, vol. 1 (New York: H. W. Wilson, 1987), p. 679.

38. Frank S. Nugent, review of *Tovarich*, *New York Times*, 31 December 1937, p. 9.

39. Pauline Kael, *Kiss Kiss Bang Bang* (New York: Simon and Schuster, 1969), p. 59.

40. Baxter, *Hollywood in the Thirties*, p. 33.

41. Bosley R. Crowther, review of *Once in a Blue Moon, New York Times*, 16 February 1936, sec. 9, p. 5.

42. Richard Averson and David White, *The Celluloid Weapon: Social Comment in the American Film* (Boston: Beacon, 1972), p. 58.

43. Jean-Pierre Coursodon with Pierre Sauvage, *American Directors*, vol. 1 (New York: McGraw-Hill, 1983), p. 77.

44. Andre Sennwald, review of *British Agent, New York Times*, 20 September 1934, p. 20.

45. Mordaunt Hall, review of *After Tonight, New York Times*, 3 November 1933, p. 23.

46. Bosley R. Crowther, review of *The Emperor's Candlesticks, New York Times*, 9 July 1937, p. 18.

47. Sarris, *Interview With Filmmakers*, p. 288.

48. Baxter, *Hollywood in the Thirties*, p. 127.

49. Andre Sennwald, review of *We Live Again, New York Times*, 2 November 1934, p. 27.

50. Richard Koszarski, *Hollywood Directors, 1914–1940* (New York: Oxford University Press, 1976), p. 287.

51. J.T.M., review of *Espionage, New York Times*, 17 May 1937, p. 23.

52. John Baxter, *Sixty Years of Hollywood* (New York: A. S. Barnes, 1973), p. 114.

53. Frank S. Nugent, review of *The Charge of the Light Brigade, New York Times*, 2 November 1936, p. 24.

54. Frank S. Nugent, review of *Balalaika, New York Times*, 15 December 1939, p. 33.

55. Robert Wilson, ed., *The Film Criticism of Otis Ferguson* (Philadelphia: Temple University Press, 1971), p. 333.

56. John Wakeman, ed., *World Film Directors*, vol. 1 (New York: H. W. Wilson, 1987), pp. 1130–31.

57. Robert Fyne, "From Hollywood to Moscow," *Film Library Quarterly* 16, nos. 1–2 (1983): 32.

Chapter 2

1. *Life* 14, no. 13 (March 1943): 23.

2. Charles E. Bohlen, *Witness to History, 1929–1969* (New York: W. W. Norton, 1972), p. 123.

3. Wilson D. Miscamble, "The Foreign Policy of the Truman Administration: A Post-Cold War Appraisal," *Presidential Studies Quarterly* 24, no. 3 (summer 1994): 480.

4. Robert Beitzell, *The Uneasy Alliance: America, Britain, and Russia, 1941–1943* (New York: Alfred A. Knopf, 1972), p. 375.

5. Miscamble, "The Foreign Policy of the Truman Administration," p. 480.

6. Robert Dallek, *The American Style of Foreign Policy: Cultural Politics and Foreign Affairs* (New York: Oxford University Press, 1983), p. 150.

7. John G. Stoessinger, *Crusaders and Pragmatists: Movers of Modern American Foreign Policy* (New York: W.W. Norton, 1985), p. 52.

8. Robert H. Jones, *The Roads to Russia: U.S. Lend-Lease* (Norman: University of Oklahoma Press, 1969), p. 3.

9. Karl W. Ryavec, *U.S.-Soviet Relations* (New York: Longman, 1989), p. 4. Jones, *The Roads to Russia*, pp. 281–91. Selected total aid figures, 1941–45: 16,429,800 long tons of supplies; 14,062 aircraft; 427,284 vehicles; 5,374 tanks; 35,170 motorcycles; 131,633 machine guns; 13,000 pistols; 532,845 tons of sugar; 485,181 tons of canned meat; 640,628 gallons of aviation gasoline; 1,055 tons of cigarettes; 388,449 tons of ethyl alcohol.

10. Peter G. Boyle, *American-Soviet Relations: From the Russian Revolution to the Fall of Communism* (New York: Routledge, 1993), p. 44.

11. Stoessinger, *Crusaders and Pragmatists*, p. 53.

12. Dallek, *American Style of Foreign Policy*, p. 139.

13. Stoessinger, *Crusaders and Pragmatists*, p. 60.

14. David McCullough, *Truman* (New York: Simon and Schuster, 1994), pp. 44–47.

15. Ibid., pp. 55, 141–42.

16. Ibid., p. 293.

17. Ibid., p. 371.

18. Ibid., p. 375.

19. Ibid., pp. 382, 447.

20. Clayton R. Koppes and Gregory D. Black, *Hollywood Goes to War: How Politics, Profits and Propaganda Shaped World War II Movies* (Berkeley: University of California Press, 1987), p. vii.

21. Melvin Small, "Buffoons and Brave Hearts: Hollywood Portrays the Russians, 1939–1944," *California Historical Quarterly* 52: no. 4 (Winter 1973): 326.

22. Stanford psychologist Steven Kull points out that "everything is simplified in wartime, thinking becomes black and white, mental health improves, health in general improves, suicides go down by half." In an interview from the PBS video, Sam Keen, *Faces of the Enemy* (Berkeley: Catticus, 1987).

23. Robert Fyne, *The Hollywood Propaganda of World War II* (Metuchen, N.J.: Scarecrow, 1994), p. 110.

24. Bernard F. Dick, *The Star-Spangled Screen: The American World War II Film* (Lexington: University Press of Kentucky, 1985), p. 159.

25. Small, "Buffoons and Brave Hearts," p. 333.

26. Victor Navasky, *Naming Names* (New York: Viking, 1980), p. 406.

27. Koppes and Black, *Hollywood Goes to War*, p. 210.

28. Ibid., pp. 209–10.

29. John Baxter, *Hollywood in the Thirties* (New York: A. S. Barnes, 1969), p. 96.

30. Bosley R. Crowther, review of *The North Star*, *New York Times* (8 November 1943), p. 24.

31. Adam Hochschild, *The Unquiet Ghost* (New York: Bantam, 1994) p. 141.

32. Robert L. Conquest, *The Harvest of Sorrow: Soviet Collectivization and the Terror-Famine* (New York: Oxford University Press, 1986).

33. Joseph R. Millichap, *Lewis Milestone* (Boston: Twayne, 1981), p. iii.

34. Review of *The North Star*, *New York Times*, 4 April 1943, p. 3 (II).

35. Stephen J. Whitfield, *The Culture of the Cold War* (Baltimore: Johns Hopkins University Press, 1991), p. 132.

36. Jay Hyams, *War Movies* (New York: Gallery Books, 1984), p. 86.

37. Koppes and Black, *Hollywood Goes to War*, p. 217.

38. Ibid.

39. Bosley R. Crowther, review of *Song of Russia*, *New York Times*, 14 March 1944, p. 37.

40. Small, "Buffoons and Brave Hearts," p. 331.

41. David Culbert, "Our Awkward Ally: *Mission to Moscow*," in ed. John E. O'Connor and Martin A. Jackson, *American History/American Film: Interpreting the Hollywood Image* (New York: Frederick Ungar, 1985), p. 130.

42. Hochschild, *The Unquiet Ghost*, p. xv.

43. Ibid., p. 162.

44. Culbert, "Our Awkward Ally," p. 135.

45. James Agee, review of *Mission to Moscow*, *Nation*, 22 May 1943, pp. 749–50.

46. Culbert, "Our Awkward Ally," p. 126.

47. David Culbert, *Mission to Moscow* (Madison: University of Wisconsin Press, 1980), p. 37.

48. Ibid., pp. 13, 37.

49. Bosley R. Crowther, review of *Counter Attack*, *New York Times*, 17 May 1945, p. 15.

50. Sam Keen, *Faces of the Enemy: Reflections of the Hostile Imagination* (San Francisco: Harper and Row, 1986).

Chapter 3

1. Mel Gusow, "Oscar-Winning Screenwriter of the Classic 'Casablanca' " *New York Times*, 19 August 1995, p. 23.

2. Victor Navasky, *Naming Names* (New York: Viking, 1980), p. xiv.

3. Ibid., p. 106.

4. Douglas Miller and Marion Nowak, *The Fifties: The Way We Really Were* (New York: Doubleday, 1977), pp. 3–4.

5. Jacqueline Hess, *U.S.-Soviet Relations* (Washington, D.C.: Close-Up Foundation, 1983), p. 22.

6. Peter G. Boyle, *American-Soviet Relations: From the Russian Revolution to the Fall of Communism* (New York: Routledge, 1993), p. 69.

7. Robert Dallek, *The American Style of Foreign Policy: Cultural Politics and Foreign Affairs* (New York: Oxford University Press, 1983), p. 157.

8. Wilson D. Miscamble, "The Foreign Policy of the Truman Administration: a Post-Cold War Appraisal," *Presidential Studies Quarterly* 24, no. 3 (summer 1994): 481–82.

9. John Lewis Gaddis, *Strategies of Containment* (New York: Oxford University Press, 1982), p. ix.

10. Ibid., pp. 89–90.

11. Ibid., p. 109.

12. Gaddis, *Strategies of Containment*, p. 127.

13. Dallek, *American Style of Foreign Policy*, p. 187.

14. Ibid., pp. 198, 220.

15. Named for the room in the White House where its sessions were first held.

16. Gaddis, *Strategies of Containment*, pp. 151, 134.

17. John G. Stoessinger, *Crusaders and Pragmatists: Movers of Modern American Foreign Policy* (New York: W. W. Norton, 1985), p. 98.

18. Boyle, *American-Soviet Relations*, p. 117.

19. Stoessinger, *Crusaders and Pragmatists*, p. 134.

20. Ibid., p. 135.

21. Gaddis, *Strategies of Containment*, p. 212.

22. Stoessinger, *Crusaders and Pragmatists*, p. 135.

23. Dallek, *American Style of Foreign Policy*, p. 225.

24. Boyle, *American-Soviet Relations*, p. 142. Much of this information became public at the 1992 Havana Conference on the Cuban missile crisis.

25. Stoessinger, *Crusaders and Pragmatists*, p. 152.

26. Gabrielle Brussel, *Cuban Missile Crisis: U.S. Deliberations and Negotiations at the Edge of the Precipice*, Pew Case No. 334 (Washington, D.C.: Pew Case Study Center, Georgetown University, 1993), p. 6.

27. Evan Thomas, *The Very Best Men: Four Who Dared: The Early Years of the CIA* (New York: Simon and Schuster, 1995).

28. William Kuhns, *Movies in America* (Dayton, Ohio: Pflaum, 1972), p. 185.

29. John Fell, *A History of Films* (New York: Holt, Rinehart and Winston, 1979), p. 321.

30. John Baxter, *Sixty Years of Hollywood* (New York: A. S. Barnes, 1973), p. 190.

31. Gordon Gow, *Hollywood in the Fifties* (New York: A. S. Barnes, 1971), p. 17.

32. Kuhns, *Movies in America*, p. 189.

33. Gow, *Hollywood in the Fifties*, p. 195.

34. Kuhns, *Movies in America*, p. 196.

35. Nora Sayre, *Running Time: Films of the Cold War* (New York: Dial, 1982), p. 26.

36. Douglas Brode, *The Films of the Fifties* (Secaucus, N.J.: Citadel, 1976), p. 9.

37. Krin and Glen Gabbard, *Psychiatry and the Cinema* (Chicago: University Chicago Press, 1987), p. 84.

38. Stuart Samuels, "Invasion of the Body Snatchers," in ed. John E. O'Connor and Martin Jackson, *American History/American Film: Interpreting the Hollywood Image* (New York: Frederick Ungar, 1979), pp. 204–15.

39. Frederick S. Perls, *Gestalt Therapy: Excitement and Growth in Human Personality* (New York: Bantam, 1977); Albert Ellis, *New Guide to Rational Living* (New York: Wilshire, 1971); Carl Rogers, *Client-Centered Therapy*

(Boston: Houghton-Mifflin, 1971); Eric Berne, *Transactional Analysis* (New York: Grove, 1971).

40. Siegfried Kracauer, "National Types as Hollywood Presents Them," in ed. Arthur F. McClure, *The Movies: An American Idiom* (Rutherford, N.J.: Farleigh Dickinson University Press, 1985), pp. 178–91.

41. Stephen J. Whitfield, *The Culture of the Cold War* (Baltimore: Johns Hopkins University Press, 1991), p. 127.

42. Ibid., pp. 130–31.

43. C. Eckert, "The Anatomy of a Proletarian Film: Warner's *Marked Woman*," *Film Quarterly* 27 (1974): 10–24.

44. Susan Sontag, *Against Interpretation* (New York: Dell, 1967), p. 222.

45. The eight critical films: *Behind the Iron Curtain, Red Planet Mars, The World in His Arms, California Conquest, Never Let Me Go, Prisoner of War, The Red Danube, The Journey*. The six middling pictures: *Anastasia, Berlin Express, Jet Pilot, The Iron Petticoat, Silk Stockings, A Time to Love and a Time To Die*.

46. David Shipman, *The Great Movie Stars: The Golden Years* (New York: Hill and Wang, 1987), p. 339.

47. Ibid., p. 580.

48. "Rivkin Says Army Praised His Film," *New York Times*, 20 March 1954, p. 11.

49. "P.O.W. Film Denied Army Publicity Aid," *New York Times*, 18 March 1954, p. 24.

50. Bosley R. Crowther, review of *Never Let Me Go*, *New York Times*, 11 June 1953, p. 37.

51. Patricia King Hanson, "Delmer Daves," in ed. Christopher Lyon, *The International Dictionary of Films and Filmmakers: Volume 1* (New York: St. J Press, 1989), p. 572.

52. Crowther, review of *Never Let Me Go*, p. 37.

53. Stephen L. Hanson, "Raoul Walsh," in *The International Dictionary of Films and Filmmakers: Volume 1*, p. 471.

54. Jean-Pierre Coursodon, *American Directors* (New York: McGraw-Hill), pp. 351–54.

55. Bosley R. Crowther, review of *The World in His Arms*, *New York Times*, 10 October 1952, p. 21.

56. Stephen L. Hanson, "William Wellman," in *The International Dictionary of Films and Filmmakers, Volume 1*, p. 585.

57. Patricia King Hanson, "George Sidney," in *The International Dictionary of Films and Filmmakers, Volume 1*, p. 499.

58. Peter Cowie, ed., *Fifty Major Filmmakers* (New York: A. S. Barnes, 1975), p. 99.

59. H.H.T., review of *California Conquest, New York Times*, 7 June 1952, p. 22.

60. Baxter, *Sixty Years of Hollywood*, p. 181.

61. Bosley R. Crowther, review of *Jet Pilot, New York Times*, 5 October 1957, p. 8.

62. ———, review of *The Iron Petticoat, New York Times*, 2 February 1957, p. 12.

63. ———, review of *Romanoff and Juliet, New York Times*, 9 July 1961, p. 26.

64. ———, review of *Taras Bulba, New York Times*, 26 December 1962, p. 5.

65. Navasky, *Naming Names*, p. 20.

66. Dorothy B. Jones, "Communism and the Movies: A Study of Film Content," in *Reporting on Blacklisting, Volume I, The Movies*, ed. John Cogley (New York: Arno, 1972).

67. Nora Sayre, "Cold War Cinema II," *The Nation* (March 1979): 245.

68. Robert V. Daniels, *The End of the Communist Revolution* (New York: Routledge, 1993), pp. 152, 150.

Chapter 4

1. Ralph B. Levering, *The Cold War, 1945–1972* (Arlington Heights, Ill: Harlan Davidson, 1982), p. 132.

2. Cf. William E. Griffith, *Cold War and Coexistence: Russia, China and the United States* (Englewood Cliffs, N.J.: Prentice-Hall, 1971); Harrison E. Salisbury, *War between Russia and China* (New York: Norton, 1969).

3. John G. Stoessinger, *Crusaders and Pragmatists: Movers of Modern American Foreign Policy* (New York: W. W. Norton, 1985), pp. 174–202.

4. Michael Beschloss, *The Crisis Years: Kennedy and Khrushchev, 1960–1963* (New York: HarperCollins, 1991), pp. 673, 680.

5. Robert Dallek, *The American Style of Foreign Policy: Cultural Politics and Foreign Affairs* (New York: Oxford University Press, 1983), p. 242.

6. Peter G. Boyle, *American-Soviet Relations: From the Russian Revolution to the Fall of Communism* (New York: Routledge, 1993), p. 153.

7. James David Barber, "Presidential Character and Foreign Policy Performance," in *The Domestic Sources of American Foreign Policy: Insights and Evidence*, ed. Eugene W. Wittkopf (New York: St. Martin's Press, 1994), pp. 324–39.

8. Dallek, *The American Style of Foreign Policy*, p. 262.

9. Joan Hoff-Wilson, " 'Nixingerism,' NATO and Detente," *Diplomatic History* 12, no. 4 (1989): 520.

10. Stoessinger, *Crusaders and Pragmatists*, p. 240.

11. Dan Caldwell, *American-Soviet Relations from 1947 to the Nixon-Kissinger Grand Design* (Westport, Conn: Greenwood, 1981), pp. 57–70.

12. Alber Auster and Leonard Quart, *American Film and Society since 1945* (New York: Praeger Special Studies, 1984), p. 75.

13. Lawrence Suid, "The Pentagon and Hollywood," in *American History/American Film: Interpreting the Hollywood Image*, ed. John E. O'Connor and Martin Jackson (New York: Frederick Ungar, 1979), p. 251.

14. James Monaco, *American Film Now: The People, the Power, the Money, the Movies* (New York: Oxford University Press, 1979), pp. 1–48.

15. Suid, *Pentagon and Hollywood*, p. 220.

16. Terry Christensen, *Reel Politics: American Political Movies From 'Birth of a Nation' to 'Platoon'* (New York: Blackwell, 1987).

17. Roger Manvell, ed., *The International Encyclopedia of Film* (New York: Crown, 1972), p. 345.

18. Bosley R. Crowther, review of *Fail Safe, New York Times*, 21 September 1964, p. 36.

19. Seth Cagin and Philip Dray, *Hollywood Films of the Seventies* (New York: Harper and Row, 1984), p. 7.

20. Thomas Bohn and Richard Stromgren, *Light and Shadows: A History of Motion Pictures* (Port Washington, N.Y.: Alfred, 1975), p. 467.

21. Norman Kagan, *The Cinema of Stanley Kubrick* (New York: Holt, Rinehart and Winston, 1972), p. 191.

22. Peter Cowie, ed., *50 Major Film-Makers* (New York: A. S. Barnes, 1975), p. 143.

23. Charles Maland, "*Dr. Strangelove*: Nightmare Comedy and the Ideology of Liberal Consensus," in *Hollywood as Historian: American Film in a Cultural Context*, ed. Peter C. Rollins (Lexington: University Press of Kentucky, 1983), p. 191.

24. Kagan, *Cinema of Stanley Kubrick*, p. 120.

25. Nora Sayre, *Running Time: Films of the Cold War* (New York: Dial, 1982), p. 217.

26. Robert Brustein, "Out of This World," *New York Review of Books*, 6 February 1970.

27. Kagan, *Cinema of Stanley Kubrick*, p. 132.

28. Stanley Kauffman, *The World on Film* (New York: Harper and Row, 1966), p. 19.

29. Cagin and Dray, *Hollywood Films*, p. 6.

30. Richard Averson and David White, *The Celluloid Weapon: Social Comment in the American Film* (Boston: Beacon, 1972), p. 204.

31. Robert Alden, review of *The Russians Are Coming, The Russians Are Coming, New York Times*, 26 May 1966, p. 55.

32. Bosley R. Crowther, review of *The Bedford Incident, New York Times*, 3 November 1965, p. 43.

33. Stephen J. Whitfield, *The Culture of the Cold War* (Baltimore: Johns Hopkins University Press, 1991), p. 217.

34. Gene D. Phillips, *Major Filmmakers of the American and British Cinema* (Bethlehem, Pa: Lehigh University Press), p. 250.

35. Ibid., p. 246.

36. Manvell, *International Encyclopedia of Film*, p. 424.

37. Bosley R. Crowther, review of *The Billion Dollar Brain, New York Times*, 23 December 1967, p. 29.

38. Since a Polish pope was elected in the 1970s, the idea of a Russian pope in this 1969 film seems at least moderately less implausible.

39. Pauline Kael, *Going Steady* (Boston: Little, Brown, 1970), pp. 179–81.

40. Joel W. Finler, *All-Time Box Office Hits* (London: Columbus Books, 1985), p. 174.

41. Susan Sackett, *Hollywood Reporter Book of Box Office Hits* (New York: Watson-Guptil, 1990), p. 333.

42. "All-Time Box Office Champions," *Variety*, 21–28 February 1994, p. 19.

43. Phillips, *Major Filmmakers*, p. 187.

44. David Lean, interview by Gerald Pratley, in *Interviews With Film Directors*, ed. Andrew Sarris (Indianapolis: Bobbs-Merrill, 1967), p. 264.

45. Richard Schickel, *Second Sight* (New York: Simon and Schuster, 1972), p. 46.

46. David Lean, interview by Gerald Pratley, in *Interviews With Film Directors*, ed. Andrew Sarris, 1967, p. 264.

47. Phillips, *Major Filmmakers*, p. 181.

48. John G. Tomlinson, review of *Dr. Zhivago*, in *Magill's Survey of Cinema*, ed. Frank N. Magill (Englewood Cliffs, N.J.: Salem, 1980), p. 470.

49. Pauline Kael, *Deeper into Movies* (Boston: Little, Brown, 1973), p. 328.

50. Ibid., p. 368.

51. Marc Ferro, *Nicholas II: Last of the Tsars* (New York: Oxford University Press, 1995).

52. Kael, *Deeper into Movies*, p. 367.

53. Vincent Canby, review of *Nicholas and Alexandra*, *New York Times*, 19 December 1971, p. 3 (II).

Chapter 5

1. Karl W. Ryavec, *United States-Soviet Relations* (New York: Longman, 1989), p. 50.

2. Cf. Raymond L. Garthoff, *Detente and Confrontation: American-Soviet Relations from Nixon to Reagan* (Washington: Brookings Institution, 1985), p. 70; William G. Hyland, *Mortal Rivals: Understanding the Hidden Pattern of Soviet-American Relations* (New York: Simon and Schuster, 1987), p. 5.

3. Dan Caldwell, *American-Soviet Relations from 1947 to the Nixon-Kissinger Grand Design* (Westport, Conn.: Greenwood, 1981), pp. 106–8.

4. Robert W. Turner, "I'll Never Lie to You," in *Jimmy Carter in His Own Words* (New York: Ballantine, 1976).

5. John G. Stoessinger, *Crusaders and Pragmatists: Movers of Modern American Foreign Policy* (New York: W. W. Norton, 1985), p. 283.

6. Jerel A. Rosati, *The Carter Administration's Quest for Global Community: Beliefs and Their Impact on Behavior* (Columbia: University of South Carolina Press, 1987), p. 10.

7. Ibid., p. 81.

8. Peter G. Boyle, *American-Soviet Relations: From the Russian Revolution to the Fall of Communism* (New York: Routledge, 1993), p. 191.

9. "An Interview with Brezhnev," *Time*, 22 January 1979, pp. 16–19.

10. Walter Lafeber, *America, Russia and the Cold War, 1945–1980* (New York: John Wiley, 1980), p. 300.

11. Boyle, *American-Soviet Relations*, p. 186.

12. Ibid., p. 194.

13. Terry Christensen, *Reel Politics: American Political Movies from 'Birth of a Nation' to 'Platoon'* (Cambridge, Mass.: Basil Blackwell, 1987), pp. 142–44.

14. Albert Auster and Leonard Quart, *American Film and Society since 1945* (New York: Praeger Special Studies, 1984), p. 104.

15. Daniel J. Leab, "The Blue Collar Ethnic in Bicentennial America: *Rocky*," in *American History/American Film: Interpreting the Hollywood Image*, ed. John E. O'Connor and Martin Jackson (New York: Frederick Ungar, 1979), p. 258.

16. Michael J. Strada, "The Cinematic Bogy Man Comes Home: American Popular Perceptions of External Threat," *The Midwest Quarterly*, 28, no. 2 (Winter 1987): 248–70.

17. Auster and Quart, *American Film and Society*, p. 103.

18. Seth Cagin and Philip Dray, *Hollywood Films of the Seventies* (New York: Harper and Row, 1984), p. 255.

19. William J. Palmer, *The Films of the Seventies: A Social History* (Metuchen, N.J.: Scarecrow, 1987), p. 117.

20. While avoiding the war itself from 1970 to 1977, Hollywood made the following generally depressing, violent, and psychologically disturbing pictures about Vietnam veterans: *Clay Pigeon* (1971), *The Hard Ride* (1971), *Slaughter* (1972), *Welcome Home, Soldier Boys* (1972), *Gordon's War* (1973), *The Stone Killer* (1973), *Trained to Kill* (1973), *Mean Johnny Barrows* (1976), *Tracks* (1976), *Taxi Driver* (1976), *Rolling Thunder* (1977), *Twilight's Last Gleaming* (1977). See Jay Hyams, *War Movies* (New York: Gallery, 1984), pp. 195–99.

21. Ibid., p. 196.

22. The films favorable toward Russians include *Earth II, The 500 Pound Jerk, Bear Island, The Spy Who Loved Me, Meteor, The Golden Moment*. The only overtly critical entry is *Night Flight from Moscow*. Middling pictures include *Embassy, Colossus: The Forbin Project, Kremlin Letter, Mackintosh Man, The Girl from Petrovka, The Sell Out, Telefon, Brass Target, The President's Mistress, Russian Roulette, Final Assignment, Love and Death, For the Love of It*.

23. The spy movies are *Embassy, Kremlin Letter, Mackintosh Man, Night Flight from Moscow, Russian Roulette, The Sell Out, The Spy Who Loved Me, Telefon, The President's Mistress*.

24. *Colossus: The Forbin Project, Earth II, Bear Island*, and *Meteor* are cooperative venture films; *Love and Death* and *For the Love of It* are light comedies; *The 500 Pound Jerk, The Girl from Petrovka*, and *the Golden Moment* are East-West love stories; *Brass Target* is a war movie, and *Final Assignment* is a citizen cooperation film.

25. Frank Rich, review of *The Spy Who Loved Me, New York Times*, 21 August 1977, p. 11 (B).

26. Janet Maslin, review of *The Spy Who Loved Me, New York Times*, 28 July 1977, p. 17.

27. William F. Luce, "The Man You'll Love to Hate," *New York Times*, 27 July 1977, p. 15 (III).

28. This film appears shortly after Steven Spielberg's hugely successful *Jaws*, whose killer shark must have inspired its human counterpart, played by Richard Kiel in this James Bond film.

29. Susan Sackett, *Hollywood Reporter Book of Box Office Hits* (New York: Watson-Guptil, 1990), p. 351.

30. "All-Time Box Office Champions," *Variety*, 21–28 February 1994, p. 19.

31. Richard Schickel, *Second Sight* (New York: Simon and Schuster, 1973), p. 301.

32. Andrew Sarris, *The Primal Screen* (New York: Simon and Schuster, 1973), p. 202.

33. Janet Maslin, review of *Meteor, New York Times*, 19 October 1979, p. 6 (C).

34. Nora Sayre, review of *The Girl From Petrovka, New York Times*, 23 August 1974, p. 16.

35. Vincent Canby, review of *Telefon, New York Times*, 17 December 1977, p. 20.

36. Roger Manvell, ed., *The International Encyclopedia of Film* (New York: Crown, 1972), p. 454.

37. Vincent Canby, review of *The Kremlin Letter, New York Times*, 2 February 1973, p. 26.

38. Manvell, *International Encyclopedia of Film*, p. 274.

39. Andrew Sarris, ed., *Interviews with Film Directors* (Indianapolis: Bobbs-Merrill, 1967), p. 224.

40. Jean-Pierre Coursodon, *American Directors* (McGraw-Hill, 1983), p. 185.

41. Pauline Kael, *Deeper into Movies* (Boston: Little, Brown, 1973), p. 104.

42. John Simon, review of *Love and Death, New York Times*, 29 June 1975, p. 15 (II).

43. Christopher Lasch, *The Culture of Narcissism* (New York: Warner, 1979); Tom Wolfe, *In Our Time* (New York: Farrar, Strauss, and Giroux, 1982).

44. Cagin and Dray, *Hollywood Films*, p. 256.

Chapter 6

1. Peter G. Boyle, *American-Soviet Relations: From the Russian Revolution to the Fall of Communism* (New York: Routledge, 1993), p. 199.

2. Lou Cannon, *Reagan* (New York: G.P. Putnam's Sons, 1982), p. 32; Anne Edwards, *Early Reagan: The Rise to Power* (New York: William Morrow, 1987), p. 56.

3. Edwards, *Early Reagan*, p. 144.

4. Ibid., pp. 14, 16, 74, 92.

5. John G. Stoessinger, *Crusaders and Pragmatists: Movers of Modern American Foreign Policy* (New York: W. W. Norton, 1985), p. 289.

6. Cannon, *Reagan*, p. 23.

7. Boyle, *American-Soviet Relations*, p. 201.

8. Ibid., p. 209.

9. Coral Bell, *The Reagan Paradox: American Foreign Policy in the 1980s* (New Brunswick, N.J.: Rutgers University Press, 1989), p. 6.

10. Ibid., pp. 9–16.

11. Ibid., p. 52.

12. Ibid., p. 13.

13. David E. Kyvig, *Reagan and the World* (New York: Greenwood, 1990), p. 19.

14. Ibid., p. 29.

15. Michael Schaller, *Reckoning with Reagan: America and Its President in the 1980s* (New York: Oxford University Press, 1992), p. 129.

16. Kyvig, *Reagan and the World*, p. 22.

17. Helen Caldicott, *Missile Envy: The Arms Race and Nuclear War* (New York: William Morrow, 1984), pp. 26–32. Caldicott writes that her 6 December 1982, 75-minute interview with the president left her "shocked" and "profoundly concerned" by Reagan's misinformation concerning numerous basic realities of the nuclear military situation.

18. Boyle, *American-Soviet Relations*, p. 203.

19. Schaller, *Reckoning with Reagan*, p. 119.

20. Michael Mandelbaum and Strobe Talbott, *Reagan and Gorbachev* (New York: Vintage, 1987), p. 125: "In 1940 Reagan starred in a Warner Brothers spy picture, *Murder in the Air*. He played Brass Bancroft, a double agent assigned to help protect a vital U.S. military secret, the 'Inertia Projector,' an airborne death-ray that could destroy enemy aircraft before they could bomb the United States. This new 'super-weapon,' according to the film, 'not only makes the United States invincible in war, but in so doing promises to become the greatest force for world peace ever discovered, which is the hope and prayer of all thinking people, regardless of race, creed, or government.' "

21. John Lewis Gaddis, "Reagan and the World: A Roundtable Discussion," in *Reagan and the World*, p. 151.

22. Christopher Andrew and Oleg Gordievsky, *From KGB: The Inside Story* (New York: HarperCollins, 1990).

23. Boyle, *American-Soviet Relations*, pp. 213–14.

24. Gaddis, "Reagan and the World," p. 18.

25. Tom O'Brien, *The Screening of America: Movies and Values from Rocky to Rain Man* (New York: Frederick Ungar, 1990), p. 29.

26. Ibid., p. 130.

27. Pauline Kael, *Taking It All In* (New York: Holt, Rinehart and Winston, 1984), p. xiii.

28. Jonathan Halperin and Robert English, *The Other Side: How Soviets and Americans Perceive Each Other* (New Brunswick, N.J.: Rutgers University Press, 1987), pp. 119, 12.

29. Six films involve competitive spies, five are based on Cold War vigilantism, and four entail U.S. citizens escaping from Soviet oppression. Others are Soviets invade U.S. (3), antigovernment trust yourself (3), cooperative spies (2), spy comedies (2), U.S. students fight Cold War (2), Russians defect to freedom (2), U.S. corporate spies (2), and one each for cooperative joint ventures, historical epics, and brave Soviet dissidents.

30. Susan Sackett, *Hollywood Reporter Book of Box Office Hits* (New York: Watson-Guptil, 1990), p. 335.

31. "All-Time Box Office Champions," *Variety*, 21–28 February 1994, p. 20.

32. David Denby, review of *Rocky IV*, *New York*, 9 December 1985, p. 90.

33. Jack Kroll, review of *Rocky IV*, *Newsweek*, 9 December 1985, p. 92.

34. Rex Reed, review of *Rocky IV, New York Post,* 27 November 1985, p. 38.

35. Mike McGrady, review of *Rocky IV, Newsday,* 27 November 1985, p. 93 (II).

36. Nigel Floyd, review of *Rocky IV, Monthly Film Bulletin,* (February 1986): 48.

37. Cf. Jerry Hough, "Rocky, Rambo, and the American Mood," *Christian Science Monitor,* 24 February 1986, p. 23.

After defeating Drago, Rocky says to the cheering crowd, "When I came here I didn't know what to expect. All I seen is a lot of people hating me and I guess I didn't like you too much neither. During this fight I seen a lot of changing in the way you felt about me and the way I felt about you. . . . If I can change and you can change, everybody can change."

38. Tom Milne, review of *Invasion, USA, Monthly Film Bulletin* (November, 1985): 342.

39. Archer Winston, review of *Invasion, USA, New York Post,* 27 September 1985, p. 17.

40. Milne, review of *Invasion, USA,* p. 342.

41. "All-Time Top Grossing Independent Films," *Variety,* 21–27 February 1994, p. 52 (A).

42. Terry Christensen, *Reel Politics: American Political Movies From 'Birth of a Nation' to 'Platoon,'* (Cambridge, Mass.: Basil Blackwell, 1987), p. 201.

43. Richard Combs, review of *Red Dawn, Sight and Sound* (winter 1984/85): 66.

44. David Sterritt, review of *Red Dawn, Christian Science Monitor,* 30 August 1984, p. 21.

45. Lenny Rubinstein, review of *Red Dawn, Cineaste* 13, no. 4 (1984): 41.

46. Kevin Thomas, review of *Red Dawn, Los Angeles Times,* 10 August 1984, p. 15.

47. Armond White, review of *Red Dawn, Films in Review* (October 1984): 498.

48. Anthony T. Allegro, "On Milius," in *The International Dictionary of Films and Filmmakers: Volume II,* ed. Christopher Lyon (New York: St. J, 1989), p. 372.

49. It seems ironic for *Firefox* to get so exercised over the destabilizing effects of a Soviet radar-proof jet fighter. It assumes the U.S.'s right to steal the filmic Soviet technology at the same time that the U.S. was actually developing such an aircraft in the form of the B-2 Stealth bomber. Also worrying about Soviet stealth technology in this period was Tom Clancy's best-selling novel, *The Hunt for Red October*—but in the form of a Soviet submarine invisible to U.S. sonar detection.

50. Vincent Canby, review of *Firefox, New York Times,* 18 June 1982, p. 23.

51. Sackett, *Hollywood Reporter,* p. 352.

52. Christensen, *Reel Politics,* p. 200.

53. Thomas Doherty, review of *Rambo: First Blood, Part 2, Film Quarterly* (Spring 1986): 51.

54. Gaylyn Studlar and David Desser, "Never Having to Say You're Sorry: *Rambo's* Re-Writing of the Vietnam War," in *From Hanoi to Hollywood,* ed.

Linda Dittmar and Gene Michaud (New Brunswick, N.J.: Rutgers University Press, 1990), pp. 101–3.

55. Sackett, *Hollywood Reporter*, p. 352.

56. Vincent Canby, review of *Moscow on the Hudson*, *New York Times*, 6 April 1984, p. 12 (C).

57. Janet Maslin, review of *Gorky Park*, *New York Times*, 16 December 1984, p. 6 (III).

58. Stanley Kauffmann, *Field of View: Film Criticism and Comment* (New York: PAJ, 1986), p. 143.

59. Milton Cantor, review of *Reds*, *American Historical Review* (December 1982): 1484.

60. Sackett, *Hollywood Reporter*, p. 352.

61. Cantor, review of *Reds*, p. 1484.

62. "All-Time Box Office Champions," p. 21.

63. Vincent Canby, review of *2010*, *New York Times*, 7 December 1984, p. 15 (III).

Chapter 7

1. Robert Dallek, "American Reactions to Changes in the USSR," in *Soviet-American Relations After the Cold War*, ed. Seweryn Bialer and Robert Jervis (Durham, N.C.: Duke University Press, 1991), p. 56.

2. "Reagan toned down the invective for a variety of reasons that had little to do with any change in his perceptions or convictions and a great deal to do with what the moment required and his sense of what would please his audience." Michael Mandelbaum and Strobe Talbott, *Reagan and Gorbachev* (New York: Vintage, 1987), p. 44.

3. Mr. Reagan frequently tried to deflect responsibility for the absence of meetings with the Soviets in his first term using one-liners to make light of the "frequent funerals over there." In reality, though, his administration showed no real interest in any kind of meaningful communication with the Soviets during his first term.

4. Morris H. Morley, ed., *Crisis and Confrontation: Ronald Reagan's Foreign Policy* (Totowa, N.J.: Rowman and Littlefield, 1988), p. 4.

5. Robert V. Daniels, *The End of the Communist Revolution* (New York: Routledge, 1993), p. 138.

6. Peter G. Boyle, *American-Soviet Relations: From the Russian Revolution to the Fall of Communism* (New York: Routledge, 1993), p. 217.

7. David E. Kyvig, *Reagan and the World* (Westport, Conn.: Greenwood, 1990), p. 11.

8. Mandelbaum and Talbott, *Reagan and Gorbachev*, p. 175.

9. Ibid., p. 174.

10. Francis Fukuyama, *The End of History and the Last Man* (New York: Free Press, 1993).

11. Michael Mandelbaum, "The Bush Foreign Policy," *Foreign Affairs* 70, no. 1 (1991): 5.

12. Raymond L. Garthoff, "The Bush Administration's Foreign Policy toward the Soviet Union," *Current History* 90 (October 1991): 311–16.

13. Boyle, *American-Soviet Relations*, p. 228.

14. Eight of the critical films of the late 1980s are clones of earlier violent films from the early eighties.

Late 1980s CRI Films:	Progenitors:
No Return, No Surrender	*Rocky IV, Karate Kid*
Streets of Gold	*Rocky IV*
Amerika	*Red Dawn, Invasion USA*
Black Eagle	Bruce Lee films
Defense Play	*Red Dawn, Born American*
Rambo III	*Rambo, First Blood II*
	Rocky IV
Red Scorpion	*Rambo, First Blood II*
No Retreat, No Surrender II	*No Retreat, No Surrender*
	Rocky IV

15. "All-Time Box Office Champions," *Variety*, 21–27 February 1994, p. 22.

16. Richard Schickel, review of *Rambo III, Time*, 30 May 1988, p. 64.

17. David Denby, review of *Rambo III, New York*, 6 June 1988, p. 60.

18. Martin Burden, review of *Rambo III, New York Post*, 25 May 1988, p. 25.

19. Anne Billson, review of *Superman IV: The Quest for Peace, Monthly Film Bulletin* (September 1987): 283.

20. David Sterritt, review of *Superman IV: The Quest for Peace, Christian Science Monitor*, 2 September 1987, p. 21.

21. Vincent Canby, review of *Russkies, New York Times*, 6 November 1987, p. 12 (III).

22. Ibid.

23. Vincent Canby, review of *Red Heat, New York Times*, 17 June 1988, p. 17.

24. Roger Ebert, review of *Red Heat, New York Post*, 17 June 1988, p. 26.

25. Canby, review of *Red Heat*, p. 17.

26. The character of Viktor Rostavili is the first Soviet Georgian to appear as a Soviet citizen in American cinema, and one of very few non-Slavic (Russian, Ukrainian, or Byelorussian) characters in Hollywood films.

27. Michael Wilmington, review of *Red Heat, Los Angeles Times*, 17 June 1988, p. 1.

28. "The cult of Rustaveli in Georgia is spontaneous and universal. In Feudal and Tsarist times, many an illiterate peasant could recite whole stanzas of 'The Knight in the Panther's Skin' by heart. Rustaveli's poem provided the common people and the nobility alike with a fund of inspiration and folk wisdom which kept the torch of Georgian culture alight through many a century of alien oppression." Venera Urushadze, translator from Georgian of Shota Rustaveli's *The Knight in the Panther's Skin* (Tbilisi: Publishing House, 1986), p. 10.

29. Suzanne Moore, review of *Red Heat, New Statesman and Society*, 20 January 1989, p. 42.

30. Martin Burden, review of *Iron Eagle II*, *New York Post*, 12 November 1988, p. 18.

31. William H. Honan, "Can the Cold War Be a Hot Topic for a Movie?" *New York Times*, 25 February 1990, pp. 17–18: "A message at the beginning of the film, says McTiernan, tells the audience that those events took place before Gorbachev came to power. Also, we added a few lines in which we gently tried to hint that this incident, or some incident like it, might have been what shocked the Soviet hierarchy into changing. He cited the final scene in which Baldwin remarks, 'there will be hell to pay in Moscow, when the dust settles from all of this,' and Connery replies: 'perhaps some good will come of it.' "

32. David Sterrit, review of *The Hunt for Red October*, *Christian Science Monitor*, 12 March 1990, p. 15.

33. "All-Time Box Office Champions," *Variety*, 21–27 February 1994, p. 22.

34. Janet Maslin, review of *The Fourth Protocol*, *New York Times*, 28 August 1987, p. 19 (C).

Cold War Coda

1. Vlasovite: General Andrei A. Vlasov led a "Russian liberation army" of POWs who fought for the Nazis against Stalinist Russia at the end of World War II with the avowed goal of getting rid of Stalin. They were turned back over to Soviet authorities by the Allies in 1945 to predictably brutal treatment by Stalin.

2. Ticket purchases represent votes in a quasi-democratic expression of popular will. Hollywood executives cater to popular (i.e., negative and violent) films rather than pictures about international cooperation.

3. Karen S. Johnson-Cartee and Gary A. Copeland, *Negative Political Advertising: Coming of Age* (Hillsdale, NJ: Lawrence Erlbaum Associates, 1991), p. 15. The negativity effect is defined as the "tendency for negative information to be weighted more heavily than positive information when forming evaluations of social stimuli. Across widely varying events, settings, and persons, positive experiences or positive aspects of stimuli have been found to be less influential in the formation of judgments than are negative aspects of stimuli."

4. Herschell Gordon Lewis, "The Power of Negative Thinking," *Direct Marketing* 51, no. 4 (August 1988): 60–62.

5. Michael Pfau and Henry C. Kenski, *Attack Politics: Strategy and Defense* (Westport, Conn.: Praeger Studies in Political Communication, 1990), p. 1.

6. Paul Monaco, *Ribbons in Time: Movies and Society since 1945* (Bloomington: Indiana University Press, 1988), p. 1.

7. Siegfried Kracauer, "National Types As Hollywood Presents Them," *Public Opinion Quarterly* (1949).

8. Harry Hann, "Seeing Red: How Hollywood Movies Handle the Russians," *New York Daily News*, 11 December 1983, p. 17.

9. Sam Keen, *Faces of the Enemy: Reflections of the Hostile Imagination* (San Francisco: Harper and Row, 1986).

10. Michael Paul Rogin, *Ronald Reagan, the Movies, and Other Episodes of Political Demonology* (Berkeley: University of California Press, 1987), p. viii.

11. Frederick Hartmann, *The Conservation of Enemies* (Westport, Conn.: Greenwood, 1982).

Filmography

After Tonight, George Archainbaud (1933)-------------- MID
British Agent, Michael Curtiz (1934) ------------------ MID
Catherine the Great, Paul Czinner (1934)-------------- MID
The Scarlet Empress, Joseph von Sternberg (1934) --------- CRI
We Live Again, Rouben Mamoulian (1934)*------------- MID
I Stand Condemned, Anthony Asquith (1935)* ----------- MID
Charge of the Light Brigade, Michael Curtiz (1936) --------- MID
Once in a Blue Moon, Ben Hecht (1936) --------------- MID
The Emperor's Candlesticks, George Fitzmaurice (1937)------ MID
Espionage, Kurt Neumann (1937)-------------------- MID
The Soldier and the Lady, George Nichols Jr. (1937) -------- FAV
Tovarich, Anatole Litvak (1937)-------------------- MID
Spawn of the North, Henry Hathaway (1938) ----------- CRI
Balalaika, Reinhold Schunzel (1939) ----------------- FAV
Confessions of a Nazi Spy, Anatole Litvak (1939)*---------- CRI
Ninotchka, Ernst Lubitsch (1939)-------------------- MID
Comrade X, King Vidor (1940) --------------------- CRI
He Stayed for Breakfast, Alexander Hall (1940) ---------- MID
Public Deb Number 1, Gregory Ratoff (1940)* ---------- MID
Action in the North Atlantic, Lloyd Bacon (1943) --------- FAV
Miss V. from Moscow, Albert Herman (1943)* ---------- FAV

*Film not viewed; evaluation based on print reviews and screenplays (obtained from the New York State Motion Picture Archives, Albany, N.Y.).

Mission to Moscow, Michael Curtiz (1943)– – – – – – – – – – – – FAV
Three Russian Girls, Fedor Ozep and Henry Kesler (1943) – – – – FAV
Days of Glory, Jacques Tourneur (1944) – – – – – – – – – – – – – FAV
The North Star, Lewis Milestone (1944) – – – – – – – – – – – – – FAV
Song of Russia, Gregory Ratoff (1944) – – – – – – – – – – – – – – FAV
Counter Attack, Zoltan Korda (1945) – – – – – – – – – – – – – – – FAV
Behind the Iron Curtain, William Wellman (1948)– – – – – – – – – – CRI
Berlin Express, Jacques Tourneur (1948)– – – – – – – – – – – – – – MID
The Red Danube, George Sidney (1950)*– – – – – – – – – – – – – – MID
Red Planet Mars, Harry Horner (1952) – – – – – – – – – – – – – – CRI
The World in His Arms, Raoul Walsh (1952) – – – – – – – – – – – CRI
California Conquest, Lew Landers (1953)– – – – – – – – – – – – – – CRI
Never Let Me Go, Delmer Daves (1953) – – – – – – – – – – – – – – CRI
Prisoner of War, Andrew Marton (1954) – – – – – – – – – – – – – CRI
Anastasia, Anatole Litvak (1956) – – – – – – – – – – – – – – – – – MID
War and Peace, King Vidor (1956)– – – – – – – – – – – – – – – – – FAV
The Iron Petticoat, Ralph Thomas (1957) – – – – – – – – – – – – – MID
Jet Pilot, Joseph von Sternberg (1957) – – – – – – – – – – – – – – MID
Silk Stockings, Rouben Mamoulian (1957) – – – – – – – – – – – – MID
The Journey, Anatole Litvak (1959)*– – – – – – – – – – – – – – – – CRI
Romanoff and Juliet, Peter Ustinov (1961) – – – – – – – – – – – – FAV
The Manchurian Candidate, John Frankenheimer (1962)– – – – – – CRI
Taras Bulba, J. Lee Thompson (1962) – – – – – – – – – – – – – – FAV
From Russia with Love, Terence Young (1963) – – – – – – – – – – MID
Dr. Strangelove, Stanley Kubrick (1964) – – – – – – – – – – – – – FAV
Fail Safe, Sidney Lumet (1964) – – – – – – – – – – – – – – – – – FAV
Seven Days in May, John Frankenheimer (1964) – – – – – – – – – FAV
The Bedford Incident, John Harris (1965) – – – – – – – – – – – – FAV
Dr. Zhivago, David Lean (1965) – – – – – – – – – – – – – – – – – MID
Funeral in Berlin, Guy Hamilton (1966)– – – – – – – – – – – – – – CRI
The Russians Are Coming, The Russians Are Coming,
     Norman Jewison (1966) – – – – – – – – – – – – – – – – – – – FAV
Billion Dollar Brain, Ken Russell (1967) – – – – – – – – – – – – – FAV
You Only Live Twice, Lewis Gilbert (1967)– – – – – – – – – – – – MID
Ice Station Zebra, John Sturges (1968) – – – – – – – – – – – – – – MID
The Shoes of the Fisherman, Michael Anderson (1968) – – – – – – FAV
The Chairman, J. Lee Thompson (1969) – – – – – – – – – – – – – FAV
Topaz, Alfred Hitchcock (1969) – – – – – – – – – – – – – – – – – CRI
Fiddler on the Roof, Norman Jewison (1971)– – – – – – – – – – – CRI
Nicholas and Alexandra, Franklin Shaffner (1971) – – – – – – – – CRI
Colossus: The Forbin Project, Joseph Sargent (1972) – – – – – – – MID
Earth II, Tom Gries (1972)– FAV
Embassy, Gordon Hessler (1972) – – – – – – – – – – – – – – – – MID
The 500 Pound Jerk, William Kronnick (1973)– – – – – – – – – – FAV

Kremlin Letter, John Huston (1973)– – – – – – – – – – – – – – – – – MID
The Mackintosh Man, John Huston (1973)– – – – – – – – – – – – – MID
Night Flight from Moscow, Henry Verneuil (1973)– – – – – – – – – – CRI
The Girl from Petrovka, Robert Miller (1974) – – – – – – – – – – – MID
Love and Death, Woody Allen (1975) – – – – – – – – – – – – – – – MID
Russian Roulette, Lou Lombardo (1975) – – – – – – – – – – – – – FAV
The Sell Out, Peter Collinson (1976) – – – – – – – – – – – – – – – MID
The Spy Who Loved Me, Lewis Gilbert (1977) – – – – – – – – – – – FAV
Telefon, Don Siegel (1977) – MID
Bear Island, Don Sharp (1978) – – – – – – – – – – – – – – – – – – MID
Brass Target, John Hough (1978) – – – – – – – – – – – – – – – – – MID
The President's Mistress, John L. Moxey (1978) – – – – – – – – – – MID
Meteor, Ronald Neame (1979) – – – – – – – – – – – – – – – – – – FAV
Final Assignment, Paul Almond (1980)– – – – – – – – – – – – – – – MID
For the Love of It, Hal Kanter (1980) – – – – – – – – – – – – – – – MID
The Golden Moment, Richard Sarafian (1980)– – – – – – – – – – – FAV
Condorman, Charles Jarron (1981) – – – – – – – – – – – – – – – – MID
Berlin Tunnel 21, Richard Michael (1981) – – – – – – – – – – – – – CRI
For Your Eyes Only, John Glen (1981) – – – – – – – – – – – – – – – MID
Reds, Warren Beatty (1981) – – – – – – – – – – – – – – – – – – – FAV
Coming Out of the Ice, Waris Hussein (1982) – – – – – – – – – – – CRI
Firefox, Clint Eastwood (1982)– – – – – – – – – – – – – – – – – – CRI
The Soldier, James Glickenhaus (1982) – – – – – – – – – – – – – – CRI
World War III, David Greene (1982)– – – – – – – – – – – – – – – – CRI
Enigma, Jeannot Swarcz (1983)– – – – – – – – – – – – – – – – – MID
Octopussy, John Glen (1983) – – – – – – – – – – – – – – – – – – MID
Cowboy and the Ballerina, Jerry Jameson (1984) – – – – – – – – – FAV
Gorky Park, Michael Apted (1984) – – – – – – – – – – – – – – – – MID
Gotcha! Jeff Kanew (1984) – – – – – – – – – – – – – – – – – – – CRI
The Jigsaw Man, Freddie Francis (1984)– – – – – – – – – – – – – MID
Red Dawn, John Milius (1984) – – – – – – – – – – – – – – – – – – CRI
The Delos Adventure, Joseph Purcell (1985) – – – – – – – – – – – CRI
Moscow on the Hudson, Paul Mazursky (1985) – – – – – – – – – – MID
Secret Weapons, Don Taylor (1985) – – – – – – – – – – – – – – – CRI
The Belarus File, Robert Markowitz (1985) – – – – – – – – – – – MID
Born American, Renny Harlin (1985) – – – – – – – – – – – – – – – CRI
The Falcon and the Snowman, John Schlesinger (1985) – – – – – – CRI
Gulag, Robert Young (1985) – – – – – – – – – – – – – – – – – – – CRI
Invasion, USA, Joseph Zito (1985)– – – – – – – – – – – – – – – – CRI
Keeping Track, Robin Spry (1985)– – – – – – – – – – – – – – – – MID
Lethal, Dwight Little (1985) – – – – – – – – – – – – – – – – – – – MID
Orion's Belt, Tristan da Vere Cole (1985) – – – – – – – – – – – – CRI
Rambo: First Blood, Part II, Ted Kotcheff (1985) – – – – – – – – – CRI
Rocky IV, Sylvester Stallone (1985) – – – – – – – – – – – – – – – CRI

Sakharov, Jack Gold (1985)– CRI
Spies like Us, John Landis (1985) – – – – – – – – – – – – – – – – – – MID
2010, Peter Hyams (1985) – FAV
White Nights, Taylor Hackford (1985) – – – – – – – – – – – – – – MID
A View to a Kill, John Glen (1985)– – – – – – – – – – – – – – – – FAV
No Retreat, No Surrender, Corey Yuen (1986) – – – – – – – – – – – CRI
Streets of Gold, Joe Roth (1986) – – – – – – – – – – – – – – – – – – CRI
Yuri Nosenko, KGB, Mitch Jackson (1986) – – – – – – – – – – – – MID
Amazing Grace and Chuck, Mike Newell (1987) – – – – – – – – – – FAV
Amerika, Donald Wrye (1987) – – – – – – – – – – – – – – – – – – – CRI
Dancers, Herbert Ross (1987) – – – – – – – – – – – – – – – – – – – FAV
The Fourth Protocol, John MacKenzie (1987) – – – – – – – – – – – CRI
The Living Daylights, John Glen (1987)– – – – – – – – – – – – – – FAV
Morgan Stewart's Coming Home, Paul Aaron and
    Jerry Winsor (1987)– CRI
No Way Out, Roger Donaldson (1987) – – – – – – – – – – – – – – MID
Russkies, Richard Rosenthal (1987) – – – – – – – – – – – – – – – – FAV
Superman IV: The Quest for Peace, Sidney J. Furie (1987) – – – – – FAV
Young Nurses in Love, Chuck Vincent (1987) – – – – – – – – – – – MID
Black Eagle, Eric Carson (1988) – – – – – – – – – – – – – – – – – – CRI
Defense Play, Monte Markham (1988)– – – – – – – – – – – – – – – CRI
Intrigue, David Drury (1988)– MID
Iron Eagle II, Sidney J. Furie (1988) – – – – – – – – – – – – – – – FAV
Little Nikita, Richard Benjamin (1988)– – – – – – – – – – – – – – MID
Rambo III, Peter MacDonald (1988) – – – – – – – – – – – – – – – CRI
Red Heat, Walter Hill (1988)– – – – – – – – – – – – – – – – – – – FAV
The Experts, Dave Thomas (1989)– – – – – – – – – – – – – – – – MID
Just Another Secret, Lawrence G. Clark (1989) – – – – – – – – – – FAV
No Retreat, No Surrender II, Corey Yuen (1989) – – – – – – – – – – CRI
The Package, Andrew Davis (1989) – – – – – – – – – – – – – – – – MID
Price of the Bride, Tom Clegg (1989) – – – – – – – – – – – – – – – MID
Red King, White Knight, Geoff Murphy (1989)– – – – – – – – – – FAV
Red Scorpion, Joseph Zito (1989) – – – – – – – – – – – – – – – – – CRI
The Fourth War, John Frankenheimer (1990) – – – – – – – – – – – MID
By Dawn's Early Light, Jack Sholder (1990) – – – – – – – – – – – MID
Full Fathom Five, Carl Franklin (1990)– – – – – – – – – – – – – – FAV
The Hunt for Red October, John McTiernan (1990)– – – – – – – – MID
The Russia House, Fred Schepisi (1990) – – – – – – – – – – – – – FAV
Company Business, Nicholas Meyer (1991) – – – – – – – – – – – – FAV
Death Has a Bad Reputation, Lawrence G. Clark (1991) – – – – – – CRI
The Inner Circle, Andrei Konchalovsky (1991)– – – – – – – – – – – MID
Terminator II, James Cameron (1991) – – – – – – – – – – – – – – – MID

Bibliography

Auster, Albert, and Leonard Quart. *American Film and Society since 1945*. New York: Praeger Special Studies, 1984.

Averson, Richard, and David White. *The Celluloid Weapon: Social Comment in the American Film*. Boston: Beacon, 1972.

Baxter, John. *Hollywood in the Thirties*. New York: A. S. Barnes, 1968.

———. *Sixty Years of Hollywood*. New York: A. S. Barnes, 1973.

Beitzel, Robert. *The Uneasy Alliance: America, Britain, Russia, 1941–1943*. New York: Alfred A. Knopf, 1972.

Bell, Coral. *The Reagan Paradox: American Foreign Policy in the 1980s*. New Brunswick, N.J.: Rutgers University Press, 1989.

Belton, John. *American Cinema-American Culture*. New York: McGraw-Hill, 1993.

Bennett, Edward M. *Franklin D. Roosevelt and the Search for Security: American-Soviet Relations, 1933–1939*. Wilmington, Del.: Scholarly Resources, 1985.

Beschloss, Michael. *The Crisis Years: Kennedy and Khrushchev, 1960–1963*. New York: HarperCollins, 1991.

Biskind, Peter. *Seeing Is Believing: How Hollywood Taught Us to Stop Worrying and Love the Fifties*. New York: Pantheon, 1983.

Bohlen, Charles E. *Witness to History: 1929–1969*. New York: W. W. Norton, 1977.

Bohn, Thomas, and Richard Stromgren. *Light and Shadows: A History of Motion Pictures*. Port Washington, N.Y.: Alfred, 1975.

Boyle, Peter G. *American-Soviet Relations: From the Russian Revolution to the Fall of Communism*. New York: Routledge, 1993.

Brode, Douglas. *The Films of the Fifties*. Secaucus, N.J.: Citadel, 1976.

Brownstein, Ronald. *The Power and the Glitter: The Hollywood-Washington Connection*. New York: Random House, 1992.

Brussel, Gabrielle. *Cuban Missile Crisis: U.S. Deliberations and Negotiations at the Edge of the Precipice*. Pew Case No. 334. Washington: Georgetown University, 1993.

Cagin, Seth, and Philip Dray. *Hollywood Films of the Seventies*. New York: Harper and Row, 1984.

Caldwell, Dan. *American-Soviet Relations From 1947 to the Nixon-Kissinger Grand Design*. Westport, Conn.: Greenwood, 1981.

Cannon, Lou. *Reagan*. New York: G.P. Putnam's Sons, 1982.

Carnes, Mark C., ed. *Past Imperfect: History According to the Movies*. New York: Henry Holt, 1995.

Christensen, Terry. *Reel Politics: American Political Movies from "Birth of a Nation" to "Platoon."* New York: Blackwell, 1987.

Conquest, Robert L. *The Harvest of Sorrow: Soviet Collectivization and the Terror-Famine*. New York: Oxford University Press, 1986.

Coursodon, Jean-Pierre. *American Directors*. New York: McGraw Hill, 1983.

Cowie, Peter. *Fifty Major Filmmakers*. New York: A. S. Barnes, 1975.

Culbert, David. *Mission to Moscow*. Madison: University of Wisconsin Press, 1980.

Dallek, Robert. *Franklin D. Roosevelt and American Foreign Policy, 1932–1945*. New York: Oxford University Press, 1995.

———. *Ronald Reagan: The Politics of Symbolism*. Cambridge, Mass.: Harvard University Press, 1981.

———. *The American Style of Foreign Policy: Cultural Politics and Foreign Affairs*. New York: Oxford University Press, 1983.

Daniels, Robert V. *The End of the Communist Revolution*. New York: Routledge, 1993.

Davies, Philip, and Brian Neve, eds. *Cinema, Politics, and Society in America*. New York: St. Martin's Press, 1981.

Davis, T.R., and S.M. Lynn-Jones. "City Upon a Hill." *Foreign Policy* 66 (Spring 1987): 20–38.

Deibel, Terry L. "Bush's Foreign Policy: Mastery and Inaction." *Foreign Policy* 84 (Fall 1991): 1–19.

Dick, Bernard F. *The Star Spangled Screen: The American World War II Film*. Lexington: University Press of Kentucky, 1985.

Divine, Robert A. *Roosevelt and World War II*. Baltimore: Johns Hopkins University Press, 1969.

Dulles, John Foster. "A Policy of Boldness." *Life* 19 (May 1952).

Edwards, Anne. *Early Reagan: The Rise to Power*. New York: William Morrow, 1987.

Eubank, Keith. *Summit At Teheran: The Untold Story*. New York: William Morrow, 1985.

Fell, John. *A History of Films*. New York: Holt, Rinehart and Winston, 1979.

Finler, Joel W. *All-Time Box Office Hits*. London: Columbus Books, 1985.

Fyne, Robert. "From Hollywood to Moscow." *Film Library Quarterly* 16, nos. 1–2 (1983).

——— *The Hollywood Propaganda of World War II*. Metuchen, N.J.: Scarecrow, 1994.

Gabbard, Krin and Glen Gabbard. *Psychiatry and the Cinema*. Chicago: University of Chicago Press, 1987.

Gaddis, John Lewis. *Strategies of Containment*. New York: Oxford University Press, 1985.

———. *The United States and the End of the Cold War*. New York: Oxford University Press, 1994.

Garthoff, Raymond L. *Detente and Confrontation: American-Soviet Relations from Nixon to Reagan*. Washington: Brookings Institution, 1985.

———. "The Bush Administration's Policy Toward the Soviet Union." *Current History* 90 (October 1991).

George, Alexander L., and Juliette L. George. *Woodrow Wilson and Colonel House: A Personality Study*. New York: Dover, 1956.

Goldman, Eric. *The Tragedy of Lyndon Johnson* New York: Knopf, 1969.

Gow, Gordon. *Hollywood in the Fifties*. New York: A. S. Barnes, 1971.

Grayson, Benson Lee, ed. *The American Image of Russia, 1917–1977*. New York: Ungar, 1978.

Halperin, Jonathan J., and Robert D. English, eds. *The Other Side: How Americans and Soviets Perceive Each Other*. New Brunswick, N.J.: Transaction, 1987.

Hann, Harry. "Seeing Red: How Hollywood Movies Handle the Russians." *New York Daily News*, 11 December 1983.

Hartmann, Frederick. *The Conservation of Enemies*. Westport, Conn.: Greenwood, 1982.

Herring, George. *Aid to Russia: 1941–1946*. New York: Columbia University Press, 1973.

Hochschild, Adam. *The Unquiet Ghost: Russians Remember Stalin*. New York: Penguin, 1994.

Hoff-Wilson, Joan. "Nixingerism, NATO and Detente." *Diplomatic History* 13, no. 4 (1989).

Hollows, Joanne, and Mark Jancovich, eds. *Approaches to Popular Film*. New York: St. Martin's Press, 1995.

Holston, Kim. *The English-Speaking Cinema*. Jefferson, N.C.: McFarland, 1994.

Honan, William H. "Can the Cold War Be a Hot Topic for a Movie?" *New York Times*, 25 February 1990.

Hoopes, Townsend. *The Devil and John Foster Dulles*. Boston: Little, Brown, 1975.

Hyams, Jay. *War Movies*. New York: Gallery, 1984.

Hyland, William G. *Mortal Rivals: Understanding the Hidden Pattern of Soviet-American Relations*. New York: Simon and Schuster, 1987.

Isaacson, Walter, and Evan Thomas. *The Wise Men: Six Friends and the World They Made*. New York: Simon and Schuster, 1986.

Izod, John. *Hollywood and the Box Office*. New York: Columbia University Press, 1988.

Janis, Irving L. *Victims of Groupthink*. Boston: Houghton-Mifflin, 1982.

Jeffords, Susan. *Hard Bodies: Hollywood Masculinity in the Reagan Era*. New Brunswick, N.J.: Rutgers University Press, 1993.

Jones, Dorothy B. "Communism and the Movies: A Study of Film Content" in John Cogley, ed. *Reporting on Blacklisting: Volume I, The Movies*. New York: Arno, 1972.

Jones, Robert H. *The Roads to Russia: U.S. Lend-Lease*. Norman: University of Oklahoma Press, 1969.

Kael, Pauline. *Kiss Kiss Bang Bang*. New York: Simon and Schuster, 1969.

———. *Going Steady*. Boston: Little, Brown, 1970.

———. *Deeper Into Movies*. Boston: Little, Brown, 1973.

———. *Taking It All In*. New York: Holt, Rinehart, and Winston, 1984.

Kagan, Norman. *The Cinema of Stanley Kubrick*. New York: Holt, Rinehart, and Winston, 1972.

Kauffman, Stanley. *Field of View: Film Criticism and Comment*. New York: PAJ Publications, 1986.

———. *The World on Film*. New York: Harper and Row, 1966.

Kearns, Doris. *Lyndon Johnson and the American Dream*. New York: Signet, 1977.

Keen, Sam. *Faces of the Enemy: Reflections of the Hostile Imagination*. San Francisco: Harper and Row, 1986.

Kerry, Richard J. *The Star-Spangled Mirror: America's Image of Itself and the World*. Savage, Md.: Rowman and Littlefield, 1990.

Koppes, Clayton R., and Gregory D. Black. *Hollywood Goes to War: How Politics, Profits and Propaganda Shaped World War II Movies*. Berkeley: University of California Press, 1987.

Koszarski, Richard. *Hollywood Directors, 1914–1940*. New York: Oxford University Press, 1976.

Kracauer, Siegfried. "National Types as Hollywood Presents Them." In *The Movies: An American Idiom*. Edited by Arthur F. McClure, Rutherford, N.J.: Farleigh Dickinson University Press, 1971.

Kuhns, William. *Movies in America*. Dayton: Phlaum, 1972.

Kyvig, David E. *Reagan and the World*. New York: Greenwood, 1990.

Lafeber, Walter. *America, Russia and the Cold War*. New York: Alfred A. Knopf, 1990.

Larson, Deborah W. *Origins of Containment: A Psychological Explanation*. Princeton: Princeton University Press, 1985.

Levering, Ralph B. *The Cold War, 1945–1972*. Arlington Heights, Ill.: Harlan Davidson, 1982.

Lifton, Robert J., and Eric Olson. *Explorations in Psychohistory*. New York: Simon and Schuster, 1975.

Lundestad, Geir. *The American Empire and Other Studies of U.S. Foreign Policy in a Comparative Perspective*. New York: Coronet, 1990.

Lyon, Christopher, ed. *The International Dictionary of Films and Filmmakers*. New York: St. J Press, 1989.

Maland, Charles, "*Dr. Strangelove*: Nightmare Comedy and the Ideology of Liberal Consensus." In *Hollywood as Historian: American Film in a Cultural Context*. Edited by Peter C. Rollins, Lexington: University Press of Kentuky, 1983.

Maltby, Richard. *Harmless Entertainment: Hollywood and the Ideology of Consensus*. Metuchen, N.J.: Scarecrow, 1983.

Mandelbaum, Michael. "The Bush Foreign Policy." *Foreign Affairs* 70, no. 1 (1991).

Mayers, David. *The Ambassadors and America's Soviet Policy*. New York: Oxford University Press, 1995.

Mazlish, Bruce. *Kissinger: The European Mind in American Foreign Policy*. New York: Basic Books, 1976.

———. *In Search of Nixon*. Baltimore: Penguin, 1973.

Mazlish, Bruce, and Edwin Diamond. "Thrice-Born: A Psychohistory of Jimmy Carter's Rebirth." *New York Times*, 30 August 1976.

McCullough, David. *Truman*. New York: Simon and Schuster, 1992.

McMahan, Jeffrey. *Reagan and the World: Imperial Policy in the New Cold War*. New York: Monthly Review, 1985.

Miller, Douglas, and Marion Nowak. *The Fifties: The Way We Really Were*. New York: Doubleday, 1977.

Miller, Richard, ed. *The Kaleidoscopic Lens: How Hollywood Views Ethnic Groups*. New York: Ozer, 1980.

Millichap, Joseph R. *Lewis Milestone*. Boston: Twayne, 1981.

Miscamble, Wilson D. "The Foreign Policy of the Truman Administration: A Post-Cold War Appraisal." *Presidential Studies Quarterly* 24, no. 3 (Summer 1994).

Monaco, James. *American Film Now: The People, The Power, The Money, The Movies*. New York: Oxford University Press, 1979.

Monaco, Paul. *Ribbons in Time: Movies and Society since 1945*. Bloomington: Indiana University Press, 1988.

Morley, Morris H., ed. *Crisis and Confrontation: Ronald Reagan's Foreign Policy*. Totowa, N.J.: Rowman and Littlefield, 1988.

Navasky, Victor. *Naming Names*. New York: Viking, 1980.

Nisbet, Robert A. *Roosevelt & Stalin: The Failed Courtship*. Washington, D.C.: Regnery Gateway, 1988.

O'Brien, Tom. *The Screening of America: Movies and Values from Rocky to Rain Man*. New York: Ungar, 1990.

O'Connor, John E., and Martin Jackson, eds. *American History/American Film: Interpreting the Hollywood Image*. New York: Frederick Ungar, 1979.

Palmer, William J. *The Films of the Seventies: A Social History*. Metuchen, N.J.: Scarecrow, 1987.

Paris, Barry. *Garbo*. New York: Alfred Knopf, 1995.

Phillips, Gene D. *Major Film Directors of the American and British Cinema*. Bethlehem, Penn.: Lehigh University Press, 1990.

Reed, Rex. *Big Screen Little Screen*. New York: MacMillan, 1971.

Rogin, Michael Paul. *Ronald Reagan, the Movies, And Other Episodes in Political Demonology*. Berkeley: University of California Press, 1987.

Rollins, Peter C., ed. *Hollywood As Historian: American Film In a Cultural Context*. Lexington: University Press of Kentucky, 1983.

Rosati, Jerel A. *The Carter Administration's Quest for Global Community: Beliefs and their Impact on Behavior*. Columbia: University of South Carolina Press, 1987.

———. *The Politics of United States Foreign Policy*. New York: Harcourt, Brace, 1992.

Ryavec, Karl W. *United States-Soviet Relations*. New York: Longman, 1989.

Sackett, Susan. *Hollywood Reporter Book of Box Office Hits*. New York: Watson-Guptill, 1990.

Sainsbury, Keith. *The Turning Point: Roosevelt, Stalin, Churchill, Chiang Kai-Shek, 1943*. New York: Oxford University Press, 1985.

Sarris, Andrew, ed. *Interviews With Film Directors*. Indianapolis: Bobbs-Merrill, 1967.

———. *The Primal Screen*. New York: Simon and Schuster, 1972.

Sayre, Nora. *Running Time: Films of the Cold War*. New York: Dial Press, 1982.

Schaller, Michael. *Reckoning With Reagan: America and Its President in the 1980s*. New York: Oxford University Press, 1992.

Schatz, Thomas. *Hollywood Genres: Formulas, Filmmaking, and the Studio System*. Philadelphia: Temple University Press, 1981.

Schickel, Richard. *Second Sight*. New York: Simon and Schuster, 1972.

Sennett, Ted. *Hollywood's Golden Year: 1939*. New York: St. Martin's Press, 1989.

Shepley, James. "Brinkmanship." *Life* 16 (January 1956).

Shipman, David. *The Great Movie Stars: The Golden Years*. New York: Hill and Wang, 1988.

Small, Melvin. "Buffoons and Brave Hearts: Hollywood Portrays the Russians, 1939–1944." *California Historical Quarterly* 52, no. 4 (Winter 1973): 326–37.

———. "How We Learned to Love the Russians: American Media and the Soviet Union During World War II." *The Historian* 36, no. 3 (May 1974): 455–78.

———. "Hollywood and Teaching About Russian-American Relations." *Film and History* 10 (1980): 1–8.

Smith, Hedrick. *The New Russians*. New York: Random House, 1991.

Steigerwald, David. *Wilsonian Idealism in America*. Ithaca: Cornell University Press, 1994.

Stoessinger, John G. *Henry Kissinger: The Anguish of Power*. New York: Norton, 1976.

———. *Crusaders and Pragmatists: Movers of Modern American Foreign Policy*. New York: W. W. Norton, 1985.

Strada, Michael. "A Half Century of American Cinematic Imagery: Hollywood's Portrayal of Russian Characters, 1933–1988." *Coexistence* 26 (Winter 1989): 333–50.

———. "The Cinematic Bogy Man Comes Home: American Popular Perceptions of External Threat." *The Midwest Quarterly* 28, no. 2 (Winter 1987).

Studlar, Gaylyn, and David Desser. "Never Having to Say You're Sorry: *Rambo's* Re-Writing of the Vietnam War." In *From Hanoi to Hollywood.* Edited by Linda Dittmar and Gene Michaud, New Brunswick, N.J.: Rutgers University Press, 1990.

Talbott, Strobe, and Michael Mandelbaum. *Reagan and Gorbachev.* New York: Vintage, 1987.

Thomas, Evan. *The Very Best Men: Four Who Dared: The Early Years of the CIA.* New York: Simon and Schuster, 1995.

Thompson, Kenneth W., ed. *Foreign Policy in the Reagan Presidency.* Lanham, Md.: University Press of America, 1993.

Turner, Robert W. *Jimmy Carter in His Own Words.* New York: Ballantine Books, 1976.

Vermilye, Jerry. *The Films of the Thirties.* Secaucus, N.J.: Citadel, 1982.

Wakeman, John, ed. *World Film Directors.* New York: H. W. Wilson, 1987.

White, Ralph K. *Fearful Warriors: A Psychological Profile of US-Soviet Relations.* New York: Free Press, 1984.

Whitfield, Stephen J. *The Culture of the Cold War.* Baltimore: Johns Hopkins University Press, 1991.

Wilson, Robert, ed. *The Film Criticism of Otis Ferguson.* Philadelphia: Temple University Press, 1971.

Index

Titles of films are in italics and are followed by their dates of production in parentheses. Titles of books are in italics and are followed by their author names in parentheses. Titles of other works (magazines, TV shows, etc.) are in italics. Names of characters are entered as personal names (last, first), with the name of the actor who portrayed them following in parentheses. References followed by "n" or "nn" indicates notes.

About the Authors

Michael Strada has taught international studies courses at West Liberty State College since 1969 and West Virginia University since 1985, where he also serves as co-director of the WV Consortium for Faculty and Course Development in International Studies. His articles have appeared in journals like *Coexistence, Journal of Popular Culture, Peace Research, International Review of History and Political Science,* and *The Midwest Quarterly*; Prentice-Hall will publish *Through the Global Lens* in 1997. Strada has visited more than forty countries and led ten travel-study groups to Russia. In 1990, he and Harold Troper met while teaching aboard the Semester at Sea program.

Harold Troper holds a Ph.D. from the University of Toronto and is professor of the History of Education at the Ontario Institute for Studies in Education at the University of Toronto. His special interests include the history of North American immigration, ethnicity, and culture. He is a widely published author and his award-winning books include *Immigrants: A Portrait of the Urban Experience* (1975), *None Is Too Many: Canada and the Jews of Europe, 1933–1948* (1982), and *Old Wounds: Jews, Ukrainians, and the Hunt for Nazi War Criminals in Canada* (1988). This is his first book exploring issues of film history, but he is no stranger to the magic of a darkened movie theater. His preteen Saturdays were seldom complete without an afternoon double bill. If he eventually graduated from black licorice to hot buttered popcorn, his passion for movies is as strong as ever.